MW00715975

Concepts of
Information Retrieval

CONCEPTS OF
INFORMATION RETRIEVAL

Miranda Lee Pao

1989
LIBRARIES UNLIMITED, INC.
Englewood, Colorado

Copyright © 1989 Miranda Lee Pao
All Rights Reserved
Printed in the United States of America

No part of this publication may be reproduced, stored in a retrieval
system, or transmitted, in any form or by any means, electronic,
mechanical, photocopying, recording, or otherwise, without the prior
written permission of the publisher.

LIBRARIES UNLIMITED, INC.
P.O. Box 3988
Englewood, CO 80155-3988

Library of Congress Cataloging-in-Publication Data

Pao, Miranda Lee.
    Concepts of information retrieval / Miranda Lee Pao.
    xvi, 285 p. 17x25 cm.
    Includes index.
    ISBN 0-87287-405-2
    1. Information retrieval. 2. Information technology. 3. Library
science--Technological innovations. I. Title.
Z699.P29 1988   88-39271
025.5'24--dc 19   CIP

Dedicated to my sister
MARGARET SHOU-SING LEE

Contents

Part I
BASIC PHENOMENA

Part II
INFORMATION RETRIEVAL SYSTEMS

Illustrations

FIGURES

xi

FIGURES *(Continued)*

TABLES

TABLES *(Continued)*

Preface

This book is intended as a text for an introductory course in document-based information retrieval. Although increasingly the retrieval of documents in full text is available, most often this type of retrieval results in information indicating the locations of the actual documents sought. Since the study of information and its transmission is basic to all retrieval problems, this book is also concerned with information science. Unfortunately, the term *information science* has been used to denote many aspects of the study of information in several related disciplines. At the moment, the term is too broad and too vague to be meaningful. Some brief discussion of information science is included in the text only to provide a broad framework to show the functions of retrieval systems.

Readers will note that I have restricted specific technology issues to only a few system's functions. Although computing, telecommunication, and laser technologies have become the driving forces in our field, many of us believe that the centrality of our discipline should be enhanced and served by this new technology and should not be driven by them. Indeed, some believe that the increased accessibility of information via advanced technology has been in part responsible for the information glut. In other words, accessibility becomes the cause of inaccessibility. It is easy to lose sight of what our main concern is by the dazzling capabilities of computers and optical discs. Technologies and instrumentations have an essential, but not independent, role in the development of a discipline, such as information science. The rapid advances in information technologies should be viewed as exploding opportunities for the realization of retrieval systems with greatly enhanced capabilities.

We also believe that there is a definable domain for our discipline that is not covered by nor of primary concern to information professionals in other disciplines. More significantly, even though there is a paucity of theories and laws in the strictest scientific sense, there is a body of concepts, principles, and ideas that are uniquely our own. These abstract constructs and methods have been developed, by and large, independently of the available technologies.

In addition to presenting the concepts underlying existing document-based retrieval systems, I have included selected experimental techniques developed as alternatives to achieving traditional retrieval functions. Many are based on sound principles. With the continuing development of better and more powerful tools, their applications have become realizable.

Lastly, although my main concern is with document-based retrieval systems, I share the view that it is not only a specific type of information retrieval system, but it is also the most complex form of retrieval system. Certainly all retrieval systems including data, record management systems, and knowledge base systems must address the same set of functions, each of which may receive more or less emphasis. Many of the problems and issues associated with these major functions are also common to all information retrieval processes.

This book is divided into three parts. The first deals with basic phenomena involved in our brand of information science. They are information, users, and the concept of relevance. Information is taken to mean literature which are published information resources. The second part presents the main functions of any information retrieval system. Although selection, information representation, file organization, question analysis and search strategy, and dissemination are divisions arbitrarily chosen, they provide an outline for discussion. Readers will note that there is an apparant unevenness in the amount of treatment of each chapter. For example, the chapter on information representation appears to be longer than other chapters. By and large, this is a reflection of the amount of works and attention paid to each area in the past. The third part of the book contains a brief treatment on evaluation. Although one chapter on testing and evaluation is grossly inadequate, it adds to the completeness of the text. Readers are referred to several excellent books on the subject by Kantor, King, Lancaster, and others.

The content and organization of this book is based on my experience in teaching a course originally developed by Tefko Saracevic while he was at Case Western Reserve University. Although I have made numerous changes through the years, his course has served as the basic structure for this book. Dr. Saracevic has reviewed the manuscript and made many constructive comments.

Obviously this book is influenced by the thinking of my former colleagues at Case, specially William Goffman. Collectively, the faculty and students at the Matthew A. Baxter School of Information and Library Science for many years provided an intellectually exciting and challenging environment which has benefited me immeasurably.

The writing of this text has helped to consolidate my own thinking in the field. I am grateful to the National Library of Medicine for the very generous Research Career Development Award. During the five years of support, I have been able to devote my time to study as well as to research some of the works reported here. I owe a particular debt of gratitude to my friend and former colleague, Sarah S. Gibson, who reviewed an earlier version of the manuscript. Her suggestions and insightful criticisms have helped to clarify my presentation. I am also grateful to Laurie S. McCreery. For many years, I have relied upon her for her expert editing. She has made many suggestions in the text. The final version has benefited greatly from their constructive comments, reactions, and suggestions. They have been most generous with their time in helping to make the book more readable. Lastly, I thank my husband, Richard, who is a constant source of challenge and support.

Part I
BASIC PHENOMENA

1
Communication and Information

DEFINITION

Information science was first defined at the Conference on Training Science Information Specialists held in 1961 and 1962 at the Georgia Institute of Technology as

> the science that investigates the properties and behavior of information, the forces governing the flow of information, and the means of processing information for optimum accessibility and usability. The processes include the origination, dissemination, collection, organization, storage, retrieval, interpretation, and use of information. The field is derived from or related to mathematics, logic, linguistics, psychology, computer technology, operations research, the graphic arts, communication, library science, management, and some other fields. (Taylor, 1966)

This statement was quoted by Robert S. Taylor in his article in the 1966 inaugural volume of the *Annual Review of Information Science and Technology*. Although this definition provides a base from which to start, it did not and still does not represent a consensus opinion. Information is the basis of the works of all scholars regardless of their subject matter. The practice of all professions including those of medicine, law, business, and social services, also relies on information. Information forms the foundation of all human existence. In spite of its pervasive presence, its basic nature, properties, and associated processes are not well understood. As a result, one tends to view information from one's own perspective, and to focus on those aspects of the broader field of information as they relate to one's specific discipline, or one's professional activities and concerns. The study of information is often linked with specific types of systems, such as information flow in biological systems, and information management in business information systems. Even among the fields in which the concept of information is central, such as artificial intelligence, cognitive science, communication science, computer science, epistomology, library science, linguistics,

3

neurophysiology, and psychology, there is a wide discrepancy in the terms used to denote similar concepts, and to describe individuals engaged in information-related work. Each field focuses on some properties of information or on aspects of the information transfer process.

Taylor himself recognizes the apparent confusion concerning the extent and scope of the field. He asserts that the field can be viewed in two different, but not incompatible ways: operationally and pedagogically. Operationally, it is seen in a spectrum from services such as libraries through systems design to basic investigations in the supporting sciences. Pedagogically, two components are discerned: an applied science, and a pure science component. He explicitly states that they are "information engineering or technology, and the information sciences." The former is concerned with the development, design, and operation of information systems, including libraries, indexing and abstracting services, and information and data centers. The latter explicates systems and their components and is concerned with the basic sciences underlying system development: neurophysiology, linguistics, mathematics, logic, psychology, sociology, and epistemology. This concept is aptly expressed by Goffman:

> The aim of a discipline of information science must be that of establishing a unified scientific approach to the study of various phenomena involving the notion of information whether such phenomena are found in biological processes, in human existence, or in machines created by human beings. Consequently, the subject must be concerned with the establishment of a set of fundamental principles governing the behavior of all communication processes and their associated information systems. (Goffman, 1970)

Taylor further emphasizes the theoretical, experimental, and operational study of the interface between man and document or organized knowledge, between man and man, and between man and machine, in other words, the behavioral aspects of information processing. Yet the intellectual content of information science as a study area remains a topic of hot debate as evidenced in the writings contained in a collected volume *The Study of Information: Interdisciplinary Messages* (Machlup and Mansfield, 1983). These contributors are eminent scholars from a diverse array of fields − artificial intelligence, cognitive psychology, computer science, cybernetics, general systems, information science, library science, linguistics, and neuroscience. They present many different ways of interpreting the concept of information. One can only deduce that there are numerous disciplines, interdisciplines, metadisciplines, and subdisciplines in which information is the central or peripheral concern.

THE COMMON VIEW
OF INFORMATION

The key to a discussion of the definition of information science is what the word *information* means. Unfortunately, the word has multiple meanings. It is used in different ways by different people in different disciplines. There is little consistency in the way the term is used and defined. Some view it as the product of a mysterious act of the intellect. Others construct information systems to supply specialized needs so that information is viewed as a utility, supplied on a pay-as-you-go basis. Some view it as a commodity supplied on-demand as a documentary product or a service. Although there is no agreement on its meaning, the key role of information in modern society is undisputed. That there is a rapidly growing percentage of the GNP of this nation directly related to the generation, production, processing, and distribution of information has been noted by Bell (1973), Machlup (1979), Price (1963), Branscomb (1979), and others. The term *information age* is frequently used to characterize the present information-oriented society. The high-technology industries of electronics and communication have dominated the economy. Represented by such giants as IBM, AT&T, and others, these information-oriented corporations have not only captured a major market share of business but have also created an unparallel need for information in developing products, and in operating businesses and organizations. For the first time, information resources along with human and capital resources are recognized as indispensable. Harnessing information as a resource means increased productivity. The contribution of information is recognized to be just as significant to business strategy as the financial aspects.

The emphasis on the value of information also has changed the work of the information professionals. New top-level positions with titles such as "chief information manager" or "information officer" signal the rise in the value and status of information systems in the corporate culture (Keefe, 1987). The job of an information officer is no longer that of knowing how the technology works, but what it can do. This is an individual who has access to the chief executive, and may be responsible for the largest capital expenditure in the company. There is an increasing awareness that a commitment in specific information technology for the organization means a substantial investment in the form of hardware and software together with the expertise needed to operate, maintain, and to get the most out of the system. These resources chosen will be with the organization for a very long time.

In managing basic resources such as energy, capital, and human resources, the challenge is to maximize their limited supply. The resource of information is quite different in that it is in surplus. It must therefore be managed in a different way. There appears to be more information around than any one person can use effectively (Branscomb, 1979). The key is to identify and retrieve those relevant and accurate pieces of information and deliver them in a timely fashion. This is known as information retrieval.

Although the scope of the field of information science is difficult to delineate, the subarea, information retrieval, is more well defined. According to Borko (1968), it is an interdisciplinary science primarily concerned with the pragmatic and system-oriented area and with conceptual work directly applicable to information processes. Indeed, in his recent writings, Borko has advocated the term *information library science* to denote the close relationship between these two areas (Borko, 1984). In this text, concepts and applications in information retrieval, particularly those applicable to document retrieval, are presented. Only information embodied in recorded form, notably in paper and machine-readable media, is considered.

In the remaining part of this chapter, the most well-known information theory is briefly introduced together with the problems identified in most communication processes.

SHANNON'S INFORMATION THEORY

It was Claude Shannon who formulated a strict mathematical definition of information in precise quantitative terms. Shannon, a Bell Telephone engineer, was concerned with the engineering problems associated with the transmission of messages via telephone lines. Parameters such as the number of relays, coding, bandwidth, and noise in the channel would have immediate consequences on the design and cost of better communication channels for the telephone company. In 1948, he proposed an information theory in which the parameters needed in the production and transmission of information could be predicted based on the statistical nature of the originating message source. His paper together with a paper on communication theory by Warren Weaver has been published as a single volume, *The Mathematical Theory of Communication*, now a classic in information theory (Shannon and Weaver, 1949).

In a much simplified version, all communication processes can be generalized in a simple model consisting of five parts (see Figure 1.1). These five parts are:

1. Information source produces messages which are transmitted to the receiving destination. Messages may be of various types, for example, a sequence of letters as in telegraphic transmission.

2. Transmitter operates on the message in some way to produce a signal suitable for transmission over the chosen channel, for example, in telegraphy, this entails an encoding of dots and dashes.

3. Channel is the medium used to transmit the signal from the transmitter to the receiver. It can be a beam of light, a band of radio frequency, etc. Noise in the channel can distort the quality of signals.

4. Receiver performs the reverse function of the transmitter. It accepts and decodes signals into information.

5. Destination is the person or thing for whom the message is intended.

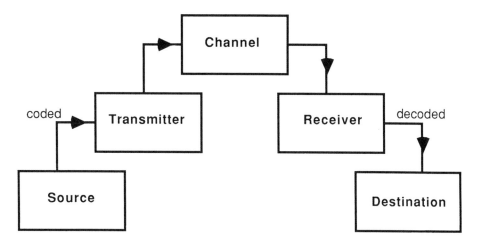

Fig. 1.1. Shannon-Weaver communication model (adaptation).

Weaver warned that the information in Shannon's theory is used in a special sense that must not be confused with its ordinary usage (Shannon and Weaver, 1949). In particular, information must not be confused with meaning. Two ideas are central to Shannon's notion of information. In the first place, the informativeness of a message is that property which reduces uncertainty in the intended recipient. In any situation, information about something one already knows is informationally worthless. If one considers only those messages intended by a specific originating source to be informative to a specific receiver, those messages can be more or less informative depending on how much they are able to remove uncertainty in the recipient. In other words, information is concerned with the degree of change to the knowledge state of the recipient as compared with the original state prior to the exposure of the message. The change in the recipient's cognitive state is a reflection of the informational content of a message received. This adjustment of one's cognitive framework is predicated upon certain conditions. First, the messages must be physically receivable by the recipient. They must be understood, and finally, the recipient should be able to validate them.

This notion may be illustrated by an example. If a student who is already a skillful programmer is compelled to attend introductory lectures on Pascal programming, the lectures would be of no informational value to him. Information about something already known to the individual is worthless information. On the other hand, if the individual is not familiar with computer programming, has some logical reasoning aptitude, and is able to attend the classes, these lectures on Pascal could be very informative. This implies that the transmitted message must lie within the receiver's field of experience. Simply stated, for the message to have some utility, it should be appropriate for the receiver in terms of his or her background so that it is comprehensible.

The second idea is that "information is a measure of one's freedom of choice when one selects a message." The measure of information is associated with the available number of messages when a specific one is chosen. Shannon's measure of information is based on the size of the reservoir or pool of possible messages from which the appropriate ones are eventually selected and transmitted. This is an unusual way to think about information. Unlike the concept of meaning, which is applicable to individual messages, this concept of information applies to the total information source as a whole which is expressed in statistical terms. Hence, it is possible to describe the capacity of the communication channel in terms of the amount of information it can transmit. This is the most reduced form of communication, namely, the transmission of signals without regard to what is being transmitted, or how effective it is to the destination. However limited this notion of information is, this theory became extremely useful particularly to Shannon in his capacity as a communication engineer. For the first time, information, more precisely, signal flow, could be measured.

To illustrate, suppose only three symbols, A, B, and C are available at an information source. Also suppose if each message must consist of three relays of symbols, there are a total of 27 messages possible from the information source. They are:

AAB	AAC	BBA	BBC	CCA	CCB
BAA	CAA	ABB	CBB	BCC	ACC
ABA	ACA	BAB	BCB	CAC	CBC
ABC	BAC	CAB	ACB	BCA	CBA
AAA	BBB	CCC			

Mathematically, the total number of possible messages is computed as p^n where p is the number of available symbols and n is the number of relays per message. At the time of the systems design, the messages eventually selected for transmission would be unknown. Thus, the transmitting system must be designed to accommodate every possible message available for selection, and not merely the actual one(s) chosen. Since the number of messages in a given set is always finite, this number, or some function of it, can be viewed as a measure of information produced for any one message chosen from this particular set. In a broad sense, Shannon's measure is based on the statistical structure of the message source or the potentiality of the information source.

THREE LEVELS OF THE COMMUNICATION PROBLEM

The opening statement of Weaver's article, "Recent Contributions to the Mathematical Theory of Communication," contained in the text by Shannon and Weaver states that "the word communication will be used here in a very broad sense to include all of the procedures by which one mind may affect another" (Shannon and Weaver, 1949). He noted that there are three levels of problems in dealing with communication which must be overcome: the technical or physical problems, the semantic or representational problems, and the effectiveness or behavioral problems (see Figure 1.2).

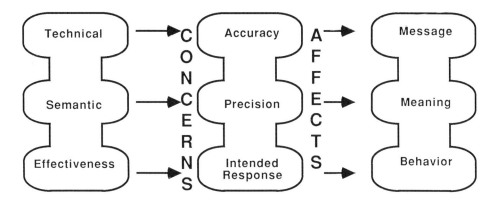

Fig. 1.2. Three levels of the communication problem.

The technical or physical problems have to do with the accuracy with which the symbols of communication are transmitted. Concern is strictly with the engineering problems associated with the transmission of codes, messages, waves, or symbols which, in turn, affect the channel capacity for a chosen transmitting source, the coding process, the capacity of the equipment used, and the tolerable noise level.

The semantic or representational problems have to do with the precision with which the transmitted symbols convey the intended meaning. Focus is on the words used in the message, and the interpretation of meaning by the receiver as compared to the meaning intended by the sender. Words have different shades of meaning. It is entirely possible for the intended meaning to be interpreted differently by the receiver. Thus, depending on the inflection used, *yes* can be interpreted as a question, an affirmative response, or a final definite affirmation.

The effectiveness or behavioral problems have to do with the success with which information conveyed from the sender to the destination affects some desired conduct at the destination. It is concerned with the effect of the conveyed message. Clearly, even when the problems at the technical and semantic levels are solved, there is no guarantee that the desired outcome will be achieved. The behavioral problems depend on factors not controlled at all by the information system. Yet the behavioral outcome is the ultimate aim of any effective communication.

At the technical level, Shannon's theory neatly summarized and clarified the engineering considerations of message transmission. Shannon provided the communication engineer with a useful measure of the commodity, information, which is transmitted. He showed how to measure the information rate of a message source, such as the output of a television camera transmitted per second. He also showed how to measure the capacity of a channel used for communication, such as a telephone line. As a result, better transmission systems can be designed. His theory is universal in application to all forms of messages, all media of transmission, and all modes of communication. This major step toward the understanding of the properties of information has formed the foundation of modern communication theory. His theory has yet to be superceded. However, it is important to note that it was never meant to solve the semantic nor the effectiveness problems of communication. These are irrelevant to the engineering considerations of communication. On the other hand, the technical aspects are necessary preconditions for the success of the other two levels of communication. Inaccurately transmitted messages cannot be expected to convey the intended meaning nor to affect desired conduct. Information in Shannon's theory is meant to be quantified for the purpose of accurate signal transmission. In its limited sense, his theory is elegant in its formulation and powerful in its applications. A broader treatment of communication and information can be found in the landmark publication by Cherry (1978).

Before concluding this section, it should be pointed out that it would be grossly inadequate to limit the study of information to the narrow definition used in Shannon's theory. The meaning of the message sent and how it is received and used are legitimate concerns of anyone interested in information and communication. The reader only needs to scan through the collected volume edited by Fritz Machlup and Una Mansfield to see that several groups of scholars are deeply involved in *cognitive information* as opposed to *information*. Cognitive scientists are concerned with the study of the principles by which intelligent entities interact with their environment and with the activity of knowing. The field of cognitive science is a relatively young discipline. It has several subareas including those of cognitive psychology. Individuals in other disciplines, such as information science and artificial intelligence, not only are closely monitoring developments from cognitive sciences, but also are inching toward different aspects of the same direction. Although quantifiable results are still lacking, much insight has been gained in how people learn and how information is processed and utilized.

INFORMATION IN
KNOWLEDGE COMMUNICATION

Philosophers from Aristotle on have attempted to distinguish between the related concepts of ideas, data, information, and knowledge. An idea is said to be an atomic unit of our intellect. Data are sets of symbols representing captured evidence of activities, transactions, and events. Information can be viewed as that which carries ideas, or as selected and manipulated data. Knowledge is processed information which has produced a change in the intellectual framework of learning within an individual. It is understood that not all contacts between information and individuals result in knowledge acquisition.

Clearly, these are circular definitions. One cannot clearly distinguish between *idea, data, information*, and *knowledge*. In the epilogue to *The Study of Information* (1983), Machlup eloquently explained the meaning of information and presented a list of definitions for *cognitive information* that incorporated the concept of meaning. Nevertheless, information may be reasonably considered a primitive concept, as are energy, electricity, distance, power, and work. One understands each of them intuitively, but there are no adequate definitions for them. Their lack of precise definition has not prevented men and women from studying their properties, behaviors, and interrelationships within systems and organizations. As a result of better understanding, these intuitive concepts have been adequately harnessed and have become measurable commodities serving society. A parallel may be made for information.

Although most information activities occur in the mind, some of them do take on physical manifestations. People communicate by writing and by conversing. Even though recorded forms of communication are only crude forms of representing what goes on in the mind, they do serve an important role in formal scholarly communication. Historically, pioneers in information science have been concerned with documentation and bibliographic control of the graphic records of human communication. Therefore, their works have concentrated on the phenomena of information within the arena of knowledge communication processes, that is, formal communication by means of publications of journal articles and books, and all other forms of scholarly exchange of information. In other words, the chief concern of these individuals was to provide better access to available literature resources, thus disseminating information more effectively. Issues of selectivity, organization, identification, control, storage, retrieval, and dissemination of knowledge are central to the design and development of information retrieval systems. Recently, developments in electronic technology have revolutionized the concept of information, and have introduced many new physical forms of communication.

For better understanding of the phenomena of communication and information that are basic to information transfer, flow, and use, characteristics of literature have been systematically studied. Literature is often regarded in the context of specific subjects. So far, research in information retrieval has focused on specific subject literatures that are the recorded representations of a field of knowledge as created by individuals. Such publications are published, reviewed, read, cited, borrowed, explained, copied, circulated, abstracted, and indexed. Thus, each of these processes can be studied in terms of its relevant observable parameters. In the next chapter, the major findings of the studies of literature will be presented as well as some of the analytic methods utilized.

REFERENCES

Bell, D. 1973. *The Coming of the Post-Industrial Society*. New York: Basic Books.

Borko, H. 1968. "Information Science: What Is It?" *American Documentation*, 19(1):3-5.

Borko, H. 1984. "Trends in Library and Information Science Education." *Journal of the American Society for Information Science*, 35(3):185-193.

Branscomb, L.M. 1979. "Information: The Ultimate Frontier." *Science*, 203(4376):143-147.

Cherry, C. 1978. *On Human Communication*. Cambridge, Massachusetts: MIT Press.

Goffman, W. 1970. "Information Science: Discipline or Disappearance." *Aslib Proceedings*, 22(12):589-595.

Keefe, L.M. 1987. "More Room at the Top." *Forbes*, 139:102-104.

Kochen, M. 1984. "Information Science Research: The Search for the Nature of Information." *Journal of the American Society for Information Science*, 35(3):194-199.

Machlup, F. 1979. *The Production and Distribution of Knowledge in the United States*. 2nd edition. Princeton, New Jersey: Princeton University Press.

Machlup, F., and U. Mansfield., eds. 1983. *The Study of Information: Interdisciplinary Messages*. New York: John Wiley and Sons.

Price, D.J.D. 1963. *Little Science, Big Science*. New York: Columbia University Press.

Price, D.J.D. 1965. "Networks of Scientific Papers." *Science,* 149(3683):510-515.

Shannon, C.E., and W. Weaver. 1949. *The Mathematical Theory of Communication*. Urbana, Illinois: University of Illinois Press.

Taylor, R.S. 1966. "Professional Aspects of Information Science and Technology." *Annual Review of Information Science and Technology*, edited by Carlos A. Cuadra. Vol. 1, 15-40. Chicago: Encyclopaedia Britannica.

2

Literature

BIBLIOMETRICS

Bibliometrics is a term introduced by Alan Pritchard in his article, "Statistical Bibliography or Bibliometrics," (Pritchard, 1969), to denote the field of study which uses mathematical and statistical methods to investigate and to quantify the processes of written communication. He noted that literature is a key ingredient in the present knowledge communication process. The attributes of the units of literature which exist in published form, that is, journal articles and books, can be studied in statistical terms. For example, a publication is often authored by an individual. Therefore, an author can be associated with the document. This document is meant to be read by people. One may observe the use of this document by its circulation records within an institution, by the number of times reprints were requested, by the number of photocopies made, or by the number of times it was cited, and so on. A specific publisher is usually responsible for publication. It is possible to examine and predict the probability that publications on similar topics would be published by the same publisher. In the case of journal articles, the subject coverage of specific journals may be detected. One might even study the author's output in the specific subject domain. Therefore, publications, authors, users, citations, and journals are some of the observable parameters in literature studies. Bibliometric studies seek to quantify, describe, and predict the processes of written communication.

Bibliometric studies of literature are important for the following reasons:

1. Quantification and measurement of activities and processes can identify areas of deficiency within existing information systems whose major concern is documents. Such data can then be used for better planning and management of information services. Systematic analysis can also provide improved design of document retrieval systems.

2. Past statistics can offer clues for predicting future use and trends so that needed services may be anticipated.

3. Basic and applied research can advance the knowledge of communication. It can also foster understanding of the underlying mechanism governing the generation and transmission of information, thus contributing to a science of information.

Bibliometric studies may be classified according to three essential attributes of literature: (1) the physical object of the literature unit; (2) its creation and subject content; and (3) its use. This chapter covers the first two attributes, but, since there is such a large volume of studies regarding users and literature use, the entire third chapter will be devoted exclusively to this third attribute.

SPECIFIC PROPERTIES OF LITERATURE INVESTIGATED

Object: Nature of Scientific Literature

Historically bibliometric studies have concentrated on the literature of the physical and biological sciences. Following the extraordinarily intensive scientific activities surrounding the secret development of the atomic bomb, peaceful application of such knowledge was delayed, although many saw much potential use of the knowledge. With normal information dissemination resumed beginning with the postwar period, attention shifted swiftly to industrial and commercial applications of nuclear power and other scientific knowledge. Additionally, generous funding from both private and public sources has stimulated an increased outpouring of research. Consequently, the rapid growth of scientific and technical literatures after World War II has exacerbated storage and access problems. For the scientist, the problem of keeping up with the growing volume of new knowledge threatens both productivity and research quality. Therefore, methods must be developed to identify and retrieve needed information and to weed out the nonessential. This is the primary function of information retrieval systems.

There are three forms of scientific publications:

1. Primary publications
   - Periodicals – general and specialized
   - Books – monographs, dissertations, patents, and technical reports
   - Data – numeric, statistical, textual, and coded

2. Secondary publications
   - Abstracts
   - Indexes
   - Bibliographies

3. Tertiary publications
   - Reviews – periodic and irregular review articles
   - Encyclopedias, dictionaries, manuals, and handbooks
   - Textbooks

Science is totally dependent on the present system of communication via the primary literature. Ziman (1969) claimed that the preeminence of science in the western world can be attributed to the establishment of the scientific journal as the primary means of communication. He has noted three essential characteristics of scientific literature. This literature is *fragmentary*, *derivative*, and *edited*.

Examination of a typical scientific paper will show that its contribution is often modest. The author usually attempts to explain, analyze, or verify a small definable piece of a grander scheme. Historically, by amalgamating these individual fragmentary efforts, the totality of scientific knowledge has been able to progress at a rapid pace. The scientific journal has provided an efficient means for the exchange and sharing of information. This interdependent behavior is unique with scientists. In contrast, although artistic and humanistic works are obviously affected by the contemporary social milieu, artists and scholars in the humanities tend to work alone and produce independent contributions.

Secondly, scientific papers are derivative for they rely heavily on previous research. The most obvious evidence of this is the list of bibliographic references at the end of every paper. These references provide a context within which the work is placed. Unlike the arts, in which insights and understanding may only be indirectly traced, scientific works almost always draw upon previous principles, methods, apparatus, techniques, or theories.

Thirdly, as Watson's *The Double Helix* (1968) and Zuckerman's work on Nobel laureates (Zuckerman, 1967) indicate, research often stumbles and takes wrong turns, yet one has never heard of a journal of unsuccessful experiments. All reported works appear to lead from well-thought-out plans to infallible successes. Therefore, scientific papers are heavily edited and contrived. This same editing process also incorporates a rigorous quality control mechanism. Peer review is built into the process of scientific publication. By and large, this external censorship in the form of anonymous referees insures the accuracy and honesty of research, so that one can build on works by others without having to replicate and verify previous works. The fact that worthwhile works must be written and published insures the availability of information to one's peers and promotes information exchange.

Since individual papers are scattered among different journals, the problems of retrieval and access are staggering. Secondary publications are designed to organize and to provide access to primary literature. Due to this piecemeal approach to scientific communication, there is a need for several stages of intellectual synthesis. These are accomplished in the form of state-of-the-art reviews and monographs. Such secondary publications are also scrutinized by peer reviews. Experts are usually commissioned to write reviews, so that they can filter out the significant and influential ideas and place them in perspective within a larger framework. In time, textbooks, encyclopedias, and other tertiary publications are published. Each forms another level of synthesis that extracts key ideas in the primary literature and gives them another organized and logical presentation.

Object: Size and Growth

In *Little Science, Big Science*, a seminal work in information science, Price (1963) first presented concrete statistical data on the phenomenon of the exponential growth of literature. Between 1660 and 1960, that is, from the establishment of the first known scientific journals, the *Philosophical Transactions of the Royal Society* and *Journal des Sçavans*, to the writing of *Little Science, Big Science*, the number of scientific papers has been doubling every 15 years. So powerful is this compounding effect that if one had started with merely a single paper in 1660, by 1977, there would have been an accumulation of nearly 2.3 million papers (see Figure 2.1). Although definitive data on the actual growth of scientific journal literature is lacking, there is strong evidence to support Price's projection. For example, Bearman reported that there were 2.2 million documents processed by members of the National Federation of Abstracting and Indexing Services alone in 1977. Such exponential growth is also corroborated by the King report (King, Lancaster, McDonald, Roderer, and Wood, 1976) which estimated 18,800 journal titles in the world in 1960 growing to 49,440 in 1974, and 6,335 in 1960 in the United States growing to 8,460 in 1974. Thus, this rate of growth cannot be attributed to any single event. One may conclude that it is part of the nature of science.

What is even more startling is Price's conclusion that most of the scientists who have ever lived are presently alive at any given point in time (Price, 1965). As a result, over 80 percent of the totality of scientific activities that has ever occurred is happening within our living memory. Price named this the immediacy factor of science, and it is the direct result of the consistent compounding growth of literature over the last three centuries. Figure 2.2 provides an illustration.

Suppose the number of scientists doubles every 15 years. At year t, the total number of scientists is x. Fifteen years later, at year $(t + 15)$, there should be $2x$ number of scientists; 30 years later at year $(t + 30)$, there should be $4x$ number of scientists; at year $(t + 45)$, there should be $8x$ (or 2 to the power of 3) number of scientists accumulated. Assuming that the active life of a scientist is 45 years, at year $(t + 45)$, the first group of x number of scientists would have retired from active professional lives. Thus, $8x - x$ (or $7x$) number of scientists would have been left active at that time. Since the total number of scientists who ever lived at year $(t + 45)$ is $8x$, proportionally speaking, for every eight scientists who have ever lived, seven are alive today. Since publishing is an integral part of scientific career, the volume of literature is directly proportional to the number of active scientists. Therefore, today's problem regarding the oversupply of information has been a problem for three centuries. And it will probably continue. One recalls that the motivation for the establishment of the first scientific journal was to monitor and digest the learned publications of that time. Thus, the urgency of the literature problem did not start with the World Wars. In fact, Price's data shows that the influence of war on the loss of personnel and the suppression of scientific results due to secrecy of information had only a slight, lateral displacement effect. Except for the two brief pauses, the rate of growth was unaffected.

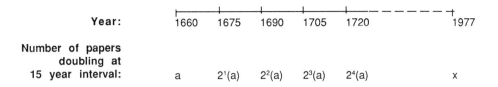

Number of papers
doubling at
15 year interval:

$$x = 2^{(1977-1660)/15}$$

$$= 2^{21.133}$$

$$= 2,299,677$$

Assuming that a = 1, or there was only one paper published in 1660,
the total number of papers accumulated in in 1977 would be

Fig. 2.1. Doubling effect of scientific literature.

	15 years	15 years	15 years	15 years	
Year:	t	t+15	t+30	t+45	t+60

Number of Scientists: x $2^1(x)$ $2^2(x)$ $2^3(x)$ $2^4(x)$

At year = (t+ 45), the number of scientists who ever lived = $2^3(x)$

= 8x

At the same time, the number of scientists retired = x

The number of active scientists = 8x - x
= 7x

Therefore, 7x/8x or 87.5% of all scientists who ever lived
are active at any given point in time.

Fig. 2.2. Immediacy factor in the growth of science.

Object: Half-life and Obsolescence

The term *half-life* has been borrowed from physics (Line, 1970). It is defined as the time required for half of the atoms of a radioactive substance present to become disintegrated. Information and literature do not become disintegrated. Instead, the value of information increases with usage. In terms of the use of literature, half-life has been interpreted as the time during which half of the total use of individual items has been or is expected to be made. Some investigators interpret use as the number of times these items are circulated in a library, or as the number of citations made to these items. Half-life may also be quantified as the number of years in which half of all bibliographic references of a given subject are cited. For example, half of all references cited in the literature of chemistry were reported to be papers less than eight years old. Half of all references in physics were made to writings less than five years old. If these figures were still true today, physicists tend to draw on more recent publications than chemists (Price, 1963).

In terms of the availability of literature in a subject, half-life is interpreted as the time required for half of all currently active literature in the subject to be published. That is, if one examines the publication dates of all the literature of a subject, one will find that half of the total literature is usually published within the last few years. For example, considering all the literature that has ever been published in the subject of computational musicology up to 1977, half of that amount had been published within the previous seven years (see Table 2.1). Therefore, the half-life of literature in computational musicology is seven. For physics, the half-life is ten; for mathematics, the half-life is between twenty and twenty- five years. One may conclude that the publication rate of physics is much higher than that of mathematics.

The concept of useful half-life has many applications. For example, it has been applied to the library use of bound journals in an attempt to evaluate their worth. Half-life and obsolescence are related (Line and Sandison, 1974, 1975). In scientific libraries, the useful half-life of all journals is about ten years. In other words, half of all circulated bound journals are concentrated in those published within the last ten years. The other half are drawn from the vast collection of older journals. That is, after ten years, bound journal volumes are hardly used. It is most tempting to utilize such data in establishing guidelines for a library policy on weeding, retention, microform substitution, and secondary storage designations. Additionally, since the growth of literature is geometric and available shelf space is finite, a logical use of the most accessible space is to display the most used items. Others have used the concept of half-life to evaluate journal titles by comparing the time elapsed between the publications of articles in a given journal and their being cited by others. The implication is that if they are cited shortly after they are published, then they are being used and read with intense interest.

Another way of looking at literature obsolescence is that current publications tend to be more circulated, browsed through, and cited because there are proportionally more of such current materials. Studies have shown indeed that older works are less used.

Table 2.1
Half-life of the Subject Literature of Computational Musicology

Year of Publication	# of Publications	Cumulative # of Publications	% Cumulation
1975	20	20	2.15
1974	35	55	5.92
1973	45	100	10.75
1972	59	159	17.10
1971	89	248	26.67
1970	114	362	38.93
1969	88	450	48.39
1968	70	520	55.91
1967	87	607	65.27
1966	55	662	71.18
1965	66	728	78.28
1964	36	764	82.15
1963	28	792	85.16
1962	32	824	88.60
1961	18	842	90.54
1960	17	859	92.37
1959	21	880	94.62
1958	14	894	96.13
1957	8	902	96.99
1956	17	919	98.82
1955	1	920	98.93
1954	1	921	99.03
1953	5	926	99.57
1951	3	929	99.89
1949	1	930*	100.00

*Excluding 8 undated publications.

Object: Citations

One important attribute of literature is that most scholarly publications contain a list of bibliograhic references. This practice of citation has provided information scientists with a convenient and handy measure of subject relationship (Smith, 1981). The relevance of a publication is usually judged by scanning its content. Since authors cite to substantiate claims and to acknowledge the use of previously proposed theories or results, citation is an explicit acknowledgement by the author of the influence of specific previous scholarship (Garfield, 1979). It gives an unobtrusive link between related documents. In addition to the use of references to relate one's work to a larger framework of science, the practice of citation also allows the author to lay claim to newly discovered knowledge and to set priority by such acts. One cites to give credence to one's work. It is a time-honored tradition in all scholarly writings.

Since the terms *reference* and *citation* tend to be used interchangeably, the following example will be used to clarify their differences. Paper *A* contains a reference to paper *P*. By necessity, paper *P* is published prior to paper *A*. Paper *P* is cited by paper *A*. *A* contains a reference *P*; *P* has a citation from *A*. The number of references a paper has is measured by the number of items in its bibliographic list. The number of citations a paper has up to year *t*, is found by looking up the paper in a citation index from its year of publication to year *t*. One checks to see in how many papers it may have been cited.

Since citations are explicit, frequency distributions of citations over a given period can easily be ascertained. Focusing on citations to a given item over a given time can be graphed. One item's relation with another item can be established by the common references contained in both items (Kessler, 1963). Their relation can also be viewed by their being cited together in subsequent publications (Small, 1973). By analyzing the cocitation relationship of journals and publications in a given discipline, the structure of the subject could be graphically displayed in terms of highly interactive conceptual classes of documents (Small and Griffith, 1974; Griffith, Small, Stonehill, and Dey, 1974). More recently, the technique of cocitation analysis of authors has been used to create a realistic map of contributors active in information science (White and Griffith, 1981).

Since a citation establishes a relation between two items, that is, item *A* cites item *B*, the linkage is directional in that two papers cannot cite each other. A network of citation can be represented by a directed graph. In sum, citation offers a ready means for quantification if one accepts the premise that a citation link normally implies a certain subject relationship, even if the specific relationship is unspecified (Smith, 1981). Citations can provide an unobtrusive, objective means of measurement of subject relatedness among scholarly documents. In the last twenty years, the *Science Citation Index* and its companion indexes have made citation studies possible.

Price (1965) has identified two populations of references which appear to reflect certain characteristics of citations in science. He noted that 50 percent of all citations were found to refer to an exceptionally hyperactive group of publications of rather recent vintage. This increased use of current papers over and above the natural growth of the literature forms a special core. This is known as the research front which has been found to be largely responsible for major advances in scientific knowledge. It appears to be unique in science. A small group of authors and a small group of publications exert major influence in a given scientific subject. These individuals are leaders in the field. They are much cited, and citations to their works follow unusual patterns. The rest of the citations are distributed fairly evenly over all of the past literature with decreasing frequency. Content in this large body of much less used literature can be repackaged into a more compact and usable textbook form to facilitate usage. At the same time, an alerting service to disseminate papers from the research front can keep scientists up-to-date with the latest advances in their subject.

Creation and Content: Authors and Their Productivity

Lotka's Law of author productivity states that the total number of authors y in a given subject, each producing x publications, is inversely proportional to some exponential function n of x (Lotka, 1926), i.e.,

$$x^n . y = C \tag{1}$$

where x = number of publications,

y = number of authors credited with x publications,

n = constant,

C = constant.

For scientific subjects, n is approximately equal to 2, i.e.,

$$x^2 . y = C$$

Therefore, in a comprehensive bibliography of a subject, one can expect to find a small core of authors who are responsible for a large number of its publications. The number of authors publishing x number of papers is roughly equal to the total number of authors producing one paper divided by the square of x. This is known as the inverse square law of scientific productivity.

	Number of authors produced x papers
If number of single paper author is ($x = 1$)	100,
Then number of authors producing 2 papers is ($x = 2$)	100/4 or 25.
(total number of papers by authors each with 2 papers = 50)	
number of authors producing 3 papers is ($x = 3$)	100/9 or 11.
(total number of papers by authors each with 3 papers = 33)	
number of authors producing 4 papers is ($x = 4$)	100/16 or 6.
(total number of papers by authors each with 4 papers = 24)	
number of authors producing 5 papers is ($x = 5$)	100/25 or 4.
(total number of papers by authors each with 5 papers = 20.)	

Subsequent values for x may be substituted in a like manner.

In the studies reported, as few as 5 percent of the total number of authors may be producing half of the total literature of a given subject. On the average, less than 10 percent of the authors in a field are responsible for half of the literature, and as a group, 75 percent of the total group of authors produce less than 25 percent of the literature. There are a few higher producers among many less productive authors. There is a great disparity of productivity among workers in a field.

Lotka's Law has been tested by several investigators on several sets of data. So far, except for a few data sets sampled by unorthodox methods, conformity to the law has been consistent (Pao, 1985a). It has been shown that the inverse square law is a specific case. The two constants n and C should be optimally determined from the data set to be tested. This test is illustrated with Chemical Abstract data and data taken from Auerbach's bibliography originally shown in Lotka's paper. The values of n are computed by the least square method using the logarithmic values of the numbers or percentages of authors who have made 1, 2, 3, ... contributions to the chosen subject and the logarithmic values of these numbers 1, 2, 3, ... of contributions (see Tables 2.2 and 2.3, pages 23-24).

Table 2.2
Calculation of n for Chemical Abstract Data

1	2	3	4	5	6
x	y	$X = \log x$	$Y = \log y$	XY	XX
1	3991	0.0000	3.6011	0.0000	0.0000
2	1059	0.3010	3.0249	0.9106	0.0906
3	493	0.4771	2.6929	1.2848	0.2276
4	287	0.6021	2.4579	1.4798	0.3625
5	184	0.6990	2.2648	1.5830	0.4886
6	131	0.7782	2.1173	1.6476	0.6055
7	113	0.8451	2.0531	1.7351	0.7142
8	85	0.9031	1.9294	1.7424	0.8156
9	64	0.9542	1.8062	1.7235	0.9106
10	65	1.0000	1.8129	1.8129	1.0000
11	41	1.0414	1.6128	1.6795	1.0845
12	47	1.0792	1.6721	1.8045	1.1646
13	32	1.1139	1.5052	1.6767	1.2409
14	28	1.1461	1.4472	1.6586	1.3136
15	21	1.1761	1.3222	1.5551	1.3832
16	24	1.2041	1.3802	1.6620	1.4499
17	18	1.2305	1.2553	1.5446	1.5140
18	19	1.2553	1.2788	1.6052	1.5757
19	17	1.2788	1.2305	1.5734	1.6352
20	14	1.3010	1.1461	1.4912	1.6927
21	9	1.3222	0.9542	1.2617	1.7483
22	11	1.3424	1.0414	1.3980	1.8021
23	8	1.3617	0.9031	1.2298	1.8543
24	8	1.3802	0.9031	1.2465	1.9050
25	9	1.3979	0.9542	1.3340	1.9541
26	9	1.4150	0.9543	1.3502	2.0022
27	8	1.4314	0.9031	1.2927	2.0488
28	10	1.4472	1.0000	1.4472	2.0943
29	8	1.4624	0.9032	1.3207	2.1386
30	7	1.4771	0.8451	1.2483	2.1819
		32.4236	46.9721	43.2991	38.9988

$$n = \frac{N\Sigma XY - \Sigma X \, \Sigma Y}{N \Sigma X^2 - (\Sigma X)^2}$$

$$= \frac{30(43.2991) - (32.4236)\,(46.9721)}{30(38.9988) - (32.4236)^2}$$

$$= -1.8878$$

Table 2.3
Calculation of n for Auerbach's Data

1	2	3	4	5	6
x	y	$X = \log x$	$Y = \log y$	XY	XX
1	784	0.0000	2.8943	0.0000	0.0000
2	204	0.3010	2.3096	0.6953	0.0906
3	127	0.4771	2.1038	1.0038	0.2276
4	50	0.6021	1.6990	1.0229	0.3625
5	33	0.6990	1.5185	1.0614	0.4886
6	28	0.7782	1.4472	1.1261	0.6055
7	19	0.8451	1.2788	1.0807	0.7142
8	19	0.9031	1.2788	1.1548	0.8156
9	6	0.9542	0.7782	0.7426	0.9106
10	7	1.0000	0.8451	0.8451	1.0000
11	6	1.0414	0.7782	0.8104	1.0845
12	7	1.0792	0.8451	0.9120	1.1646
13	4	1.1139	0.6021	0.6707	1.2409
14	4	1.1461	0.6021	0.6900	1.3136
15	5	1.1761	0.6990	0.8221	1.3832
16	3	1.2041	0.4771	0.5745	1.4499
17	3	1.2305	0.4771	0.5871	1.5140
		14.5511	20.6337	13.7993	14.3658

$$n = \frac{17(13.7993) - (14.5511)(20.6338)}{17(14.3659) - (14.5511)^2}$$

$$= -2.0210$$

The constant C may be estimated by substituting the absolute value of n into the following formula:

$$C = 1/\left[\sum_{1}^{P-1} 1/x^n + 1/(n-1)(P^{n-1}) + 1/2P^n + n/24(P-1)^{n+1} \right]$$

Where P is estimated to be 20, and x assumed the value from 1 to 20. The constants n and C for the Chemical Abstract data set were found to be 1.878 and 0.5669 respectively; and for the Auerbach data 2.021 and 0.6151. The statistical test, Kolmogorov-Smirnov test, appears to be the most appropriate test of goodness-of-fit between a set of actual data and the theoretical construct according to Lotka. Tables 2.4 (pages 26-27) and 2.5 (page 28) show the results. Since the maximum D value for the Chemical Abstract data falls outside of the critical value 0.0196, the null hypothesis that this set of data conforms to Lotka's Law is rejected. On the other hand, the maximum D value for the Auerbach data is 0.0253 which lies within the critical value of 0.0448. Thus Lotka's inverse power law does apply to the Auerbach data. For further detail on the procedure for testing for conformity, the reader is referred to Pao's paper (1985) published in *Information Processing and Management*, listed in the reference section at the end of this chapter.

There are two schools of thought regarding the role of the individual scientist in the advancement of science. Ziman (1969) and Kuhn (1962) have both emphasized the collaborative achievements of scientists as the unique hallmark of science. They believe that the work of all scientists in filling the missing bits according to a paradigm and in discovering pieces in an existing system is necessary for the production of major scientific advancements. On the other hand, Price (1963), Crane (1972), Crawford (1971), Cole and Cole (1972), and Griffith and Mullins (1972) have found evidence of elites and elitism in science. They found that the "invisible college" in any field is the powerful moving force in any scientific area. Its members are the most influential and productive. They are the gatekeepers who serve on national reviewing committees that determine research funding and accceptance for publication in professional journals. They control research direction and funding. Their usual association with quality academic departments also allows them to shape the educational programs and the training of young scientists. Thus, they play key roles in information dissemination and exchange. Characteristics of both forces seem to be at work.

Table 2.4

Kolmogorov-Smirnov Test of Observed and Expected Distributions
of Senior Authors in Chemical Abstracts

Observed				Theoretical		
1	2	3	4	5	6	7
# Paper	# Author	% Authors	Cum of Authors	Expected % Authors	Expected Cum of Authors	D
x	y	$f_o(y_x) = y_x/\Sigma y_x$	$\Sigma f_o(y_x)$	$f_e(y_x)^*$	$\Sigma f_e(y_x)$	$\|\Sigma f_o(y_x) - \Sigma f_e(y_x)\|$
1	3991	0.5792	0.5792	0.5669	0.5669	0.0123
2	1059	0.1537	0.7328	0.1532	0.7201	0.0127
3	493	0.0715	0.8044	0.0712	0.7913	0.0131
4	287	0.0416	0.8460	0.0414	0.8327	0.0133
5	184	0.0267	0.8727	0.0272	0.8598	0.0129
6	131	0.0190	0.8917	0.0192	0.8791	0.0126
7	113	0.0164	0.9081	0.0144	0.8935	0.0146
8	85	0.0123	0.9205	0.0112	0.9047	0.0158
9	64	0.0093	0.9298	0.0090	0.9136	0.0162
10	65	0.0094	0.9392	0.0073	0.9209	0.0183
11	41	0.0060	0.9451	0.0061	0.9271	0.0180
12	47	0.0068	0.9520	0.0052	0.9323	0.0197
13	32	0.0046	0.9566	0.0045	0.9367	0.0199
14	28	0.0041	0.9607	0.0039	0.9406	0.0201
15	21	0.0030	0.9637	0.0034	0.9440	0.0197
16	24	0.0035	0.9672	0.0030	0.9471	0.0201
17	18	0.0026	0.9698	0.0027	0.9498	0.0200
18	19	0.0028	0.9726	0.0024	0.9522	0.0204
19	17	0.0025	0.9750	0.0022	0.9544	0.0206
20	14	0.0020	0.9771	0.0020	0.9563	0.0208**
21	9	0.0013	0.9784	0.0018	0.9581	0.0203
22	11	0.0016	0.9800	0.0017	0.9598	0.0202
23	8	0.0012	0.9811	0.0015	0.9613	0.0198
24	8	0.0012	0.9823	0.0014	0.9627	0.0196
25	9	0.0013	0.9836	0.0013	0.9640	0.0196
26	9	0.0013	0.9849	0.0012	0.9652	0.0197
27	8	0.0012	0.9861	0.0011	0.9663	0.0198
28	10	0.0015	0.9875	0.0011	0.9674	0.0201
29	8	0.0012	0.9887	0.0010	0.9684	0.0203
30	7	0.0012	0.9897	0.0009	0.9693	0.0204
31	3	0.0004	0.9901	0.0009	0.9702	0.0199
32	3	0.0004	0.9906	0.0008	0.9710	0.0196
33	6	0.0009	0.9914	0.0008	0.9718	0.0196
34	4	0.0006	0.9920	0.0008	0.9725	0.0195
36	1	0.0001	0.9922	0.0007	0.9732	0.0190
37	1	0.0001	0.9923	0.0006	0.9738	0.0185
38	4	0.0006	0.9929	0.0006	0.9744	0.0185
39	3	0.0004	0.9933	0.0006	0.9749	0.0184

Table 2.4 — *Continued*

Observed				Theoretical		
1	2	3	4	5	6	7
# Paper	# Author	% Authors	Cum of Authors	Expected % Authors	Expected Cum of Authors	D
x	y	$f_o(y_x) = y_x/\Sigma y_x$	$\Sigma f_o(y_x)$	$f_e(y_x)^*$	$\Sigma f_e(y_x)$	$\|\Sigma f_o(y_x) - \Sigma f_e(y_x)\|$
40	2	0.0003	0.9936	0.0006	0.9755	0.0181
41	1	0.0001	0.9938	0.0005	0.9760	0.0178
42	2	0.0003	0.9941	0.0005	0.9765	0.0176
44	3	0.0004	0.9945	0.0005	0.9770	0.0175
45	4	0.0006	0.9951	0.0004	0.9773	0.0178
46	2	0.0003	0.9954	0.0004	0.9778	0.0176
47	3	0.0004	0.9958	0.0004	0.9781	0.0177
49	1	0.0002	0.9959	0.0004	0.9785	0.0174
50	2	0.0003	0.9962	0.0004	0.9789	0.0173
51	1	0.0002	0.9964	0.0003	0.9792	0.0172
52	2	0.0003	0.9967	0.0003	0.9795	0.0172
53	2	0.0003	0.9970	0.0003	0.9798	0.0172
54	2	0.0003	0.9972	0.0003	0.9801	0.0171
55	3	0.0004	0.9977	0.0003	0.9804	0.0173
57	1	0.0002	0.9978	0.0003	0.9807	0.0171
58	1	0.0002	0.9980	0.0003	0.9810	0.0170
61	2	0.0003	0.9983	0.0002	0.9812	0.0171
66	1	0.0002	0.9984	0.0002	0.9814	0.0170
68	2	0.0003	0.9987	0.0002	0.9816	0.0171
73	1	0.0002	0.9988	0.0002	0.9818	0.0170
78	1	0.0002	0.9990	0.0002	0.9819	0.0171
80	1	0.0002	0.9991	0.0001	0.9821	0.0170
84	1	0.0002	0.9993	0.0001	0.9822	0.0171
95	1	0.0002	0.9994	0.0001	0.9823	0.0171
107	1	0.0002	0.9996	0.0001	0.9824	0.0172
109	1	0.0002	0.9997	0.0001	0.9825	0.0172
114	1	0.0002	0.9999	0.0001	0.9826	0.0173
346	1	0.0002	1.0000	0.0000	0.9826	0.0174

6891

*Calculated with $f_e(y_x)$ $= 0.5669 (1/x^{1.8878})$

**$D_{max} = 0.0208$

At the 0.01 level of significance,

the critical value $= 1.63/\sqrt{\Sigma\ y_x}$

$= 0.0196.$

Table 2.5
Kolmogorov-Smirnov Test of Observed and Expected Distributions
of Senior Authors in Auerbach's Data

Observed				Theoretical		
1	2	3	4	5	6	7
# Paper	# Author	% Authors	Cum of Authors	Expected % Authors	Expected Cum of Authors	D
x	y	$f_o(y_x) = y_x/\Sigma y_x$	$\Sigma f_o(y_x)$	$f_e(y_x)^*$	$\Sigma f_e(y_x)$	$\|\Sigma f_o(y_x) - \Sigma f_e(y_x)\|$
1	784	0.5917	0.5917	0.6151	0.6151	0.0234
2	204	0.1540	0.7457	0.1516	0.7667	0.0210
3	127	0.0959	0.8415	0.0668	0.8334	0.0081
4	50	0.0377	0.8792	0.0373	0.8708	0.0085
5	33	0.0249	0.9042	0.0238	0.8946	0.0096
6	28	0.0211	0.9253	0.0165	0.9110	0.0143
7	19	0.0143	0.9396	0.0121	0.9231	0.0166
8	19	0.0143	0.9540	0.0092	0.9323	0.0217
9	6	0.0045	0.9585	0.0073	0.9395	0.0190
10	7	0.0053	0.9638	0.0059	0.9454	0.0184
11	6	0.0045	0.9683	0.0048	0.9502	0.0181
12	7	0.0053	0.9736	0.0041	0.9543	0.0193
13	4	0.0030	0.9766	0.0035	0.9577	0.0189
14	4	0.0030	0.9796	0.0030	0.9607	0.0189
15	5	0.0038	0.9834	0.0026	0.9633	0.0201
16	3	0.0023	0.9857	0.0023	0.9655	0.0201
17	3	0.0023	0.9879	0.0020	0.9675	0.0204
18	1	0.0008	0.9887	0.0018	0.9693	0.0193
21	1	0.0008	0.9894	0.0013	0.9706	0.0188
22	3	0.0023	0.9917	0.0012	0.9718	0.0199
24	3	0.0023	0.9940	0.0010	0.9728	0.0211
25	2	0.0015	0.9955	0.0009	0.9738	0.0217
27	1	0.0008	0.9962	0.0008	0.9745	0.0217
30	1	0.0008	0.9970	0.0006	0.9752	0.0218
34	1	0.0008	0.9977	0.0005	0.9757	0.0221
37	1	0.0008	0.9985	0.0004	0.9761	0.0224
48	2	0.0015	1.0000	0.0003	0.9763	0.0237**

1325

*Calculated with $f_e(y_x) = 0.6151 \, (1/x^{2.021})$

**$D_{max} = 0.0237$

At the 0.01 level of significance,

the critical value $= 1.63/\sqrt{\Sigma y_x}$

$= 0.0448$

Creation and Content:
Subject Dispersion

In his concern to provide efficient abstracting and indexing services to cover the ever-growing scientific literature, S.C. Bradford studied the distribution of the literature of a subject among its contributing journals. In two subject bibliographies — applied geophysics and lubrication — he found a curious relation between the number of journals and the number of articles published by these journals. He stated that

> if scientific journals are arranged in order of decreasing productivity of articles on a given subject, they may be divided into a nucleus of periodicals more particularly devoted to the subject and several groups or zones containing the same number of articles as the nucleus, when the numbers of periodicals in the nucleus and succeeding zones will be as $a : n : n^2 : n^3$ ... (Bradford, 1948)

This particular distribution has been widely known in library and information circle as the Bradford Law of Scattering. An obvious deduction from this discovery is that since the list of journal titles produces a rapidly diminishing yield of articles on a given subject, the abstracting service, subject bibliographer, or the library collection developer should focus on the publishing sources rather than attempting to cover the subject. The concentration of yield in the distribution can also suggest a reasonable cutoff based on one's budget and available staff time in the determination of coverage.

Subsequently, this law has been tested on many subject bibliographies. It has also been applied to library users and their use of library materials (Urquhart and Bunn, 1959), articles and their frequency of citation, journals and their citations of other journals, and publishers and their published monographs. An approximation of Trueswell's 20/80 rule applies (Trueswell, 1969). That is, in all cases, a concentration of at least 80 percent yield has been found in a small core of less than 20 percent of sources. Table 2.6 (page 30) shows that 8 journals on the subject of computational musicology produced 26 percent of the total literature; 26 journals produced half of the literature; and it takes an additional 248 journals to produce the other half of papers on the subject.

Bradford's Law has attracted much attention. It addresses the way a subject literature is distributed among the journals which contain it. This law has been explicated, enhanced, refined, and reformulated. In general, it can be expressed in two forms — verbal and graphic.

Bradford's original verbal formulation is illustrated in Table 2.6. The data is obtained by first ranking the journal titles according to the number of articles on the subject contained in each journal. Second, record in column 1 the number of journals with the corresponding number of articles produced by each of the journals in column 2. Then starting with the most productive journal, compute the product of columns 1 and 2, that is, the total number of articles produced by the journals, and place the values into column 3. Column 4 contains the running sums of journals in column 1, and column 5 contains the running sums of column 3.

Table 2.6
Dispersion of Publications over Publishing Sources in
Computational Musicology

1	2	3	4	5	6	
# of Sources	# of Items	Col 1 x Col 2	Cum of Sources	Cum Items	% of Cum Items	Publishing Sources
1	57	57	1	57	6.05	Computers & Hum.
2	30	60	3	117	12.42	J Acoust. Soc.
						J Mus Theory
1	29	29	4	146	15.50	Perspectives New Mus.
2	28	56	6	202	21.44	La Revue Musicale
						U of Illinois Press
1	24	24	7	226	23.99	Am Soc Univ Comp
1	22	22	8	248	26.33	Cornell Univ Press
1	18	18	9	266	28.24	CUNY Univ Press
2	16	32	11	298	31.63	Fontes Artis Musicae
						J Audio Eng Soc
1	15	15	12	313	33.23	Gustav Bosse
1	14	14	13	327	34.71	Grav Blatter
2	13	26	15	353	37.47	J Res Mus Ed
						Klub uzivatelu
4	12	48	19	401	42.57	Int'l Mus Soc
						New York Univ Press
						John Wiley
						Prentice Hall
1	11	11	20	412	43.74	Bull Con Res Mus Ed
2	10	20	22	432	45.86	Praeger Press
						Princeton Univ Press
3	9	27	25	459	48.73	Melos
						Numus-West
						Nutida Musik
1	8	8	26	467	49.57	
6	7	42	32	509	54.03	
5	6	30	37	539	57.22	
14	5	70	51	609	64.65	
16	4	64	67	673	71.55	
18	3	54	85	727	77.28	
25	2	50	110	777	82.59	
164	1	164	274	941	100.00	

274	941

The sample data in Table 2.6 shows that there are a total of 941 papers on the subject collected from 274 journals. These journals may be partitioned into a maximum of eight groups or zones. The first zone or nucleus consists of only three journals with a total of 117 papers on the subject (see Table 2.7). One hundred thirty-one papers are found in the five journals in the second zone, and the same number of papers are in the next eight journals in the following zone. The Bradford multiplier, which in theory should be a constant, is obtained by dividing the number of journals in every pair of succeeding zones. In the data in Table 2.7, the multiplier hovers around 1.60 except in one case.

Table 2.7
Maximum Divisions of Publishing Sources on the Subject
Computational Musicology

Zones	Publications	Publishing Sources	Multiplier
	A	J	b
1	117	3	-
2	131	5	1.66
3	117	8	1.60
4	123	13	1.62
5	116	21	1.62
6	117	33	1.57
7	106	77	2.33
8	114	114	1.48
Total:	941	274	

In compiling a bibliography to test for the conformity of Bradford's Law, one should meet three implicit conditions:

1. In dividing the journals into zones, the number of articles in each zone must remain constant.

2. The Bradford multiplier b must be greater than one.

3. The Bradford multiplier must remain approximately constant. (Brookes, 1969)

Problems arise when a given set of data has several ways in which the journals can be grouped. Bradford gave no reason as to the rationale for dividing his bibliographic data into three zones each. Would there be less deviation in the values of A, the number of papers in each zone, and b, the Bradford multiplier, if more zones were chosen? How does one evaluate a specific grouping?

Based on the above three conditions, it is clear that the minimum value of A which is the number of papers in each zone must be greater than $Z/2$, or half of the total number of single-article journals. Z is the number of journals each contributing only one article to the subject. Otherwise, the last two zones would each contain fewer than $Z/2$ journals resulting in $b = 1$, or the last zone would contain fewer journals than the preceding zone resulting in $b < 1$, thus contradicting the law. Therefore A, a minimum number of papers in each zone, would produce a maximum number of divisions of the journal distribution. This produces a grouping with a minimum number of journals in the nucleus as its first zone.

After the distribution has been grouped into a maximum number of zones, standard deviation of the resulting sets of values for A and b can be computed to test for conformity to the verbal formulation of Bradford's Law.

The graphic formulation of Bradford's Law is not mathematically equivalent to the verbal formulation. Drott's paper (1981) gave a good explanation. To test for conformity by the graphic representation of Bradford's Law, rank the journals according to their productivity of articles on the subject. Create a table such as Table 2.6 with column 1 containing the number of journals and column 2 with the number of papers produced by each journal. Record the cumulative number of journals (n) in column 4. Multiply the data in each corresponding row in columns 1 and 2 and put the products in column 3. Record the running sums of column 3, that is, the cumulative number of article $R(n)$ in column 5. Plot the logarithm of n on the x axis against $R(n)$ on the y axis. In other words, the number of journals and their cumulative sum of articles may be plotted on semilog paper. If the distribution conforms to Bradford's Law (Brookes, 1969), the graph known as "Bradford Bibliograph" will display the characteristics of three distinct regions: (a) a rapid rise for the first few points, (b) a major portion of linear relation between the two variables, and (c) a "droop" at the tail end of the distribution indicating the incompleteness of the bibliography (see Figure 2.3). The few highly productive journals especially devoted to the subject account for the short rise. Since most of the journals in each subject collection maintain a geometric relation to their productivity, the linearity appears in the middle section of the distribution. The droop is due to the incompleteness of the

R(n)

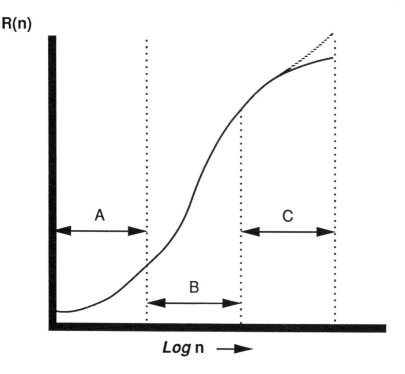

Fig. 2.3. Bradford distribution: a, nucleus; b, linear portion; c, droop.

bibliography represented, since it is nearly impossible to compile a truly complete bibliography on any subject. Mathematically, it may be expressed as:

$$R(n) = k \log(n/s)$$

where $R(n)$ is the cumulative number of articles,

   n is the cumulative number of journals,

   k is the slope of the line, and

   s is the intercept on the x axis.

The underlying explanation has been variously attempted. Most have attributed it to the "success breeds success" mechanism. That is, there are usually a few well-known journals in any subject. These usually attract most of the articles in the given subject. Yet limited space prevents them from bringing out all the manuscripts submitted. Thus, publications are spilled over to other journals. In fact, Price found that the bandwagon effect also applied to the productivity of scientific writings. He noted that if a person has successfully published a paper, the probability of his publishing his second paper is 1/3; his third paper is 2/4; his fourth paper is 3/5, and so on. It is more likely for the prolific author to write and publish than for those who rarely publish. The laws of Lotka, Bradford, and others such as Zipf, are characterized by their skewed distributions. That is, a few sources are found to be responsible for a major percentage of yield. Zipf's law is discussed in chapter 7 under automatic indexing. Several investigators including Price (1976) have attempted to explain these disparate phenomena by a unified theory.

Creation and Content: Dissemination of Ideas

Most bibliometric studies have been based on records collected in a given interval of time. For example, dispersion of relevant articles collected over ten years of a subject among a group of journals reveals a regular pattern of the subject literature at a fixed period of time. The same holds true for author productivity over a 100-year interval. Activities in a slice of time have been analyzed as if they were preserved in a frozen section under a microscope. By necessity, it is retrospective. By studying past data, activities of the future are predicted by way of statistical inference. These are called synchronous studies.

There are a handful of studies which have concentrated on the dynamic nature of subject literatures. A researcher tracks particular types of publications or authors over a period of time and offers predictions on their growth, use, and the productivity of their authors. These longitudinal tracings are known as diachronous studies. An example would be the investigation of the citation trend of a group of articles. Most items are cited after the initial period of delay of approximately six months or more. Thereafter, the number of citations tends to increase over the next five years. After reaching their peak of citation in the second or third years, most items would receive decreasing numbers of citations. Thus, those publications deviating from this pattern, and receiving more citations after five years are likely to distinguish themselves as classics in the subject.

By far the most important dynamic theory in information science is Goffman's epidemic theory of communication (Goffman and Newill, 1964) Garfield (1980) provided an excellent qualitative description of this theory. Goffman, a mathematician, observed that the dissemination of scientific ideas could be described as a process not unlike the transmission of infectious diseases. The former is a desirable condition, whereas, the latter a condition to be avoided. Mathematical models exist to describe the spread of a disease within a population and to predict its duration and intensity. Goffman draw an analogy between these two diverse phenomena. He also worked out several models from the simple, direct, one-to-one communication to a four-factor model in which the disease or idea was transmitted via intermediaries and carriers.

Elements common to all epidemics were identified and parallels were drawn. Ideas are the infectious material in intellectual epidemics. They are transmitted by direct communication between a lecturer and the audience or through conversations between an academic advisor and advisee. These ideas may also be exposed via an agent in the form of a journal in which the ideas contained in articles are transmitted to an audience.

The other important element in all epidemics is the population through which the ideas spread. At any given time, an individual in the population may belong to one of several distinct categories. Infectives are those who have carried the ideas. Authors and researchers who have the ideas to communicate are the infectives. Those who come into contact with the infectious material are the susceptibles, since they may come down with the disease. They may be journal readers and other researchers in the same field who may come across the ideas. Removals are either former infectives or those who are immune to the disease. They may be other researchers who have retired or died and are no longer active in the field.

Goffman was able to describe the epidemic process in several states. In a stable state, the number of infectives does not change over time. Then the epidemic is considered to be in an *endemic* state. In an unstable state, the number of infectives may be either increasing or decreasing. In the former case, the epidemic is spreading; in the latter case, declining.

A complex series of differential equations has been elaborated to calculate the rates of change in the number of infectives, susceptives, and removals. They describe the characteristics of the epidemic in terms of growth. They also specify the condition under which the epidemic peaks and stablizes. Finally, the equations yield the number of susceptibles beyond which the epidemic could take off. From another perspective, the epidemic could be contained by keeping the size of the susceptibles under a critical number.

Goffman tested actual data from three subject literatures, those of mast cells, symbolic logic, and schistosomiasis. First, he analyzed a comprehensive bibliography of mast cells from 1897 until 1963 compiled by Hans Selye (Goffman and Warren, 1980). The growth of this literature was considered as a two-factor epidemic process involving direct transmission of ideas between authors. The authors were classified as either infectives or removals. Individuals became infectives in the first year of publication of their papers on mast cell research. They became removals one year after the date of publication of their last paper in the Selye bibliogaphy. Goffman's analysis found that mast cell research was stable for almost 60 years after an early important discovery. After that period, a steady increase was shown. Historical data of certain key discoveries and successful chemical syntheses were found to corroborate with the outbreak of each epidemic predicted by his model.

In the literature of schistosomiasis, Warren and Goffman (1972) suggested that a four-factor model be used for its analysis. In schistosomiasis, a tropical disease, there are two hosts, definitive in human beings and intermediary in snails. The infectious agent is a parasite, whose first life cycle infects humans and whose second infects snails. The parasitic worm in a human produces eggs which leave the body with its excretion. The eggs are hatched in fresh water where they penetrate the snail. The parasite then transforms itself within the snail and leaves the snail. Free flowing in fresh water, it penetrates the skin of a human swimming in such a body of water. The cycle repeats itself. The spread of medical information is also a cyclical process involving four factors. Information in the form of ideas is the infectious material. It is developed first in the form of manuscript, and then as a published scientific paper. The definitive host is the researcher and the intermediary host is the journal. The researcher communicates his or her idea in a manuscript. If it accepted by a journal, it is revised and published as a paper. The idea may be communicated to other susceptibles via the journal. The process is repeated. Interestingly, in the four-factor model, Goffman asserted that the journal population is the controlling factor for any epidemic to occur. He found that the number of authors is directly related to the number of journals publishing on a particular subject. The number of "quality" authors is also proportional to the total number of authors in the field. It is as if there exists a delicately balanced ecosystem. If a limit is placed on the availability of journals, a decline in both the population of authors and quality research may result. From time to time, suggestions have been made to curtail the publication of journals in an effort to control the exponential growth of scientific papers. But, Goffman (Warren and Goffman, 1972) cautioned against the tampering with the present system of scientific communication since it may adversely affect the balance of quality and quantity of research literature.

The importance of this work lies in the predictive power of his theory. His mathematical analysis was able to predict the controlling conditions of the epidemic, the dimension of growth, and the rate of slowdown. He was able to define the conditions under which the epidemic would peak and stablize. The threshold value was calculated for the susceptible population in order that the epidemic take place.

In summary, major types of bibliometric studies have been surveyed. In particular, the Bradford and Lotka laws have been presented. Data have shown that literature has been growing at an exponential rate. Author productivity, citations, and subject dispersion tend to concentrate on a small group of sources. This skewed distribution of sources seem to characterize bibliograghic observables. Although the actual concentration differs in individual subjects, it seems to vary only in degrees. The general trend that a small elite is responsible for the majority of yield has been demonstrated by repeated bibliometric studies. Recent attempts have been made to unify these skewed phenomena with some success. The next chapter will be devoted entirely to literature use, and the characteristics of users of information.

REFERENCES

Bearman, T.C. 1978. "Secondary Information Systems and Services." *Annual Review of Information Science and Technology*, edited by Martha E. Williams. Vol. 13, 179-208. White Plains, New York: Knowledge Industry Publications, Inc.

Bradford, S.C. 1948. *Documentation*. London: Crosby Lockwood.

Brookes, B.C. 1969. "Bradford's Law and the Bibliography of Science." *Nature*, 224(5223):953-956.

Cole, J.R., and S. Cole. 1972. "The Ortega Hypothesis." *Science*, 178(4059):368-375.

Crane, D. 1972. *Invisible Colleges: Diffusion of Knowledge in Scientific Communities*. Chicago: University of Chicago Press.

Crawford, S. 1971. "Informal Communication Among Scientists in Sleep Research." *Journal of the American Society for Information Science*, 22(5):301-310.

Drott, M.C. 1981. "Bradford's Law: Theory, Empiricism and the Gaps Between." *Library Trends*, 30(1):41-52.

Garfield, E. 1979. *Citation Indexing — Its Theory and Application in Science, Technology, and Humanities*. New York: John Wiley & Sons.

Garfield, E. 1980. "The Epidemiology of Knowledge and the Spread of Scientific Information." *Current Contents*, 35:5-10.

Goffman, W., and V.A. Newill. 1964. "Generalization of Epidemic Theory." *Nature*, 204(4955):225-228.

Goffman, W., and K.S. Warren. 1980. *Scientific Information Systems and the Principle of Selectivity*. New York: Praeger Press.

Griffith, B.C., and N.C. Mullins. 1972. "Coherent Social Groups in Scientific Change." *Science*, 177(4053):959-964.

Griffith, B.C., H. Small, J.A. Stonehill, and S. Dey. 1974. "The Structure of Scientific Literature. II: Toward a Macro- and Micro-Structure for Science." *Science Studies*, 4(4):330-365.

Kessler, M.M. 1963. "Bibliographic Coupling Between Scientific Papers." *American Documentation*, 14(1):10-25.

King, D.W., F.W. Lancaster, D.D. McDonald, N.K. Roderer, and B.L. Wood. 1976. *Statistical Indicators of Scientific and Technical Communication (1960-1980): Vol. II. A Research Report, 125*. Rockville, Maryland: King Research Incorporated, Center for Quantitative Science.

Kuhn, T.S. 1962. *The Structure of Scientific Revolutions.* Chicago: University of Chicago Press.

Line, M.B. 1970. "Half-Life of Periodical Literature: Apparent and Real Obsolescence." *Journal of Documentation,* 26(1):46-54.

Line, M.B., and A. Sandison. 1974. " 'Obsolescence' and Changes in the Use of of Literature with Time." *Journal of Documentation,* 30(3):283-350.

Line, M.B., and A. Sandison. 1975. "Practical Interpretation of Citation and Library Use Studies." *College and Research Libraries,* 36(5):393-396.

Lotka, A.K. 1926. "The Frequency Distribution of Scientific Productivity." *Journal of the Washington Academy of Science,* 16(12):317-323.

Pao, M.L. 1985. "Lotka's Law: A Testing Procedure." *Information Processing and Management,* 21(4):305-320.

Pao, M.L. 1986. "An Empirical Examination of Lotka's Law." *Journal of the American Society for Information Science,* 37(1):26-33.

Price, D.J.D. 1963. *Little Science, Big Science.* New York: Columbia University Press.

Price, D.J.D. 1965. "Networks of Scientific Papers." *Science,* 149(3683):510-515.

Price, D.J.D. 1976. "A General Theory of Bibliometrics and Other Cumulative Advantage Processes." *Journal of the American Society for Information Science,* 27(5):292-306.

Pritchard, A. 1969. "Statistical Bibliography or Bibliometrics?" *Journal of Documentation,* 25(4):348-349.

Small, H. 1973. "Co-citation in the Scientific Literature: A New Measure of the Relationship Between Two Documents." *Journal of the American Society for Information Science,* 24(4):265-269.

Small, H., and B.C. Griffith. 1974. "The Structure of Scientific Literature. I: Identifying and Graphing Specialties." *Science Studies,* 4(1):17-40.

Smith, L.C. 1981. "Citation Analysis." *Library Trends,* 30(1):83-106.

Trueswell, R.L. 1969. "Some Behavioral Patterns of Library Users: The 80/20 Rule." *Wilson Library Bulletin,* 43(5):458-461.

Urquhart, J.A., and R.M. Bunn. 1959. "A National Loan Policy for Science Serials." *Journal of Documentation,* 15(1):21-25.

Warren, K.S., and W. Goffman. 1972. "The Ecology of Medical Literature." *American Journal of Medical Science,* 262:267-273.

Watson, J.D. 1968. *The Double Helix: A Personal Account of the Discovery of the Structure of DNA.* New York: Atheneum.

White, H., and B.C. Griffith. 1981. "Author Cocitation: A Literature Measure of Intellectual Structure." *Journal of the American Society for Information Science*, 32(3):163-171.

Ziman, J. 1969. "Information, Communication, Knowledge." *Nature* 224:318-324.

Zuckerman, H. 1967. "Nobel Laureates in Science: Patterns of Productivity, Collaboration, and Authorship." *American Sociological Review*, 32:391-402.

3

Uses and Users

TERMINOLOGY

The information need of the user is of central concern to providers of information service. The ultimate aim of any information-retrieval system is to supply and deliver the information which can precisely match the information requests. Information needs and users are studied with a view to improve the overall system of information transfer. Investigations have centered upon information searching behaviors. Researchers have explored ways in which users make use of information, the types of demands placed on the system, the impact upon the receipt of information, the flow of information, the preferred types of information channels, and the level of satisfaction expressed by the user. User studies is a multidisciplinary area of knowledge. It is primarily concerned with the *behaviors* and *experience* of users of information systems and services with regard to their *interaction*.

Obviously, the key to the success of information transfer depends largely on the accurate identification of what the user needs. The most common approach for needs assessment is simply querying the user. Satisfaction certainly is a valid yardstick by which the effectiveness of the system can be measured. Examination of users' responses to queries directed to their levels of satisfaction, degree of use, preference of types of information resources, and others allow the systems operator to detect problem areas so that deficiencies may be rectified and improvement of services provided. Since the early 1960s a flood of these kinds of studies have been conducted. Data were derived largely from judgments of preference made explicitly by users of specific information systems or libraries. However, data based on human value judgment can be unreliable. People can be emotional, forgetful, and inconsistent in their responses.

Other studies attempt to circumvent direct query of the users. Observational data based on the use of information materials and services are examined. These are called use studies. If a library collects the complete works of all the English authors in the 18th century, and it is never used, there may be something amiss in that library. On the other hand, if a collection is used often, it does not necessarily follow that it is a good collection. Nevertheless, use can be an indicator of users' satisfaction with information service.

In a recent review, Rohde (1986) found over 2,000 citations in one database alone. From the first decade of the publication of the *Annual Review of Information Science and Technology*, eight chapters were devoted to information needs and uses. Intense interest has been shown in the literature. Since 1976, only two reviews were published in the *Annual Review* (Crawford, 1978; Dervin and Nilan, 1986). The 1986 review reported that despite the large number of publications, empirical studies are limited. Furthermore, research findings with respect to actual applications and better service provided have been tenuous at best. There is no evidence that because of such studies the use of information sources and services has increased, nor has there been appreciable improvement of service to the client. Many studies were performed to solve local problems with little generalizability. There is a lack of progress in synthesis of the voluminous data collected. In part, the situation is due to methodological problems and the limited conceptual framework within which these studies have been conducted. The primary difficulty starts with a lack of agreement regarding definitions of the terms used. Even the two most important terms, *information needs* and *users* are subject to many interpretations.

Information Needs

A vague concept, *need* is often the result of some unresolved problem(s). It may be work related. It may arise when an individual recognizes that his or her current store of knowledge is insufficient to cope with the task at hand, or to resolve conflicts in a subject area, or to fill a void in some area of knowledge. This need may or may not be totally articulated. In fact, it may even exist in different levels of consciousness. That is, at certain stages, one may not even be aware of the totality of this need. Consequently, from the standpoint of the information system, an articulated demand made by a user often does not represent the true need. Hence, satisfaction of that stated demand does not, in turn, resolve the information problem.

Since it is difficult to probe the inner cognitive state of any individual to arrive at the true information need, many investigators choose to operationalize needs as the expressed preferences, or loan requests even though these do not totally represent the true need of the user. Such needs are substitutes at best, but they are quantifiable in the form of the number of reference questions asked, the number of books checked out, the number of reprints requested and so on. In interpreting the results of such studies, one infers needs from such explicit transactions. Investigators have yet to find a measure of true information need. A typical study probes the extent to which the user uses one or more kinds of information systems, the degree of difficulty or satisfaction encountered in using information services, or the characteristics of the systems contributing to the success of information transaction. Up to the present, data for need assessment studies have been derived mainly from querying users directly.

Users

There are several distinct types of users of an information system. Within the context of an organization, *potential users* can be those currently not yet served by the information service. For example, on a university campus, alumni are potential users. Likewise, all students, faculty, and staff in a university, are potential library users, even though relatively few are actual users. For the most part, library systems are staffed on the basis of serving only a fraction of potential users. Present library resources would be grossly inadequate if all potential users became actual users. *Expected users* are different from potential users in that they are those who not only have the privileges of using the service, but also have the intention of using such service. For example, those who are subscribers to a journal are expected users. Yet not all are the *actual users*. In any library environment, one can easily identify actual users. These are usually registered library users who have active loan records. Not all users who use services, such as, online database searching, benefit from the experience. *Beneficiary users* are those who have derived some benefit from information. Clearly, *users* is an ambiguous term.

TYPES OF USERS STUDIES

Historically, extensive studies have been conducted on needs of users in science and technology (Menzel, 1966; Wood, 1971; Ford, 1977). Research on the information-seeking habits of social scientists began in the 1960s (Hogeweg-de Haart, 1983). Most work on the needs of people in the humanities has appeared since the 1970s (Stone, 1982). Users studies may be grouped according to the following: (a) user oriented, (b) systems use oriented, and (c) utility oriented.

User oriented studies are focused on the characteristics of users of information. The degree of use is examined with respect of the user's age, educational level, and economic status. Personal, demographic, sociological, job, and task descriptions are sought as predictors of information use. For example, it was found that persons around the age of 25 are more likely to be information users than people at the age of 64 or older. Many of these information requirement traits were associated with subgroups of users such as chemists, humanists, and upper management personnel. Unfortunately, seldom are such descriptive data useful in formulating policy changes to improve service.

Systems use oriented studies derive their data from the system. The transactions between users and the system are investigated and examined. For example, the number of items loaned in-house and/or loaned through interlibrary channels, the number of online searches performed, and the number and types of reference questions processed can be scrutinized. Not only are frequency data sought, but such investigations also probe the reasoning process made by problem solvers and the process of research. Of prime interest is how information is used in these processes so that optimal information support may be provided. Other investigators have examined users activities associated with information seeking. Users were asked about the type of information sources most used in relation to the primary area of work, and to support current awareness activities. Comparative data on alternative mechanisms of information support such as different document-delivery systems have been also solicited. With carefully framed goals, and with the user sample carefully selected such that they are capable of making well-informed judgment, the derived data may be used to establish policy. Additionally, preferences of different information channels such as library visits, and telephone queries are examined in terms of their use frequencies. Use of formal information systems and informal communication channels are also compared. More recently, availability studies have been done. One presumes that more use can be made of materials if maximum duration is provided for materials to be used. Similarly, document-exposure time or the time spent in the system environment by the user population is an aspect studied in system-oriented investigations.

Utility oriented studies attempt to relate information use with the impact or consequence of such use. These studies are more difficult to conduct. The result of information use is not always observable nor does the consequence necessarily follow immediately after. Even directly querying the user may not yield reliable and valid data. The causal relationship between information and its resultant decision are difficult to establish. Yet reliable data on what and how information actually affect actions should be valuable input to the system manager.

Several techniques have been used. A critical incidence study is done by requiring the subjects to report on information needs and their resolution at each decision-making point of a specific research project. The project under study is normally split into several subprojects. At each decision point, alternative information-seeking strategies are identified. Each worker is asked to rate the probable success of each alternative solution each week. Presumably, as the weeks progress, relevant input information increases. The rating should become more realistic. The objective is to discover what type of information has the greatest influence on decision making. Another group of utility studies utilizes citation analysis. As one author cites another author in order to support his or her paper, one uses the content of the cited paper. Indeed, a great number of citation studies have been performed under the rubric of utility studies.

RESEARCH DESIGN

There are several general characteristics found in the research design of users studies. Despite the numerous studies done since the 1920s, there is no strong theoretical support (Wilson, 1981; Daniels, 1986). Although the experimental methods used in the 1980s are more refined and the data analysis procedures more sophisticated, many of the research methodologies used are borrowed from those of social-science research. Research has also inherited most of the problems of social-science research. Variables affecting information-seeking behaviors are many and are not easily identifiable. They are also difficult to control and the link between cause and effect is not easy to establish. Furthermore, since ultimately the information system aims to improve service, a standard of quality service must be established. Yet quality as well as service cannot be readily measured. Can one claim that a large number of reference questions answered is equivalent to a higher quality level of service? Obviously, quality can only be inferred and a number of quality indicators may be sought. Most users studies are disruptive to the normal operation of any information system. Finally, even if hard evidence is found, it is also extremely difficult to implement changes.

With the above cautionary note, the following outlines the process of research in this area:

A. Design of research plan
1. Identify a problem area or a need to study.
2. Conduct an initial literature review.
3. Define the research problem.
4. Estimate the potential for successful execution of the study.
5. Conduct a second literature review.
6. Select an appropriate research approach.
7. Formulate a hypothesis.
8. Formulate data-collection methods.
9. Formulate and develop data-collection instruments.
10. Design a data-analysis plan.
11. Design a data-collection plan.
12. Identify the population and sample.
13. Conduct pilot studies of methods, instruments, and analysis.
B. Implementation of research plan
14. Implement data-collection.
15. Implement data analysis.
16. Prepare research report.
C. Implementation of results
17. Disseminate findings and agitate for action.

Unfortunately, these processes are not exactly sequential. For example, Steps 1 through 4 may be done simultaneously requiring very little time. In selecting a research plan in Step 6 one may be constrained by the type of data-collection techniques that can be performed due to cost, time, or types of data required. A recycle of Steps 6 through 9 may be necessary. However, these steps do offer a checklist of focal points.

Obviously, identifying a problem area or generating an idea to research depends on the local condition and motivation. Literature reviews are straightforward. The collection of data should be planned carefully. This important aspect represents the means by which the degree of use of information, and the type of use are measured. In choosing a data-collection method, the selection of a measure is implied. A measure must be considered with several factors affecting the quality of the data collected.

Five factors affecting the quality of the data are:

1. *Validity* relates to the accuracy and representativeness of data and the results. Since most studies can analyze only samples of the entire population of users, high validity insures that the sample data is a good representative of the total population. The second consideration of validity of data relates to whether what is measured actually represents the concept or attribute sought. It addresses the question: will the resulting measure and the way it is measured actually reflect the concept one is trying to find? For example, accessibility of information is a concept which may be expressed in terms of the cost in dollars to the users. Here one may have only a partial measure of accessibility, since cost may also be in the effort expended by the user to reach the library. In the case of citation data, is a frequently cited paper used more than one less cited? In other words, is citation a good indicator of use? Does it exclude important aspects of use?

2. *Reliability* relates to the stability of the measure over time. Together with validity, these are two most important factors. Data collection usually extends over a period of time. For example, in gathering information from 50 interviews, can the interviewer be consistent and unambiguous in the use of words, expressions, and in attitudes with every subject? The interviewer's reaction may be easily affected by different personality types, so that an identical question may be interpreted in different ways by the interviewee depending on the manner in which the question is presented. Then the collected data cannot be reliable.

3. *Intrusiveness* relates to the degree to which data collecting interferes with normal user-system routines. When a user is asked about aspects of information seeking, the individual's original task is usually interrupted. Any disruption introduces an element of interference which may affect the truthfulness of the response given. If frequent or long periods of disturbance are imposed, low user cooperation and low validity can also be expected. Yet to obtain users' responses, a certain degree of intrusion is almost unavoidable. The researcher strives to keep the element of intrusiveness to a minimum.

4. *Efficiency* is determined by the cost in time, money, and effort of data collection in relation to the value of the study. One should face the question: is the study worth doing? Low efficiency is indicated if a massive study involving many subjects and complex data manipulation is performed which may only result in findings which could easily be obtained by canvassing a small sample of individuals.

5. *Impact* is related to the degree to which the expected results may be manipulated toward the institutional goals. If the anticipated results cannot be implemented, it appears that the study should not have been conducted in the first place. Many studies have been well designed and have produced impressive results. Yet more often than not, they have

found their way to the shelves of the director of the information service and have remained there—too impractical for implementation. For example, a library director found that the use of foreign materials would greatly help the research scientists' work if these materials were translated into English. Since regular translations of 50 journal titles would require one-third of the total budget, this important finding could hardly be implemented. Although impact does not apply directly to the process of data collection, it relates to the type of information one is attempting to seek by the investigation. Nevertheless, it is an extremely important consideration in planning a users' study.

DATA COLLECTION METHODS

Three data-collection methods are most commonly used to draw information from people. They are (1) questioning the subjects, (2) observing the subjects, and (3) studying the informational records or documents. The elaboration of each follows.

Questioning

Data obtained from questioning the subjects tend to have low validity. Such data is subjective and often not verifiable. Whether the data is obtained by direct personal interview, group interview, or by mail solicitation, personal factors from the interviewer and the subject render a wide variation in the results. It is the most intrusive form of data collection.

When utilizing data obtained from questionnaires, care must be taken to insure a large sample return. Everyone has received questionnaires. Personal experience shows that the motivation to return the form is low. However, this may be the only method available for certain types of exploratory studies. Given careful design of the questionnaire and identification of the target population, data from questioning can be useful.

Observing

Data from observing subjects is much less intrusive and the validity of the data is higher. This is an effective data- collection technique for obtaining data on nonverbalized behaviors. Yet, severe shortcoming is the limitation of available observation sites. One is handicapped in the probe of data concerning motivation and intention.

Observations can be performed by outsiders as well as by an insider such as a graduate student working in the laboratory. The insider can collect data at regular intervals, recording specific categories of activities at the moment. Reports of scientists' information seeking behavior in their laboratories by the observation method have been validated.

Studying the Informational Records
or Documents

This is the least intrusive form of data collection. In any information service, loan records, statistics, written requests, citation counts, and all types of library records are routinely kept. Researchers do not need to intrude upon the staff or the user for new data. Thus, all types of quantitative statistical analyses may be conducted. Other than the examination of the purely quantitative aspects of these records, content analysis is an acceptable technique of extracting useful data. For example, to study why bibliographic citations are made, a sample of publications may be systematically examined. Specifically, the passages in which each citation is referred to are analyzed for their content. High validity and reliability can be expected. Its limitation is that what is collected may or may not reflect what one is seeking. In probing a user's motivation and the uses for which the information content is intended, documentary records may not be adequate. In other words, validity is not always high, and the usefulness of the study with such data is often uncertain.

RESEARCH METHODOLOGY

Questionnaire Survey

Several types of research methods are commonly employed. Certainly the most common method used is the questionnaire. It is easy to administer, and it is the least expensive research method. Normally a form is used. These forms are known as survey instruments and are used to collect opinions from a sample group of subjects. It takes the least amount of time to reach a large population and this method is not constrained by subjects at widely dispersed geographic locations. The other attractive feature of a questionnaire is that the data collected can be framed in a uniform format, making data analysis relatively easy. Questionnaire design can usually benefit from a pretest of the instrument. Survey by questionnaires is the most common form of data collection used in the social sciences.

For questionnaires, the validity is low. People tend to resist giving answers regarding what they do when social acceptability or value is implied. One is reluctant to report honestly in the questionnaire. On the other hand, since it usually comes in the mail, and one responds without being watched, there is the opportunity to obtain relatively honest responses. Conversely, under unmonitored conditions, unreliable data are also common. Not only are such data generally not verifiable, but the return rate is usually low. Furthermore, there is a general belief that questionnaire returns may not be representative of the population as a whole. Since many people do not fill out questionnaires, those that do may exhibit characteristics different from the majority of the population.

Finally, it is possible to design a good questionnaire survey. One must pay special attention to the question construction. Within the questionnaire, internal consistency must be maintained, and internal cross-checking built in. Most importantly, the questions themselves should be unambiguous. Since no interaction is possible between the subject and the experimenter, the survey instrument must be self-sufficient and clear in its intended meaning. Reliability depends mostly on the instrument design. Given careful planning and pretesting of the instrument, it is possible to conduct a good questionnaire survey.

Interview

The second most commonly used technique is the interview. Its greatest strength as a technique is that it allows for in-depth probing, especially in gathering information involving complex issues. It affords flexibility and interaction in that misunderstanding and ambiguity can be totally eliminated. This technique tends to give the highest quality of data. In general the response rate is also high.

Since interviewing a subject involves an on-site visit on a one-to-one basis, it is costly. The sample size is limited by the high cost of conducting personal interviews. It is also constrained by the number of subjects in accessible locations. To minimize the variations among different interviews, training and preparation are essential. Training can reduce the influence of social interaction and reaction due to personality characteristics and bias. Preparation can also reduce the inconsistency inherent in conducting many interviews. A useful aid is a structured guide for interviewing. Valid results from both questionnaires and interviews could be obtained especially when supplemented by other methods testing the same variable (Bookstein, 1985).

Diary Methods

This is a self-administered data gathering method. It is the collection of detailed accounts of the subject's behavior in the recent past. Often, it involves a short period of time, since this method requires extensive user's participation.

There are several types of diary methods. Fixed-period diary keeping consists of requiring the subject to keep a detailed diary for a period of time. It is an extremely intrusive data collection method. Although it can contain rich informational content, both validity and reliability are low. Subjects usually start with long entries, but gradually diminishing interest results in shorter and shorter entries. Often several entries are entered at the same time at a later date.

Use of a random alarm mechanism is another data collection aid. It has been used to study the reading behaviors of scientists. The subject is given an alarm clock which has been set to go off at random intervals. During office hours, the subject carries the mechanism and is requested to record in detail the activities at the time the alarm is sounded. This acts as a reminder, and the novelty invites participation and cooperation. The researcher is also able to obtain the number of times data collection has taken place.

Another method is called the critical incidence study. It is based on the intensive study of the processes of the recent information-gathering events by the subject. One is asked to recall in detail two or three technical information acquisition instances. The subject is then queried on the nature of the use of the information, the awareness of the first information source, the intended use of the source, the degree of activity needed in order to result in information acquisition, the effect on the work, and the cognitive state of the subject.

Lastly, solution development records have also been used. These are a form of diary designed to examine the effectiveness of different information methods and sources. Via a typical case of problem solving, the subject is requested to estimate on a weekly basis the possible solution if certain sources are used. Data is recorded on dated forms. As the weeks progress, the information requirement and the development of the solution unfold. The solutions offered by different team members may be compared and evaluated.

Several of the above methods may be used simultaneously. For example, solution development records have been successfully used with critical incident techniques. By combining their use, one may discover how subjects conduct information searching in order to solve specific problems.

Group Interview and Question

The strength of group interview and discussion is that it is less labor intensive and less expensive to conduct. Due to the peer pressure of a group, there is often a 100 percent response rate. However, the classroom-like situation often inhibits response. There is a well-known form for group questioning known as the Delphi technique (Fischer, 1978; Dyer, 1979). It has been used to assess and forecast long-term trends. For example, a study of the trend of information use in the next decade may involve questioning a group of leaders in the information industry and in information science. The technique consists of asking each expert the same question. Their responses are gathered. Summary data are used as feedback to the same group. Each of them is told that, for example, 40 percent indicated a positive trend because of a number of factors, and 50 percent had a different opinion due to other influences, and so on. They are asked to revise their opinion in the second round of questioning based on the first group response. The third time, the majority opinion will be presented. Group members are again asked for revision. The idea is to allow a certain degree of indirect interaction to reach a consensus of the experts.

Observation

This is one of the classic methods of data collection. It is nonintrusive and objective. The observer is given definite guidelines to follow and a finite set of categories of activities to observe. Its strength is in its high reliability and objectivity. Its limitation is that it is relatively expensive, and one can only observe at limited locations. Furthermore, the observable data cannot reflect motivation. One should also be cautioned on the so-called *Hawthorne effect*. This refers to the situation in which normal activities of the observed subjects are affected due to the presence of the observer. As a result, the observed activities no longer typify the normal target information seeking behaviors.

Documentary Evidence

Since documents are artifacts of information, they have been used extensively as data records. Three types of documents are used: publications, statistical reports, and citations. All forms of library materials may represent information sources. The use of these materials may be examined by transaction records, such as, circulation records, interlibrary loan forms, or some other request records. These reflect explicit usage and their reliability is extremely high. Historical records, statistical data, and archival materials are also excellent data materials. Another important form of data derived from documents is citation data. Since one cites a publication usually to support one's own argument, the citing paper is using the cited document in some unspecified manner. The use of citation data is common, but still controversial. Although there are obvious abuses and misuse of citations, an assumption is made that citations are made for their relevance to the citing work.

Experiment

This is the classic scientific method of investigation of causal effect based on empirical evidence. First, a hypothesis is formulated for testing. An experimental group treated with the parameter to be tested is compared with a controlled group. It is essential that all other variables be kept constant so that the target variable will be observed. However, users studies involve many social and human variables which are impossible to control. For example, an experiment could be conducted to test whether term paper clinics conducted in academic libraries improve library use by sophomores. It is not possible to control other factors such as the instructors' research assignments, or the teaching effectiveness of individual instructors that might have a bearing on library use by these students. Therefore, experimental methods can be used under limited conditions. They are rarely done in naturalistic information-gathering and processing situations.

A SYNOPSIS OF RESEARCH RESULTS

Although many users studies have been done, the findings as a whole have not been impressive. They tend to be meaningful only within the confines of the location in which the data was collected. At best, these are case studies in which generalizability of results to all similar information-providing environments is questionable. Nevertheless, the following provides a summary of some of the findings.

Past research has pinpointed the following types of results concerning users' behaviors and patterns of information use. First, overwhelming evidence shows that if information resources are within easy reach of the user, resources at this site will always be the first to be used, even if another better source is known to exist elsewhere. A recent study by Hayes and Palmer (1983) derived similar results, thus confirming that ease of use is the single most important determining factor for the use of information.

Despite the perceived value of printed or recorded information sources, talking to knowledgeable people is the most important means of transmitting information. This informal means of communication has been the subject of several important studies (Griffith and Miller, 1970; Crane, 1972).

Next, a small percent of information sources can satisfy the majority of the users, and a small proportion of all users accounts for the major share of use (Urquhart and Bunn, 1959). This is known as the 20/80 rule. That is, 20 percent of all information resources can adequately serve 80 percent of all requests, and so on. In science and technology, only the current literature receives heavy usage. Information needs change according to different stages of research; and different classes of users such as engineers and scientists have different information needs. Consequently, information services should be sensitive to the users and the different uses of information. Most users prefer a few good publications, preferably synthesized and evaluated. Lastly, regardless of the length of the loan period, users tend to wait till the last possible date before returning the borrowed material (Shaw, 1976)!

Clearly, some of these results have obvious implications in the management of information centers. One may reconsider the loan policy, binding policy, and the arrangement of library materials on the basis of these findings. Although the experimental results may only be relevant to one specific library, the guidelines discussed are useful in planning and conducting use and users studies in general.

In Dervin's recent review (Dervin and Nilan, 1986), she reported that there are indications that a small group of investigators have conceptualized new ways of conducting users studies. Instead of examining the user from the system's view and in terms of the output from the systems, some have actually looked at what is needed by the user regardless of what the system has to offer (Hall, 1980; Krikelas, 1983). MacMullin and Taylor (1984; Taylor, 1986) attempted to identify different classes of information problems and linked them to the different information traits most valued by users. Belkin and his colleagues (1982a; 1982b) assumed that information problems could not be clearly recognized and articulated by the individual information user. However, the problem statement in the form of descriptive text passages may be statistically analyzed in terms of the actual words used. These terms are then associated with different problematic situations, and they are linked to the most effective search strategy. Clearly there is a need to better understand cognition and the knowledge framework of information users. Lastly, Dervin and Nilan (1986) adopted the "sense-making" approach to the analysis of users' needs. It is an attempt to systematize and analyze subjective and individualized information needs to improve the chance of supplying the needed information. This represents a new direction of research since qualitative and not quantitative aspects of information-seeking experience are examined and analyzed.

In summary, the area of information needs and uses is of key importance to the effective operation of information retrieval systems. However, most empirical research relies on social science research tools. Each of the methods surveyed has its weakness and bias. Several decades of experience in studying users and information uses have been accumulated, but generalizable findings are few. Although the overall purpose of such studies clearly aims to better serve information users, the direct benefit of research to practice has yet to be realized. Many studies have limited value. Most important of all, no one has found a unifying theory to provide a conceptual framework for research in this area.

Consequently, research findings have not been synthesized, compared, and correlated. There is a continuing need to develop new approaches and to test them in practice.

REFERENCES

Belkin, N.J., R.N. Oddy, and H.M. Brooks, 1982a. "ASK for Information Retrieval: I. Background and Theory." *Journal of Documentation*, 38(1): 61-71.

Belkin, N.J., R.N. Oddy, and H.M. Brooks. 1982b. "ASK for Information Retrieval: II. Results of a Design Study." *Journal of Documentation*, 38(3): 145-164.

Bookstein, A. 1985. "Questionnaire Research in Library Setting." *Journal of Academic Librarianship*, 11(1):24-28.

Crane, D. 1972. *Invisible Colleges: Diffusion of Knowledge in Scientific Communities.* Chicago: University of Chicago Press.

Crawford, S. 1978. "Information Needs and Uses." *Annual Review of Information Science and Technology*, edited by Martha Williams. Vol. 13, 61-81. Washington, D.C.: Knowledge Industry Publications, Inc.

Daniels, P.J. 1986. "Cognitive Models in Information Retrieval – An Evaluative Review." *Journal of Documentation*, 42(4):272-304.

Dervin, B., and M. Nilan. 1986. "Information Needs and Uses." *Annual Review of Information Science and Technology*, edited by Martha E. Williams. Vol. 22, 3-33. White Plains, New York: American Society for Information Science.

Dyer, E.R. 1979. "The Delphi Technique in Library Research." *Library Research*, 1(1):41-52.

Fischer, R.G. 1978. "The Delphi Method: A Description, Review, and Criticism." *Journal of Academic Librarianship*, 4(2):64-70.

Ford, G. 1977. *User Studies: An Introductory Guide and Select Bibliography.* (Occasional Paper No. 1). Center for Research on User Studies, University of Sheffield, England.

Griffith, B.C., and A.J. Miller. 1970. "Networks of Information Communication Among Scientifically Productive Scientists." *Communication Among Scientists and Engineers*, edited by C. Nelson and D. Pollack, 125-140. Lexington, Massachusetts: D.C. Heath Company.

Hall, H.J. 1981. "Patterns in the Use of Information: The Right to Be Different." *Journal of the American Society for Information Science*, 32(2):103-112.

Hayes, R.M., and E.S. Palmer. 1983. "The Effects of Distance upon Use of Libraries: Case Studies Based on a Survey of Uses of the Los Angeles Public Library—Central Library and Branches." *Library Research*, 5(1):67-100.

Hogeweg-de Haart, H.P. 1983. "Social Science and the Characteristics of Social Science Information and Its Users." *International Forum on Information and Documentation*, 8(1):11-15.

Krikelas, J. 1983. "Information-Seeking Behavior: Patterns and Concepts." *Drexel Library Quarterly*, 19(2):5-20.

MacMullin, S.E., and R.S. Taylor. 1984. "Problem Dimensions and Information Traits." *The Information Society*, 3(1):91-111.

Menzel, H. 1966. "Information Needs and Users in Science and Technology." *Annual Review of Information Science and Technology*, edited by Carlos A. Cuadra. Vol. 1, 41-69. Chicago: Encyclopaedia Britannica.

Rohde, N.F. 1986. "Information Needs." *Advances in Librarianship*, 14:49-73.

Shaw, W.M., Jr. 1976. "Loan Period Distribution in Academic Libraries." *Information Processing and Management*, 12(3):157-159.

Stone, S. 1982. "Humanistic Scholars: Information Needs and Uses." *Journal of Documentation*, 38(4):292-313.

Taylor, R.S. 1986. *Value-Added Processes in Information Systems*. Norwood, New Jersey: Ablex Publishing Corp.

Urquhart, J.A., and R.M. Bunn. 1959. "A National Loan Policy for Science Serials." *Journal of Documentation*, 15(1):21-25.

Wilson, T.D. 1981. "On User Studies and Information Needs." *Journal of Documentation*, 37(1):3-15.

Wood, D.N. 1971. "User Studies: A Review of the Literature from 1966 to 1970." *Aslib Proceedings*, 23:11-23.

4

Relevance

CONCEPT OF RELEVANCE

Relevance is one of the most important concepts in information science. It is the basis for effective communication of knowledge. As was stated in Chapter 1, communication is considered the effective contact of the source and the destination. Relevance is the factor that governs the effectiveness of each communication process. Since the purpose of information retrieval is communication, relevance is also the key ingredient in effective retrieval. A retrieval transaction is considered successful when the retrieved documents are relevant to the patron who requests them. Hence relevance may be thought of as the criterion of retrieval success. It is a measure of effectiveness between the information source and the recipient. Unfortunately, relevance is an abstract notion and an illusive property. As yet, it cannot be precisely defined nor accurately measured.

Upon examining a retrieved document, its relevance is usually quite obvious to the requestor. It seems that one can assume that the information recipient is the best qualified relevance judge. But how does one assign relevance value? How are relevance and nonrelevance determined? Relevance appears to be a subjective quality, unique between the individual and a given document supporting the assumption that relevance can only be judged by the information user. It has an individualistic quality depending on the user's cognitive state, the problem to be solved, prior knowledge of the same topic, urgency of application of the knowledge sought, and the value placed on the information. In other words, it is possible to have different relevance assessments of the identical set of documents retrieved in response to the same query from two different users. Indeed, it may even be possible to have different relevance judgments by the same individual under different circumstances and times. According to Wilson (1973), a valid notion of relevance must incorporate the individual's (a) concerns, (b) preferences over a range of alternatives, and (c) stock of knowledge at that time. The individuality of each situation introduces major variations to relevance judgment. This approach to relevance is dependent solely on the perception and practical utility considered by the information requestor.

54

On the other hand, no one can dispute that Alfred North Whitehead's *The Aims of Education* is relevant to education as a topic. Obviously, the book is not about virology or surgery. This interpretation of relevance is viewed from the standpoint of the content of the physical information unit without regard to any user. In order to organize documents for subject retrieval, information retrieval systems analyze the documents according to their relevance to a finite group of topics in the hope that users will also approach the system from a topical orientation. This system-oriented approach is less dependent on individual perspective than the former approach which relies solely on human judgment that could be inconsistent and unreliable. Interestingly, both approaches appear to be valid, though no one has yet been able to establish a definitive test for them. A naive interpretation of these two meanings of relevance is that in the former, relevance is equivalent to importance or satisfaction to the information requestor. In the latter case, that a document is relevant to topic X simply means that it is about X. In a similar way, informativeness and topicality are two other terms used to describe these two approaches (Bookstein, 1979; Boyce, 1982). The former is considered a subjectively determined property dependent on the individual who acts as the judge, and the latter, a relatively objective property assessed with respect to a particular topic.

Information professionals have long recognized the central role of relevance in retrieval. In the 1950s and 1960s, the search for better understanding of it has attracted researchers from widely different disciplines, such as philosophy, psychology, and mathematics. However, on the whole, research results have been modest. In recent years, research interest in the subject has declined. Yet in conducting evaluation of information systems, the implicit criterion of quality is relevance. The concept of relevance is equated with performance effectiveness. It is considered the effectiveness measure. Thus the issue of relevance cannot be avoided. In many retrieval experimentations, researchers often offer an operational definition of relevance as a performance measure without discussion of the concept. In this chapter, different views of relevance in information retrieval are examined briefly. Readers are encouraged to consult the extensive treatment of the topic in the review paper by Tefko Saracevic (1975).

FALSE DROP

Although logicians and philosophers have long been concerned with the notion of relevance, the conscious articulation of its importance in information retrieval started only after World War II. The early developers of mechanized information retrieval systems are pioneers such as Mortimer Taube, Hans Peter Luhn, Calvin Mooers, James Perry, and others. The basic principles of retrieval developed by these men are still used in most of today's retrieval systems (Herner, 1984). The first major thrust in work on relevance came in the early 1950s. In performing information searches, there seemed to be no way to eliminate the retrieval of nonrelevant materials. The nonrelevant retrieval were considered false drops or noise. The use of the term *noise* was influenced by Shannon's theory. The more frequently the false drop occurs, the more inefficient the information system. The prevailing belief at the time was that nonrelevance was solely the result of the malfunction of the operation of the system. The most probable culprit was thought to be the indexing component of the information system. If the document collection were indexed properly, very few nonrelevant retrievals should result. The blame was placed on the many clever indexing and coding schemes that were designed to match the records more precisely with what the user wanted. The pioneers discussed relevance in terms of nonrelevance. In effect, the notion of relevance arose from the ever-present nonrelevant retrieval (Saracevic, 1970).

Closely related to indexing schemes was the theoretical basis for the searching operation. The matching of the key concepts in a question with those contained in the relevant documents is based on prepositional calculus which found its application in Boolean algebra. The now well-known Boolean operators of AND and OR have their foundation in set theory. The description of the application of Boolean logic in retrieval will be discussed in chapter 9 which deals with search strategy. The following contains a brief description in order to illustrate the cause of false drop due to the search strategy used.

Each document in a collection is usually read by an indexer who selects one or more terms to represent the concepts found in the publication. This is known as indexing. After the document collection is indexed, the totality of terms selected represents the information content of the document collection. The set of terms is the semantic representation of the concepts contained in the physical file of documents. Associated with each term are one or more documents, each of which contains the concept as denoted by the index term. In the terminology of Boolean logic, there is a set of documents associated with each term. Operationally, a card may be posted with the term. Identification numbers for the documents associated with that particular term are listed under the term card. The set of term cards representing the concepts are then arranged in a searchable order. This is the basic input procedure used to process documents in the file in most document retrieval systems.

In searching for documents relevant to a question, the reverse process is used. Each query is analyzed in terms of its content and the sought topic identified. Then the topic is decomposed into its component concepts. Index terms are chosen, which are believed to represent these concepts in the retrieval system. In order to synthesize the index terms representing the component concepts, a Boolean expression is formulated using these index terms linked by one or more appropriate Boolean operators. In essence, by manipulating the document sets via the index terms, a new document set representing the topic sought is formed. There are three Boolean operators for three different types of relations. They are *intersection, union*, and *complement*.

The set formation resulting from an intersection of two sets consists of those documents in which the key concept found in each of the two original sets must be present simultaneously in the newly formed set. For example, the query "give me documents dealing with steel production" would be represented by 'steel AND production.' The union of two sets forms a new set in which only one concept from any one of the two sets must be found in the new set. For example, for the query "retrieve every document on steel or on copper" is represented by "steel OR copper," documents on any one of the topics, steel manufacturing, steel importing, copper mining, and copper importing are included in the new document set.

This use of Boolean operators in retrieval has been revolutionary in concept. It is simple and yet powerful. However, it has its limitations. Basically, it divides the total file into two sets. On the one hand, one finds those documents that are relevant and retrieved, and on the other, those that are not relevant and thus not retrieved. Although Boolean logic allows for coordination of concepts, it also cannot prevent false coordination. An illustration is provided by the following example. Suppose one of the documents was concerned with "the marketing of steel and the production of copper." For the first question of "give me documents dealing with the production of steel," this particular document which does not deal with steel production would be retrieved. This nonrelevant document only deals with the marketing of steel. Since the term *production* was used in conjunction with *copper* in the same document, the two terms *steel* and *production* were improperly coordinated. As long as the two concepts of steel and production were present, the document would be retrieved even though these two concepts were not related to each other in the document. This false coordination also produced a false drop even though the terms and the strategy used were both correct. It was thought that the false drop might be due to a fault in the indexing procedure, that is, the failure of the system.

DESTINATION'S VIEW VERSUS SYSTEM'S VIEW

At the International Conference for Scientific Information in 1959, Vickery made the distinction that the relevance of the document in relation to the subject matter concerned may be different from the relevance perceived by the user. Saracevic (1975) used the two expressions, *destination's view* and *system's view* to denote the two approaches to relevance. It was recognized that although human relevance judgment may be unreliable, it is an acceptable criterion. In other words, in the absence of an absolute standard of relevance, relevance established by human subjective judgment is better than no relevance standard at all. Others also advocated that more should be learned from human relevance experimentation before determining that relevance be used as performance criterion. This recognition of the user's judgment of relevance led to a new flurry of experiments in testing human relevance judgment in an attempt to answer many questions. Who should be the best judge of relevance? How does one judge relevance? How should relevance be determined?

RELATIVE VALUE OF RELEVANCE

Other properties associated with the concept of relevance were also articulated at the same conference. Bar Hillel (Saracevic, 1970) asserted that relevance is not a two-valued entity. Relevance exists on a continuous scale and should not be considered as either relevant or nonrelevant.

In theory, a perfect system would retrieve only those documents relevant to the query submitted by an individual. Since different documents may satisfy information need of different individuals to different degrees, the ideal could not be achieved. By the early 1960s, several theoretical contributions had been made. Maron and Kuhns (1960) were the first to propose that relevance may be a primitive notion which cannot be further broken down. They advocated the new notion that relevance may be expressed in probabilistic terms, that is, the likelihood that a document would satisfy a given request. This is a more realistic measure of relevance and it avoids the inevitable finality of either relevant or not relevant. Thus, in response to each query, each document in a file may be assigned a relevance number with respect to the query. Documents in the file may be ranked in descending order of their probabilities of relevance. The list of documents retrieved can be adjusted depending on the requirement specified by the requestor. For one who only wishes to examine a few highly relevant items, a cutoff of the top few relevant citations may suffice. A ranked list of all documents with a nonzero relevance number would constitute a comprehensive list of retrieval.

INFORMATION AS A MEASURE

Goffman (1964) defined relevance as a measure of information conveyed by a document relative to a query. In order to satisfy the condition of a measure, the quantity must

- Be real and a nonnegative value

- Be completely additive, i.e., the quantity must equal the sum of its parts

- Be ordered

- Have an absolute zero value

He also argued that relevance as a measure has two properties. One is a relation between the query and each document; the other is a relation existing between the documents in a file. His rationale is that the sequence with which a group of documents is presented is just as important as the identification of the documents themselves. For example, if three books are retrieved on structured computer programming, it would make no sense at all if a novice is first exposed to an advanced text on the intricacies of pointers. One should start with an introductory text.

Goffman was among the first to introduce the idea of conditional probability. That is, assuming that document A which is relevant to query Q is retrieved, what is the chance of the relevance of the next retrieved document, document B, to query Q? These theoretical considerations highlight the complex nature of the concept. A relative value rather than an absolute value of relevance has been firmly established among serious researchers. This relative value is also affected by many factors: the inherent properties or content of the documents, the interrelationship among documents, the representations of documents, and the nature of the queries and their representations. Finally, it may be viewed as a measure associated with conditional probability.

PERFORMANCE MEASURES

There were also developments relating to the pragmatic use of relevance in evaluating the performance of information retrieval systems. In the mid 1950s there was extensive use of technology and human effort in the design, development, and operation of these systems. Hence, heavy demands were made on the evaluation of these costly systems. In rigorous scientific testing and evaluation, several requirements must be met. As a prerequisite, one must articulate what it is that one is attempting to evaluate and test. The systems objective must be identified so that one is not testing something that the system was never designed to do. The criteria must be clearly defined. For example, is the speed of information delivery of prime concern? Is accuracy of information more crucial? Is utility of the information the important performance criterion? To evaluate the system according to some criteria, specific measures should be established. To measure speed, is it correct to count from the time of the request to the time of delivery of the citations? Or is it the delivery of the actual articles? How does one measure accuracy? Can accuracy of information be judged by the searcher or the requestor or the user? Or can it be judged by some other authoritative sources? Appropriate measuring instruments and methodology should be used.

The two most well-known performance measures are recall and precision. Recall measures the proportion of the relevant documents actually retrieved. That is, assuming that the collection contains 100 items on the subject being sought, how many of the 100 have been retrieved? Precision relates to the percentage of relevant documents contained in the retrieved set. In other words, when one retrieves 50 citations, how many of these are actually relevant? Naturally, it is assumed that relevance has been established by someone or some yardstick. No matter how limited these measures are, recall and precision have become the standards used by most evaluation experiments.

$$\text{RECALL} = \frac{\text{number of relevant documents retrieved}}{\text{total number of relevant documents in the file}}$$

$$\text{PRECISION} = \frac{\text{number of relevant documents retrieved}}{\text{total number of documents retrieved from the file}}$$

By the 1960s, there were several experimental testing projects on relevance. Specific methodological issues relating to experimental design were raised. They include operational definitions of relevance, variables affecting human relevance judgment, stability and reliability of human judges, and appropriate circumstances for relevance judgment.

Of special importance were two major research projects on relevance, the Cranfield experiments conducted in England, and the Comparative Systems Laboratory experiments at the Center for Communication and Documentation, Case Western Reserve University. The research team at Case Western consolidated the variables being sought in the following form:

Relevance is the _____ of a _____ existing between a _____ and a _____ as judged by a _____.

The Cranfield experiments have been credited with being the first major tests to use the recall and precision performance measures. Cyril Cleverdon was the principal investigator and his results have often been cited. One important finding was that if high recall is desired, one can expect to have lower precision, and vice versa. A example would be if a user wants all there is to know about the research on cryogenics, the search for most of the relevant materials is probably fairly easy. However, in order not to miss anything and to cover all possible sources, one would have to look at some rather unlikely sources. Many nonrelevant materials would have to be scanned, resulting in a low precision of search. On the other hand, if only a few relevant papers are needed, a quick and dirty search will suffice. In this case, one cannot expect to retrieve many relevant items. That is to say, precision is high but recall is low.

Another major finding was the identification of five major groups of variables in conducting experiments in relevance. They are people, documents, queries, relevance judges, and the way relevance is judged.

In general, if the users have greater depth of subject knowledge, they tend to agree among themselves on the relevance judgment of the materials. These subject experts also are more stringent in selecting relevant items. On the other hand, if the human judges are not themselves users of the materials to be judged, such as those delegated research assistants and information searchers, then the criteria of relevance is more lax. However, in most cases, nonrelevant documents are commonly recognized by the judges.

The subject matter of the collection of documents to be judged is also a very important consideration. The narrower the subject, the better the relevance agreement among judges. Subjects in the hard sciences are also easier to judge in terms of relevance. Moreover, writing styles also affect the relevance judgment.

The questions posed also affect the consistency and reliability of relevance judgment. If the questions are better understood, better judgment results. If the group of judges has the opportunity for discussion among themselves, the more consistent their judgment becomes. It was found that those items that were relevant to the query tend to share many semantically similar terms. Nonrelevant items do not have as many common terms found in the queries. If the judges are kept informed of the progress of the experiment on relevance, they also tend to produce better and more consistent judgment.

The conditions under which the judgment is made is the least understood aspect. There are inconclusive results from several experiments. In general, if the judges are pressured by time constraints, they tend to be more lenient in their judgments.

As for the way relevance is judged, probably the use of a ratio scale is the most reliable. Yet given a scale, most judgments are bunched at the two extreme ends. In other words, there is a high consistency among judges on nonrelevant documents and those of high relevance. For judges with subject knowledge, their agreement on the relevant documents is also high. No matter how the experiments were designed, the judges appear to prefer more categories between nonrelevant and relevant judgments. Using many judges on the same set of documents tends to result in skewed distribution. In other words, the number of documents judged in each category is uneven. It is most likely that many fall in one category.

In summary, relevance is the most important concept in information retrieval. It is also the most difficult area of investigation. Clearly relevance is the key to effective contact between the information source and the destination. As a property, it defines a relationship. It has not been formally defined nor precisely measured. Two commonly held notions of relevance exist, namely, relevance as judged by an individual and relevance as related to the subject content in question. There is much confusion between the two. Moreover, many variables are associated with the relevance of any retrieval, not all of which have been identified. Many believe that potential for progress could emerge if more experiments were performed in light of existing theoretical works in information retrieval.

REFERENCES

Bookstein, A. 1979. "Relevance." *Journal of the American Society for Information Science*, 30(5):269-273.

Boyce, B.R. 1982. "Beyond Topicality: A Two Stage View of Relevance and the Retrieval Process." *Information Processing and Management*, 18(3): 105-109.

Goffman, W. 1964. "On Relevance as a Measure." *Information Storage and Retrieval*, 2(3):201-203.

Herner, S. 1984. "Brief History of Information Science." *Journal of the American Society for Information Science*, 35(3):157-163.

Maron, M.E., and J.L. Kuhns. 1960. "On Relevance, Probabilistic Indexing, and Information Retrieval." *Journal of the Association of Computing Machinery*, 7(3):216-244.

Saracevic, T. 1970. *Introduction to Information Science.* New York: Bowker.

Saracevic, T. 1975. "Relevance: A Review of and a Framework for the Thinking on the Notion in Information Science." *Journal of the American Society for Information Science*, 26(6):321-343.

Wilson, P. 1973. "Situational Relevance." *Information Storage and Retrieval*, 9(8):457-471.

Part II
INFORMATION RETRIEVAL SYSTEMS

5

Design of
Information Retrieval Systems

Previous chapters in Part I have described various phenomena and processes found in information transfer and knowledge communication. In particular, studies of observable characteristics of literature have been shown to be of relevance and their potential application to document retrieval exhibited. Part II first introduces the considerations for systems design, and secondly, addresses the five major functions found in information retrieval systems. Underlying concepts of both operational systems and experimental approaches are included.

Systems whose purposes are the realization of communication processes are known as information systems. Human information-processing systems, electronic data processing systems, and information retrieval systems are mechanisms specifically designed to enable the retrieval of information. In this sense, libraries and information centers are specific types of information retrieval systems whose main concern is the access to the intellectual content of information records. Such systems usually function within larger and more complex social organizations. Hence, their design should be carefully planned in relation to their environment. One must be guided by the designated role of the system within the larger organizational structure, the output expected of the system, and the goals established for the system. There are a number of common approaches to systems design. For example, the Delphi Method has been used successfully to conduct technological forecasting as important data input to systems design. Master planning and strategic planning are common approaches to city and urban planning, and organizational design. In this chapter, rudimentary aspects of a specific approach, the systems approach, are introduced for the analysis and design of information retrieval systems.

SYSTEMS APPROACH

The Nature of Systems Approach

The expression, *systems approach*, has been variously defined and interpreted (Mattessich, 1982). It has been regarded as an abstract systems philosophy and as a highly rigorous mathematical simulation technique based on estimated parameters. The systems approach was first introduced and used in operations research. It is a formal procedure for examining a complex process such as an organization. Many different names are used, more or less, to denote the same approach. They include systems engineering, systems analysis, and systems design. There is a large body of literature on systems, most of which is related to operations research and cybernetics. In the context of the design of rctrieval systems, it is not a set of procedures nor a method. It is rather a concept or a way of looking at a problem. Several articles related to systems in the framework of information-retrieval systems can be found in the sixth issue of the 1982 volume of the *Journal of the American Society for Information Science* (Lunin, 1982).

Several factors have contributed to the prominent rise of the concept of systems. The most obvious is the need to cope with the emergence of increasingly large and complex organizations after the World Wars. The complexity of physical plants, operations, multilevel organizations, needed human resources and interaction, and multifaceted processes is beyond the grasp of any single individual. The design and management of such organizations require expertise in several disciplines, well coordinated to achieve a common goal. The proper functioning of such complex organizations could benefit from relevant data from various branches of the engineering sciences, human engineering, environmental sciences, aesthetics, and others. Instead of optimizing each specific area of concern, "a systems approach" attempts to look at the entire problem, the whole organization, or the process in its entirety as a unified whole and in its proper context. It is easy to see that in situations in which an integrated complex of people, facilities, equipment, and procedures are needed, an approach that has as its target the objective of the entire system is logical. The results in terms of performance output can be effective and powerful. On the other hand, there is no need to analyze with an elaborate systems approach a simple process or a small organization.

Definitions

SYSTEMS

In general, a *system* usually consists of a collection of interrelated *components interacting* to perform a specific *function* for a specific *purpose*. It is a mechanism by which a process is realized. Almost any entity can be viewed as a system. One defines and focuses on a system by placing arbitrary boundaries to the entity under study. For example, if the information service of General Motors is considered a system, one must be able to define and specify its overall purpose, its role within GM, its component parts, and the types of desired interactions between the parts. If its purpose is to support the GM research scientists with technical and scientific publications from the published literature, then the unit which processes and transmits internally produced reports is not considered as part of the service.

The concept of system is also a hierarchical one in that any system can be simultaneously a macro- and a micro-system in relationship to some other system. For example, the college or university library may be considered a part of a larger system, the university. Being one of several subsystems, the library interacts with other components such as the office of academic affairs of the central administration or the various colleges in the university within the academic community. By the same token, the university can be considered a subsystem of an even larger system, for example, the total higher educational system of a given state. The state in turn is a subsystem of the United States of America, and so on. On the other hand, the library can also be viewed as a supersystem consisting of several smaller systems, such as the circulation system, the technical service system, and so on.

SYSTEMS ANALYSIS

Systems analysis is a formal procedure established to examine a complex process or organization. It is distinguished by its attempts to reduce the process or the entity into its component parts. At the same time, these parts are viewed in relation to each other and to the entire unit as a whole with respect to an agreed-upon performance criterion.

SYSTEMS DESIGN

Systems design is a synthesizing procedure by which available resources are employed to achieve the system's established purpose. Usually the resulting new configuration of the interacting parts will emerge only after several iterations of synthesis and modifications of the design.

Characteristics of a
Systems Approach

Several distinct attributes characterize the systems approach (Churchman, 1968; Wilkerson and Paul, 1985). First, it is imperative to investigate and clarify the overall purpose of the system and to decide on the measures of quality of the final product or the criteria of effectiveness of the service goals. For example, a public library may be considered a system. "To serve the public" may be expressed as the mission for the public library, but it is not a statement of goals since service to the public as an overall goal is not measurable. Goal statements can only be measured in terms of more specific tasks and outcomes. Moreover, specific criteria of performance should be articulated and linked to the tasks identified. Most public libraries can only reach several segments of the population they profess to serve. Different groups may be served by different types of service by varying levels of intensity. There are not enough human and material resources available in any library even if "the public" really demands to be fully served. Therefore, the statement of a goal must be expressed in terms of achievable performance measures.

Performance measures may be one of two types: economic efficiency or performance efficiency. Economic or cost efficiency is interpreted as the ability to produce or process the same number of units for less cost, or the ability to produce or process more units at the same cost. Expenditure is the main concern. Performance efficiency is also known as effectiveness, which is much harder to define. In retrieval work, high quality of service is often measured by users' satisfaction. However, satisfaction is not easily measurable and quantifiable. Indicators of users' satisfaction such as the number of return visits, the number of complaints, and the number of registered users may be identified. Sometimes a number of alternative measures may also be identified. They may, however, be conflicting, and even competing with each other. For example, thoroughness of service and the number of patrons served are two desirable measures of users' satisfaction. Yet, consistent in-depth literature search may not be possible if one is also striving to serve as many patrons as possible. Realistic and complementary objectives should be explored thoroughly and negotiated between the systems designer and the systems manager. It should be noted that since the system may have subgoals, a number of performance measures may be proposed. It is only after the systems mission is explicitly articulated that any effectiveness measures of the system can have meaning. The actual process of clarification of the system's goal usually gives a better focus on the final design of the system.

Second, possible alternative overall goals need to be explored. From the outset, this analytic approach recognizes that any system exists in its environment. Each alternative must be looked at in relation to all external constraints found in its environment in terms of feasibility, risk, and cost. To do so, all environmental variables must be identified and their properties clearly distinguished so that their effects on the system can be anticipated. The feasibility of each alternative goal should be assessed and analyzed. Performance must also be balanced by the cost of such goals. In proposing designs, the emphasis is on an exploration of alternatives. These are viewed as tentative plans and subject to revision. The process of iteration is essential in the systems approach and must be built into the analytic process so that the design process is both a dynamic and responsive one. Some of the important constraints for information systems are legal, political, financial, technological, and even practical.

Third, systems analysis is viewed essentially as a problem-solving process. The system should be analyzed by dividing each unit into its component parts. Often, these parts may be responsible for the major functions of the system, or the major classes of activities required to achieve the systems' objective. To facilitate analysis, artificial boundaries may be set up for each subunit. Each part is identified with its goal in relation to its role within the system. Each unit is studied in detail, and analyzed in terms of its interactions with other parts of the total system. Several ways of analyzing the system may be employed. It may be viewed from the organizational structure, from the functional standpoint, or from the different output services perspective. A document-retrieval system is often viewed as having several major components each responsible for a major function.

In practice, the systems approach may be applied in approximately four phases: data gathering, task analysis, systems design, and systems implementation. The first phase involves intensive data collection in a nontraditional sense. The analyst works with an individual with major responsibility for the system. The aim is to identify and to establish a realistic purpose for the system. Upper and lower limits of what the system can or cannot do are explored and decided upon. The interactions between the system's analyst and the individual who is thoroughly familiar with the system is to insure that the data transmitted for the systems design is accurate. Then the analyst proceeds to specify the functions and goals of the system under review. This is followed by a process of familiarization and orientation in detail of all the component units, their organization, their function, their work content, their work flow, their activities and all documentation of their work. The environmental constraints are documented. As a result, an overall view of the system is clear and understood by all.

The second phase consists of analysis of the system by its logical subsystems. Basically, the activities and tasks of each should be schematically depicted for ease of understanding on several levels. On the systems level, the functions of each subsystem and their interrelationships can be represented by flow charts or block diagrams. The interactive parts in each subsystem can be visualized more easily in terms of work flow. The task of each subsystem can be further magnified by a detailed representation on the procedural level. As the work flow is traced, details of the steps of each major decision process are analyzed. Major alternatives are indicated. Thus, in the case of the library, the flow chart enables the tracing of the progress of a given document through the system. At a glance, it can show if the same processing has been performed on the same item. Duplication of effort or the absence of essential tasks can be identified. Similarly, the movement of people and the tasks performed can also be traced and the effort spent measured. For example, an interlibrary loan transaction may start with the patron not finding the book in the library and may end with the delivery of the book to the requestor. In addition to the flow diagrams, each task may be quantified by the amount of time spent, the dollar cost, the number of decision points needed, and the type of procedures performed.

The less tangible criteria such as tension, pressure, accessibility, availability, and convenience may not be as easy to identify. However, indicators for these elusive qualities may be found. For example, one may analyze accessibility by the distance travelled by the patron, the number of visits needed, or the number of stops made by any document.

The next stage is the design of the system. It is often conducted while analysis is still underway. One of the key ingredients of systems design is optimization. This is a process of iteration and revision based on feedback data. Within the context of the system's goals, each repetition and modification may result in new requirements and modified goals. This iterative process clarifies obtainable goals and brings one closer to a more realistic and optimal system. It is an essential part of the design phase.

The final phase is the implementation of the new system. A realistic work plan and time schedule is essential. Human factors concerning job replacement, psychological adjustments, and level of productivity must be considered. The disruption caused by new systems implementation cannot be avoided, but its adverse effects can be minimized. A phased-in plan is advised. For complex systems, often a model or prototype is built to simulate the systems operation and to test the effectiveness of planned system.

In summary, key ingredients of a systems approach consist of a carefully articulated purpose of the system based on the weighing of possible alternatives, examination of its external environmental factors and their constraints, and detailed analysis of the component parts and their interrelations. The entire process focuses on optimizing the whole unit in accordance with an agreed-upon performance criterion. Systems objectives and the classes of users served should be predetermined. The systems approach is characterized by a series of revisions. Relying on feedback data, iterations of both analysis and design aim to achieve a preselected set of goals within the limits of the available resources and constraints. The process may not result in the best system in the absolute sense, but because it is dynamic, this process provides flexibility to accommodate predicted and unforeseen changes.

INFORMATION RETRIEVAL SYSTEMS

Objectives

Turning now to the specific systems design considerations of information-retrieval systems, the most important step is to decide if a new system is indeed needed. An acceptable alternative may be the modification of an existing system to meet newly identified demands and objectives. Although management makes the final decision, the systems analyst can provide the needed data for a well-informed decision. Many systems begin with an assessment of the use of literature and/or a user study as discussed in Chapter 3. For service-oriented systems, users' input is an important consideration to be incorporated in setting the overall objective for the system. Often there are several classes of objectives. They should be ranked according to priorities. For example, in designing an optical disc system for the storage and retrieval of engineering drawings produced within an organization, one must ascertain the use to which it will be put, the actual and potential users of the materials, the extent of probable use, the types of use these drawings are intended for, and the legal requirements for the storage of the graphic documentations. In the case of a library, one may wish to serve as many patrons as possible, to provide in-depth service, to supply pertinent answers to every reference question, to support the curriculum of the college, to serve as a main source of information support for faculty research, to make available entertainment materials for the undergraduate students, and to provide a conducive environment for study. All of these may be relevant and should be considered. However, they cannot all be given the same level of priority.

The types of objectives to be considered in information retrieval systems are

- informational content of information resources collected
- utility of information resources
- users
- documentary sources
- performance criteria
- economics

INFORMATIONAL CONTENT

It is obvious that information retrieval systems exist to provide information resources to their users. Yet, the subject matter of each collection must differ. For example, the National Agricultural Library is concerned with all aspects of agricultural sciences. Therefore, as an information retrieval system, it is subject oriented. Many information systems are similarly oriented to a specific subject or group of subjects. There are other systems that are oriented toward specific missions of the institution. Take the database produced by the Environmental Protection Agency. To support the mission of the EPA, its collection or database must concern itself with several subject areas. They are not limited to chemistry, toxicity, or public health. Any materials with potential contribution to the mission of the EPA are appropriate for its database. Still others, such as the Institute for Scientific Information, collect materials on many different subjects. Its database is multidisciplinary. In general, the informational content of an information retrieval system may be subject oriented, mission oriented, multidisciplinary, or interdisciplinary.

UTILITY

Utility here means the ultimate use of the informational records gathered for the information retrieval system. Intended use and probable use should be carefully considered. Characteristics of the system must promote the intended use. An information system serving companies such as the Standard Oil Company exists to solve information problems at the parent company. It actually provides answers to specific questions regarding research conducted at the company's laboratories on oil exploration, oil refining, oil storage and transportation, or on technical or management problems.

Other types of utility can be of a current awareness nature. They provide potentially useful information to users on a continuous basis so that they are kept up-to-date in their subject fields. These systems cull the literature for items on topics matching the interests of the users they serve. Citations or full articles are then delivered. Relevant articles may even be abstracted and translated for the clients.

As information retrieval systems, most abstracting and indexing services provide a different kind of utility to their users. They are primarily devoted to gathering and organizing information in such a way that users can identify and locate bibliographic references relevant to their interests. Actual document delivery is frequently left to the device of the patron.

Lastly, there are information systems which process literature so that their output becomes acceptable input to other information retrieval systems. For example, many database producers such as PAIS (Public Affairs Information System) are themselves abstracting and indexing services producing information products. Their products are also input materials for online search services, such as DIALOG, which provides a host of other databases through which searchers can access them online. These databases are also input materials from which CD-ROM optical discs are made. Clearly, it is important for the analyst to distinguish the uses to which the information product or service is directed.

USERS

The identification of the user group is the most obvious objective that needs to be defined. One may distinguish between intended users, and actual users. Many retrieval systems, especially those within industrial and commercial companies, have specified users groups. A system with a specific user group is the Research Service of the Library of Congress which serves at the pleasure of the Congress of the United States of America.

Most information centers have less well-defined users. In particular, abstracting and indexing organizations have still less specified users. Although one could infer that the Index Medicus is intended for clinicians and biomedical researchers, it is also used by librarians, biochemists, and other allied health professionals. Actual information users differ from librarians and database searchers in that the latter group acts as an intermediary between the end-users and the system. Their role is to facilitate information retrieval for the information user. One can expect differences in the physical handling of the system by these two types of users.

DOCUMENTARY SOURCES

After the identification of the materials to be included in the retrieval system, one must determine the level at which the subjects are to be collected. Considerations are the depth of subject coverage, the types of documents, years of coverage, and languages included. Often the decision is based on a combination of constraints imposed by users' needs, storage limitations, financial resources, and personnel requirements. Does one need all published documents on a given subject? Is it desirable to collect exhaustively all technical reports? Is there a cut-off date? Should one also include trade manuals and private correspondence? Should certain languages or journals be excluded? Is the system an integrated system such that records and data other than published documents are also included? These are pertinent questions to be answered.

PERFORMANCE CRITERIA

Theoretically, the performance criterion by which the information system is judged is the key for the design of any system. For example, the effectiveness of the Patent Office should be measured by the completeness of its coverage. Unfortunately, the provision of relevant materials, which is often stated as the primary criterion, is not directly measurable. Moreover, most users do not know what to expect of an information retrieval system. Many substitute criteria are used. For example, speed of service is often cited as a performance measure. Per unit cost is another. Although commonly agreed-upon performance criteria are lacking in information systems, an articulated desirable level of service helps to establish realistic systems standards.

ECONOMICS

Although cost may often be the main determining factor in many systems designs, it should not be the sole determinant. On the basis of funding sources, the effects of whether an institution is profit-making, nonprofit, or subsidized have had a definite bearing on the design. In the early phase of the development of online information systems, 90 percent of all information retrieval systems, such as NTIS (National Technical Information Service) and Chemical Abstract, were subsidized or sponsored by nonprofit organizations. Although the need for the development of online systems was obvious, the cost and effort needed for research and development were enormous. At the same time, the payoff in the forseeable future was unlikely. There was a limited number of users who could afford the associated cost and even fewer online searchers. Clearly, a profit-making organization could ill afford to design and implement an online database search system. By the 1980s, online systems have become commercially profitable. This is not to say that without profit, retrieval systems cannot be designed or implemented. Most organizations recognize the value of information or at least the cost of not being informed. Adequate justification for the need for information systems is paramount in order to obtain assured financial support. Today, most systems are operated by profit-making organizations reflecting the increasing societal value placed on information.

Components of the System

Systems analysis necessitates the breakdown of the information system into major components. Each subsystem is expected to perform definite functions to achieve the systems' objectives. The following outline lists five functions representing the major classes of activities for any information retrieval system. Although the particular division of activities represents a structure arbitrarily imposed on the information retrieval system, it reflects a functional view of the system. There are several other models in the literature. Most of them can be compressed or expanded into the following functions:

- selection/weeding/storage
- document analysis and information representation
- file organization
- search strategy and retrieval
- service/dissemination

These functions are basic to any information retrieval system. Each of the functions appears to be self-contained and each is treated separately in the following chapters.

REFERENCES

Churchman, C. West. 1968. *The Systems Approach*. New York: The Dell Publishing Co. Inc.

Lunin, L., ed. 1982. "Perspectives on Systems Methodology and Information Research." *Journal of the American Society for Information Science*, 33(6): 373-408.

Mattessich, R. 1982. "The Systems Approach: Its Variety of Aspects." *Journal of the American Society for Information Science*, 33(6):383-394.

Wilkerson, L., and A. Paul. 1985. "Every System Should Have One: A Collection of Properties Which Can Be Used as a Criterion for Evaluating the Quality of a System." *Information Processing and Management*, 21(1): 45-49.

6

Selection of
Information Resources

In any information retrieval system, selection of materials to be included in the data file is probably the most important function for the system's operation. In order to provide information service, the system must contain information resources that may be of potential use to its users. For example, a data file could encompass an entire library system; it could be an electronic bibliographic file of citations on the subject of toxicology; it could also be a file of patient records of those who have visited a dentist. Each of the retrieval systems for those files is designed to achieve specific goals. The system may serve the information needs of the research staff of a rubber manufacturing company. It may be established to supply answers over the telephone to questions regarding poison. It may be designed as a personal information system to store reprints and bibliographic citations for future use. Whatever the system's objective, if it does not contain the appropriate subject content to serve the needs of the intended patrons, maximizing the operations of all the other functions can in no way improve the system's performance.

DEFINITIONS

The literature refers to two distinct groups of tasks in relation to the selection of information resources for information systems: selection and acquisition. *Selection* is the intellectual process of identifying the relevant and useful items from the available pool of materials, eventually making a choice based on stated and/or implied criteria. *Acquisition* is the process of procuring materials once they are identified. The former consists of a complex series of decisions based on judgment, whereas the latter is basically procedural. Selection is normally performed by the professional staff. Acquisition procedures, often spelled out in an operational manual, can be easily carried out by clerical help.

The components of selection and acquisition usually include the following:

1. *Policy statement* is a formalized document containing the rationale for selection. It articulates the types of materials and records to be included and excluded, together with the reasons for such decisions.

2. *Process of selection* relates to the actual implementation of the selection policy. It includes the use of human and information resources as aids in identifying and judging potentially useful items.

3. *Tools to aid selection* are often reference materials identified as the best sources to verify bibliographic information, to identify new and relevant materials, to locate reviews of relevant subject literatures, and to track down the necessary ordering information.

4. *Ordering procedures* consist of a set of well-defined steps to ensure the procurement of documents, records, data, and selection tools. Since a number of clerical tasks must be carried out to acquire a single document, articulating the exact procedure is intended to systematize and expedite the tasks.

5. *Feedback* is a built-in mechanism within the system to optimize the effectiveness of the selection process. Its purpose is to monitor and to upgrade the collection continuously to meet users' expectations and to respond to changes in users' needs. Users' opinions solicited on a consistent and continuous basis may be incorporated into the system as input data. An effective feedback mechanism maximizes the usefulness and relevance of the file content.

POLICY OF SELECTION

Generally speaking the process of identification and procurement of the best available materials should be guided by the objectives of the system. Since information systems seldom exist as autonomous units, the systems' objectives must agree with those of the parent organization that they serve. With clearly understood objectives, policy may be established. The systems' functions may then be articulated in accordance with policy guidelines. The selection itself should consist of tracking and scanning available sources. A decision is based on evaluative judgment with respect to topical relevance, possible usefulness, quality of content, accuracy of statements, and levels and format of presentation. Selection is intended to be a purposeful endeavor.

Selection principles are found in material selection textbooks. In the abstract, it is clear as to what should be included in the document file. As a policy, it is easy to espouse the virtue of user service, unrestricted access to information, and other principles. However, in actual practice, most systems are handicapped by (1) the constraints imposed by society and by finite resources, and (2) the lack of precise generalizable guidelines to implement lofty principles. As a result, although there is general agreement concerning the ideal method of selection, there are great discrepancies between what is desirable and what is actually done in information retrieval systems. Principles are quite different from normal practice. It is hard to articulate and pinpoint the kinds of materials that will be useful to the intended patrons. Most users do not submit recommended lists on a consistent basis. For example, one may aim to satisfy every research scientist and engineer in an organization. Yet this intention must be translated into specific journal titles, book titles, technical reports, patents, government documents, and all other pertinent items. One may simply order whatever has been recommended by the patrons. A policy of selection based solely on users' recommendations can hardly serve the needs of all users, let alone anticipate them. This example illustrates the dilemma of implementing a policy that is basically altruistic in nature. Another example is an information clearinghouse on a given subject. Although in principle, selection in this case is simply collecting every item on that subject regardless of quality, there is no easy way to keep track of every publication on a given subject. Exhaustive collecting is labor-intensive and time-consuming to a point that the final cutoff decision is usually determined by the available human and financial resources and not by the degree of comprehensiveness required. Certainly no clear-cut procedure is available.

A selection policy is a heuristic statement, a declaration of principles on the basis of which decisions should be made regarding material selection. On the other hand, it is subject to variations and interpretation in individual cases in its application. This statement does not specify the actual selection procedure. It offers a philosophy or a set of general guidelines. As a result, almost all librarians operate on the same general selection principles of high quality of information resources and use to most users, regardless of the existence of any formal selection policy.

Nevertheless, a formal selection policy is indispensable for any information system. It provides a focus and a set of general guidelines to be applied in a systematic and consistent manner. Over a period of time, the collection content can be expected to reflect the established objectives of the parent institution to a large measure. A clear direction insures a steady course of collection development. Furthermore, the mere process of establishing a selection policy heightens the awareness of the underlying purpose of the collection.

What must be contained in a policy statement?

1. It should contain a statement of the objectives and purpose of the parent organization. This is necessary to provide a framework, a relevant environment, and a sense of permanence in spite of inevitable changes in personnel and users. It charts a course.

2. It should identify the intended users. In identifying the users, priority of service can be delineated. User profiles should be drawn so that different facets and topics can be clearly stated.

3. Relevant subjects and missions should be identified. Often groups of subjects are needed. Although the core subjects are easy to define, the related or fringe areas are more difficult to specify. When interdisciplinary or multidisciplinary areas are needed, subject identification is particularly important in terms of the extent of coverage. Since topics are never truly discrete in terms of boundaries, decisions have to be made in terms of the extent of coverage. A truly exhaustive collection involves extraordinary expense that can seldom be afforded by most systems.

Operationally, the identification of subjects can be accomplished in a number of ways: (1) a committee of subject experts can produce a compromised consensus of subjects and the extent of their coverage; (2) the subjects can be defined in terms of a core group of the most heavily cited journal sources; (3) a consensus of journal sources can be reached by polling the patrons using a survey instrument; and (4) an ad hoc revision of an established position can be made. For a mission-oriented organization, the decision is more difficult to reach. For example, an information system providing information on urban problems must tackle various social, economic, political, as well as technical, issues. In the final analysis, whatever decision is made, it should be subject to periodic scrutiny and revision.

SELECTION PROCESS

This process is nebulous. Quality and value are subjectively determined. Judgment is based on years of experience selecting materials and familiarity with the published works and journal titles. Yet this mode of operation cannot be applied with consistency and objectivity. It also cannot be applied with the same degree of precision in judgment by two individuals. Research in this area is much needed. Nevertheless, several practical considerations may be noted. First, the use of the same selection tools as aids to decision making can be helpful in arriving at similar outcomes. Individuals with subject knowledge tend to be more consistent in the identification of quality items. Particularly in mission-oriented disciplines, subject expertise is a useful contributing factor. Familiarity with specialized terminology of the field can be helpful. Skills in tracking down announcements, publishers, reports, and similar items are essential. Finally, validity, reliability, and accuracy of document content dealing with qualitative and quantitative data are important aspects to consider.

SELECTION TOOLS

It is obvious that selection criteria are difficult to ascertain. Thus, one tends to concentrate on the specification of the tools and information sources that can provide some aids for selection. There are many recommended lists, review media, bibliographies, publishers' lists, and abstracting and indexing services useful for bibliographic verification of the existence and location of the items. However, in most cases, they are of minimal value in providing judgment of quality.

PROCEDURES

Ordering and subscription procedures are routinely performed by computerized systems. They do not present major problems.

FEEDBACK

As is obvious from Chapter 3, user surveys and use studies are methods by which valuable feedback information can be obtained. However, for the purpose of improving the file content, the mechanism of direct user feedback can be instituted in a variety of ways. A periodic survey can be effective. The survey results can be interpreted and then coordinated with input data such as the number of items added in each subject category. Often, such occasional formal survey instruments may be supplemented by informal exchange between the systems operators and users. Many systems may have a continuous formalized feedback mechanism in the form of a questionnaire attached to each document delivery. This method insures needed data. The only limitation is that since a questionnaire becomes a routine part of the retrieval system, its importance is diminished. Patrons may not take the time and effort to respond and to cooperate fully.

The reader is referred to books by Curley and Broderick (1985), Gardner (1981), Broadus (1981), and others for complete discussion of selection of library materials.

RESEARCH EFFORTS ON MATERIAL SELECTION

In today's environment, material selection can no longer be based purely on quality, topical relevance, and use. Budgetary constraints loom heavily as the cost of publications increases and as shelf space becomes increasingly more expensive. Since most libraries and information retrieval systems are members of some resource sharing networks, availability may not be interpreted solely as the ownership of the printed items. The shared usage of less-used items among the network membership, the electronic access of full-text journals, and the subscription of compact electronic storage containing back issues of journals are realistic alternatives to the purchase and storage of printed products. These issues are only beginning to be aired. Strategies to balance budgets, availability of information resources, patron preferences and satisfaction, and the optimal use of shelf space should be based on solid data and systematic study of the tradeoffs. These should be on the next research agenda.

As far as criteria for material selection are concerned, even though the underlying selection principles are clear, the actual process is vague. The key ingredient of selection — the quality of material — often is not discussed at all. This is understandable since the intellectual task of selection based on quality is still largely subjective. The characteristic of quality is undefined. Therefore, even with the same set of selection criteria, two selectors are likely to apply them differently, thus ending up with different groups of documents. Aside from the question of quality, topical relevancy is also dependent on the subjective judgment of experts. Again there are significant differences between judgments made by different subject specialists. Any success in research in this area holds substantial potential payoff in the improvement of systems performance.

The development of objective measurements for selection criteria would be particularly useful. Several interesting research studies have attempted to chart a more systematic and rational approach to the selection process. These researchers suggest the identification of factors that may serve as reasonable indicators for quality and usefulness. The remaining part of this chapter describes several experimental approaches. An experimental method in journal selection is also included to illustrate the application of bibliometric techniques to material selection.

Quality Judged by Reviewers

Pao (1975) proposed a method to identify quality publications based on citations received from state-of-the-art reviews. Periodic reviews of a field are often commissioned works written by authorities in the specific area. The chosen individual usually conducts a thorough review of the literature, citing all relevant items in the bibliography of the review. Occasionally a work may be cited for gross errors. On balance, most reviewers read and cite publications for relevance, quality, accuracy, influence, and controversy. It can be expected that key works in the field are repeatedly cited. Over a period of time, those papers cited repeatedly are perceived to be of greater impact and, therefore, have been shown to be of higher quality. Boyce and Primov (1977) have shown in an experiment that literature cited frequently by review articles tends to be more heavily cited by the literature at large. This objective criterion can provide a reasonable method for identifying a quality filtered group of publications. The National Library of Medicine has used this method to select its core literature for the hepatitis knowledge base project (Bernstein, Siegel, and Goldstein, 1980). This group of publications consists of articles and books frequently cited by state-of-the-art reviews.

Obsolescence Indicators

The weeding of materials in the collection is an issue closely related to selection. Since materials cannot be discarded at random, it is clear that the criteria for *not* selecting should be closely related to the criteria used for selection.

Several researchers have made important contributions in the investigation of the factors affecting the establishment of weeding criteria (Line and Sandison, 1974; Griffith, et al., 1979). An important concept studied in some depth is the aging of literature or its obsolescence. Although the precise meaning of obsolescence is unclear, its practical value in collection management is obvious. It may be explained approximately as follows: If a document becomes less and less used over the years, it is said to *obsolesce* and when it is no longer used, it is *obsolete*. This phenomenon may be due to the superseding of information contained in the document or to the document content being incorporated into later works. If the information is no longer valid, such a document should be removed from the system. A thorough review paper written by Line and Sandison (1974) noted that obsolescence may be studied from one of several indicators. These include decline in the use of the document, diminishing number of citations received, advancing document age, or other age-related factors. The reviewers also provided a list of research questions deserving of attention. Although the subject is important in terms of collection development and the maintenance of any bibliographic file, much remains to be studied. Finally, Shaw (1978) suggested a simple but effective method to monitor journal usage by placing color-coded dots on the spines of used volumes.

Determination of Topical Relevance

McGrath (1972, 1978) published several studies on selection of information resources being related to subject profiles as defined by university course offerings and departments. A particularly relevant project is concerned with the investigation of the match between the classification numbers of library books and a classified profile of the university teaching program description. He classified courses in the university's catalog into subject categories. The list of classification numbers generated could then be regarded as the university subject profile. He proceeded to examine library books corresponding to these categories. This provided a simple way to check the match between course offerings and supporting library resources. It was found that book numbers matching the course profiles were more likely to be charged out, and they were more likely to be taken off the shelves and likewise were more often charged out. Therefore, the implication is that the university subject profile can be a valid predictor of usage. It can also be used as an aid if not a criterion for a systematic selection plan in colleges and universities. This simple idea is both appealing and logical. Although such a plan does not incorporate quality, authoritativeness, and other not easily quantifiable factors, it can be a valuable selection aid.

AN EXPERIMENTAL
JOURNAL SELECTION ALGORITHM

The following presents a procedure of an objective journal selection method (He and Pao, 1986). Using citation data, the procedure is an example of the application of bibliometric techniques. The validity of the method is tested against four other objective techniques of journal ranking procedures.

Most libraries today still rely on the best subjective judgment of the librarian to determine whether the library ought to subscribe to a given journal title. Aside from the cost factor, three considerations dominate the selection decision. These are *utility* to the intended users, *quality* of the journals, and *relevance* to the disciplines and areas of interest. Relatively objective data could be obtained from usage statistics and users' surveys. However, in geographically remote areas where certain journals are inaccessible, lower use is hardly an indicator of less worth. Although journal quality and relevance are hard to define, most proposed selection methods attempt to incorporate at least one of these two aspects.

The most practical guide in journal selection for specific disciplines is the list of recommended basic titles produced by professional societies or librarians. The Brandon list for medicine is a typical example (Brandon and Hill, 1979). It is compiled as a general guide for all health sciences libraries giving equal coverage to all fields of medicine. Lists for more specialized subareas are also available. To build an entirely new medical collection, these lists are invaluable. They also serve as checklists for existing collections. Nonetheless, if money is only available to add a few titles at a time, one is left in a quandary as to which of the suggested journals to choose. For libraries with small budgets, lists of journals ranked according to quality and relevance would best meet long-range collection development needs, even if funds become available slowly.

Review of Four
Journal Selection Techniques

TOTAL NUMBER OF RELEVANT ARTICLES

Every ranking study employs at least one of three general ranking criteria: actual use, subjective user judgment, or bibliometric statistics usually based upon citations (Bennion and Karshchamroon, 1984). A Bradford distribution of journals is based on the number of articles found in a given field or discipline (Bradford, 1948). Although some experiments have shown a positive correlation between quality and quantity of yield of journals, Drott (1981) has noted that if quality is equated with numbers of citation, significant correlation is lacking. Thus, these results are inconclusive.

IMPACT FACTOR

The number of citations received often has been suggested as an objective measure of the quality of the paper cited. Although the appearance of a bibliographic reference does not specify the extent nor the type of contribution, the practice of citation is rooted in scholarly tradition. Virgo (1977) conducted the first experiment to correlate the number of citations received by journal articles with their perceived importance by subject experts. Her results were confirmed later by Lawani and Bayer (1983). Quality as expressed by experts' selection correlated positively with the number of citations received. These findings have provided a strong argument for the use of citation as a supplement if not a substitute for quality criterion.

With the appearance of the citation indexes by the Institute for Scientific Information, citation data may be collected for journal papers and for journal titles. Therefore, many studies have concentrated on the use of citations as aids in the selection of journals. Since the raw citation count associated with a given journal is subject to wide variations because of the difference in the frequency of journal issues as well as the physical size of each title, this crude measure was subsequently replaced by a normalized measure, the journal impact factor (Garfield, 1972). The impact factor of a journal is the number of citations made to a citable item in the journal. That is,

$$\text{Impact Factor of Journal } X = \frac{\text{number of citations made to Journal } X}{\text{number of citable articles contained in } X}$$

In Pan's study, the impact factor does not correlate highly with use statistics (Pan, 1978), nor does it reflect the utility of journals whose main function is to alert users to newsworthy events. Furthermore, since the impact factor of a journal is based on the number of citations made to that journal, its computation depends on the number of times the given title is cited by all other journals in the database maintained by the Institute for Scientific Information. In other words, the universe of citing journals consists of a wide variety of journals with varying emphases on research, applications, reviews, topics, etc. They range from journals of fundamental research to journals with application to very specific topics. Additionally, the citing behaviors and the relative frequency of citation are dependent on fields. Thus, the comparison of a science journal title such the *Journal of Biological Chemistry*, which has a high impact factor, with a prestigious mathematics journal such as the *Annals of Mathematics*, which has a low impact factor, is meaningless. Journals ranked according to their impact factors may offer a useful indication for journal selection within a general library. Within the context of a special library whose emphasis is on a specific discipline, journal weights must relate to the specific subject emphasis of that discipline. Therefore, the uncritical use of the impact factor is unwise.

DISCIPLINE IMPACT FACTOR

Hirst (1978) proposed a journal ranking algorithm for a small core list for a specific discipline. His *Discipline Impact Factor* is a modified version of journal impact factor in that only citations made by a number of known relevant journals in the given discipline are used in its computation. The impact to the discipline in terms of contributing citations is reflected in the measure. However, Hirst cautions that the measure has a tendency to favor long-established journals.

TOTAL CITATION INFLUENCE MEASURE

Narin's *Total Citation Influence Measure* (Narin, Pinski, and Gee, 1976) was proposed as a journal ranking weight to reflect the influence of a given journal within the totality of biomedical journals. He tested his hypothesis by using 900 journals, each of which was classified among 50 biomedical fields. This measure is a composite of several factors: influence weight, influence per publication, and total influence. It is based mainly on the number of citations received by the journal in question. In connection with his investigation, Narin brought out two points of particular interest to discipline-specific collections. First, he categorized his journals hierarchically according to their concentration on research in four levels: basic research, clinical investigation, medical research including clinical observation, and clinical observation. He found that journals dealing with fundamental basic research made minimal reference to journals with less research emphasis. In other words, research-oriented journals tend to be cited much more frequently than those journals with less research emphasis. Secondly, he found that journals within each level tend to cite journals at a higher level of research emphasis as well as journals within their own levels. Thus, a selection method based on Hirst's *Discipline Impact Factor* that generates relevant journals by a selection method based solely on cited journals would most likely miss many journals in the relevant discipline. Independently, Garfield (1978, 1982) reported that in fields such as agriculture and veterinary medicine, the journals cited by researchers are different from those in which they published most of their works. In both fields, scientists cited the same basic science journals as did other life scientists. It appears, therefore, that for a discipline-oriented collection, relevant basic science journals must be supplemented by journals dealing with the practice of the discipline. In other words, an effective selection algorithm should take into account cited journals as well as the journal citing key journals in the discipline.

A Discipline-specific
Journal Selection Algorithm

Chunpei He (He and Pao, 1986) presents a journal selection method particularly suited to disciplines that focus on application rather than on basic research, such as dentistry, veterinary medicine, and engineering. To present a ranked list of journals specific to a discipline, a two-step procedure is needed. First, a pool of candidate journals of potential contribution to that discipline is identified. This set of journals is known as the *Candidate Journal Set*. Secondly, a weighting score is computed for each journal in the Candidate Journal Set. Presumably, if the weighting scheme is accurate and valid, high scores would be assigned to those journals that are more relevant to the given discipline, thus allowing these journals to be ranked high on the list. Ideally, regardless of the size of the Candidate Journal Set, the relative position of each journal in the list would remain the same. As a practical consideration, there is no need for a truly universal Candidate Journal Set. Depending on the need of each collection, the method used to generate a Candidate Journal Set should be flexible enough to identify larger or smaller sets depending on the available manpower and budgetary resources at the time of the study.

GENERATION OF THE CANDIDATE JOURNAL SET

The method used to generate potentially relevant journals in a given discipline is based on citation data. Its objective is to identify two types of journals: those that are contributors to the research foundation of the discipline and those that are used for the professional practice of the discipline. By asking any knowledgeable individual, it is easy enough to start with one or a few key journals known to be significant to research and/or practice in a given discipline. Any such journal is known as a *seed* journal. Journals whose subject content has been heavily "used" or cited in the key journal are of potential significance to that discipline. Moreover, this is the basis for all other citation-based selection methods. If a relatively exhaustive set is desired, all journals cited by the key journals may be included. On the other hand, journals that have been only occasionally cited could be ignored.

Starting with a single journal in a topic, a complete citation network of journals can be created that reflects the intellectual structure of related subject knowledge. As a result, relevant journals in a topic can be identified. Even in an emerging subject area with poor subject indexing, Goffman and Pao (1980) were able to create such a network of papers to retrieve a group of relevant papers. Hence citation relationship may be used to generate potentially useful journals in a given subject.

Since the cited journals in a journal citation network represent the antecedent or "parent" generation of the seed journal, the antecedents of the antecedents can be identified in a similar fashion. This iterative process is suggested to assure more complete coverage in the event that the suggested seed journal may not be the most cited journal in the discipline. Research has shown that as the process of identification of the cited journal continues, more and more basic research level journals are linked, until eventually no new journals are identified in the set. In practice, one needs to identify only one or two generations of the antecedent journals.

Since only a few journals are used as seed(s), these are probably the most prestigious journals in the field. Articles in these key publications would be expected to cite basic research materials as well as the most research-oriented publications within the discipline. They are also likely to cite more fundamental works. However, Narin found that in cell biology, the key journals minimally cited other cell biology journals. Thus, limiting the Candidate Journal Set to only those cited journals would, in all likelihood, exclude most of those major application-oriented journals in the discipline. For a discipline such as agriculture or veterinary medicine, this procedure would exclude journals central to the practice of agriculture or to the diagnosis and treatment of animal diseases.

Since journals often cite other journals at the same research level, these citation interactions could be utilized to capture relevant application-oriented journals, by noting those which frequently cite the key journals in the discipline. These are, in a sense, the descendents from the seed journal. These descendent journals have utilized or relied heavily upon the key journals. Similarly, descendents of the descendents could be identified by the same process. As a result, the citation chain may be extended in both directions as shown in Figure 6.1 (see page 86). Several generations of journals may be generated from the seed journals. In theory, all journals citing and cited by the few key journals may be collected. The process may be repeated for several generations until no new journal is added to the Candidate Journal Set. It is, however, more practical to identify only those with a higher degree of contribution to the field in terms of citation.

DISCIPLINE INFLUENCE SCORE – A DISCIPLINE-SPECIFIC JOURNAL RANKING WEIGHT

The idea that a ranking score of a journal should be based on the citation influence of a selected Discipline Journal Set has been suggested by Hirst. This journal set may be taken from a list of frequently used titles, most cited titles with high impact factors, or titles selected by experts in the field. It is then possible to rank the journals in the Candidate Journal Set by the relative citation influence on the Discipline Journal Set. The Discipline Influence Score of each journal A in the Candidate Journal Set may be computed by Equation (1):

$$DIS_A = \sum_{i=1}^{n} \frac{\text{number of times } J_i \text{ cited journal A}}{\text{total number of times } J_i \text{ cited all journals}} \tag{1}$$

where DIS_A = the Discipline Influence Score of journal A in the Candidate Journal Set; J_i = a member of the Discipline Journal Set, and n = the total number of journals in the Discipline Journal Set.

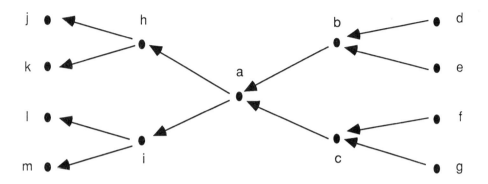

    a   the "seed" journal;

   b, c   journals directly cited by **a**, first generation of antecedents from the "seed";

d, e, f, g   journals cited by **b** or **c**, thus indirectly related to the "seed" journal, second generation of the antecedents of the "seed";

   h, i   journals citing the "seed" journal, first generation of descendents of the "seed";

j, k, l, m,   journals citing **h** or **i**, thus indirectly related to the "seed" journal, second generation of the descendents of the "seed".

Fig. 6.1. Antecedents and descendents of a *seed* journal.

The Discipline Influence Score associated with journal A is the sum of the relative frequency of citations made to journal A by each of the journals in the Discipline Journal Set. In other words, one may interpret it as the total sum of probabilities that journal A would be cited by a group of journals commonly considered relevant to the discipline. Journals in the Candidate Journal Set may then be ordered according to their associated Discipline Influence Scores.

An Experiment

The validity of this discipline-specific selection and ranking algorithm has been demonstrated in the following experiment. Veterinary medicine was chosen as the discipline for testing the procedure. This subject is of international interest since certain animal diseases are indigenous to restricted geographic locations. Yet the journals of interest to the subject consist largely of medical research literature. This discipline also encompasses most of the facets of biomedicine even though there are far fewer journals than those in human medicine. Fundamental research in biochemistry, cell biology, general medicine, and pharmacology, to a large degree, is applicable to veterinary medicine.

SEED JOURNALS

The five key journals in veterinary medicine identified by Garfield (1982) contained 25 percent of all publications in the subject as they appeared in the 1980 volume of the *Journal Citation Reports*, and accounted for 51 percent of all citations made to veterinary medicine in the Institute for Scientific Information database. The five key journals were:

Journal of Animal Science

American Journal of Veterinary Research

Veterinary Record

Journal of the American Veterinary Medical Association

Research in Veterinary Science

CANDIDATE JOURNAL SET

Antecedent journals cited in the five seed journals were identified. In order to generate a fairly small set of journals, a cutoff of 1 percent was used; that is, to be selected as an antecedent journal, the number of times it was cited by any one of the Seed documents had to exceed 1 percent of the total citations made in the seed. Citation data were derived from the Citing Journal Package contained in the 1983 volume of *Journal Citation Reports*. A total of 21 unique journals were identified as antecedents of the five seeds. A second iteration of the same procedure yielded 86 antecedents to the 21 antecedents from the first generation. Thus, 107 uniquely cited journals, derived from two parent generations, were included in the Candidate Journal Set.

Using the Cited Journal Package in the *Journal Citation Reports* published in 1983, the descendent journals of the five seed journals were identified. Each journal selected met the requirement that at least 2 percent of the bibliographic references contained in its articles were made to one of the five seed journals. The assumption was that only those journals which substantially "drew" from one of the key journals in veterinary medicine were allowed membership in the Candidate Journal Set. Unlike the cited journals, whose descendents "contributed" rather than "used" the subject content of the five known relevant journals, a more rigorous cutoff of 2 percent was selected. Eighteen journals were direct descendents of the five seeds and 43 were derived from the first generation of 18 descendents. Thus a total of 61 unique titles from the two descendent generations were added to the Candidate Journal Set. Eliminating duplicate titles, the Candidate Journal Set contained a total of 146 unique journal titles linked by citations to and from five key journals in veterinary medicine.

DISCIPLINE JOURNAL SET

Before computing the Discipline Influence Score for the journals in the Candidate Journal Set, membership in the Discipline Journal Set has to be defined. For convenience, the list of journals with high impact factors categorized under the subject "veterinary medicine" in the 1983 volume of *Journal Citation Reports* was used as the Discipline Journal Set. A total of 74 journals appeared on the list.

DISCIPLINE INFLUENCE SCORE

The next step was to compute the Discipline Influence Score for the journals in the Candidate Journal Set using equation (1). Table 6.1 shows an example of the computation of the Discipline Influence Score for the *New England Journal of Medicine*, which is a member of the Candidate Journal Set. Under the heading "Citing Journal," only 17 of the 74 titles in the Discipline Journal Set cited the *New England Journal of Medicine* in 1983. Thus, each of the remaining 57 citing journals contributed no value to the summation. The computed Discipline Influence Score was 0.1672. Finally, the 146 journals were ranked according to their Discipline Influence Scores.

Comparisons with Four
Other Ranking Techniques

To assess the validity of this discipline-specific journal selection algorithm, the ranked list of 146 journals was compared with lists of the same journals ranked by four other objective methods. Each journal in the Candidate Journal Set was ranked according to (1) the number of articles published in 1983, (2) the number of citations received during 1983, (3) the impact factor for 1983, and (4) the total citation influence measure computed for 1983. The choice of these four methods was guided by the practicality of these methods as well as by their implicit validity. For example, the ranking technique as performed by Hirst's Discipline Impact Factor was not included in the analysis because (as was expected) from the exclusive use of cited journal data, the journal list generated by this method included primarily cross-disciplinary journals and journals in general medicine, such as *Lancet* and *Nature*. Journals central to the practice of veterinary medicine were conspicuously absent.

Data used to order all four journal lists were extracted from the *Journal Citation Reports* of 1983. Spearman's rank-correlation coefficients were calculated for every other pair of the five rankings. The results are presented in Table 6.2 (see page 90).

Table 6.1
Sample Computation of a Discipline Influence Score for the
New England Journal of Medicine

Journal Code:　117
Journal Title:　New Engl J Med

Citing Journal	# of Citations Received from Citing Journal	Total # of Ref. the Citing Journal Gives to All Journals	Discipline Influence Score
Am J Vet Res	64	10040	0.0063745
J Am Vet Med Assoc	54	6195	0.0087167
J Am Anim Hosp Assoc	40	3041	0.0131535
Vet Immunol Immunop	30	2285	0.0131291
Can Vet J	18	1446	0.0124481
Lab Anim Sci	11	1167	0.0094258
Vet Pathol	11	1822	0.0060373
Comp Immunol Microb	10	667	0.0149925
J Med Primatol	10	267	0.0374531
J Small Anim Pract	10	1206	0.0082918
Adv Vet Sci Comp Med	8	2289	0.0034949
Can J Comp Med	8	1790	0.0044692
Vet Med Small Anim	8	1843	0.0043407
Vet Microbiol	7	1206	0.0058043
Deut Tierarztl Woch	6	2340	0.0025641
Kleintier Prax	6	741	0.0080971
Vet Hum Toxicol	6	713	0.0084151

Total Discipline Influence Score　=　0.1672078

Table 6.2
Spearman Rank-Correlation Coefficients for Five Rankings
of the Journals in the Candidate Journal Set

	Article Counts	Citation Counts	Impact Factor	Total Citation Influence Measure
Citation Counts	0.888*			
Impact Factor	0.619*	0.790*		
Total Citation Influence Measure	0.877*	0.931*	0.804*	
Disciplinc Influence Score	-0.016	-0.037	-0.124	-0.021

*Significant at 0.01 level.

The most obvious finding was that the list ranked according to the Discipline Influence Score did not correlate with any of the other four methods. The four other rankings showed statistically significant correlations among each other. Thus one of two opposing conclusions could be drawn: either the Discipline Influence Score was accurate as a journal weighting score or it was totally in error and that all four other ranking methods was accurate. Two evaluations were performed to arrive at the final conclusion.

Evaluation

Two types of evaluations were performed. First, a survey of professionals in veterinary medicine was conducted to assess the utility of the top 20 journals on three ranked lists. Second, the journals with high ranks on each of the five lists were compared with two recommended basic journal lists.

A questionnaire survey was designed to probe the expressed preference of journal use by subject experts in veterinary medicine. The 146 journals in the Candidate Journal Set were ranked by the Discipline Influence Score, by article counts, by citation counts, by impact factors, and by total citation influence measures. Since the rankings by article counts and by citation counts correlated significantly with those by impact factors and by total citation influence measures, only the ranked lists by impact factors, total citation influence measures, and Discipline Influence Scores were examined closely. From each of these three ranked lists, the top 20 journals were pooled. Naturally, some journal titles appeared on more than one list. As a result, 46 unique journal titles were identified and alphabetically arranged.

This list of 46 journals was submitted to researchers and professionals in a veterinary research institute and three veterinary schools in the United States. They were the National Animal Disease Center of USDA, the School of Veterinary Medicine of Purdue University, the College of Veterinary Medicine of the University of Minnesota, and the College of Veterinary Medicine of Washington State University. Each individual was asked to circle five to ten journals in the list perceived to be used most frequently in relation to the individual's teaching or research. A blank space was also provided for titles not on the list.

Researchers at the Control Institute of Veterinary Biologicals of the Ministry of Agriculture of the People's Republic of China and the Harbin Institute of Veterinary Medicine of the Chinese Academy of Agricultural Sciences were also surveyed. The former is the organization in China whose sole responsibility is the supervision of the production of vaccine, serum, antitoxin, and other veterinary biologicals. The latter is one of three national veterinary research institutes in China.

This sample from six institutions was selected to represent active professionals and researchers in developed and developing countries. In an effort to obtain a high return rate, an individual at each institution known to the primary researcher was contacted. Through this individual, other professionals were solicited for their cooperation in filling out the questionnaire. The local contacts at each site were successful in persuading the return of a total of 141 questionnaires. From each institution, a return rate of between 19 percent to 43 percent was achieved.

Totalling the returned questionnaires, each of the 46 journals was weighted by the number of selections made by the 141 experts. Thus a ranked list of 46 journal titles was compiled based on the number of selections made by the experts. Spearman's rank-correlation coefficients were computed for the associations between the rankings according to every other pair of the following: expert evaluation, Discipline Influence Score, impact factor, and total citation influence measure. The results are shown in Tables 6.3 (see page 92) and 6.4 (see page 93). It appears that the rankings according to expert evaluation correlated only with the rankings associated with the Discipline Influence Scores. The coefficient obtained was at 0.741, which is significantly higher than the 0.5 obtained from most similar studies as reported by Bennion and Karschamroon (1984) and by Chudamani (1983).

At the time of the study, there was a recommended basic list of journals in veterinary medicine published in the *Journal of Veterinary Medical Education* (Henley, 1978). A new list was submitted to the Medical Library Association for approval in 1981 (Boyd, Hull, MacNeil, Malamud, and Anderson, 1986). These two lists contained 183 and 182 journal titles respectively. Only 113 journal titles appearing on both lists were still published. Many titles from both lists were not covered by the *Journal Citation Reports*. Only 66 of the 113 titles were members of the Candidate Journal Set. Hence 58 percent of the recommended journals may also be identified through linkages by cited and citing journals.

Table 6.3
Combined List of the Top 20 Journals Ranked by Discipline Influence
Factor, Total Citation Influence Measure, and Expert Evaluation

Journal Title	Ranked by			
	Expert Evaluation	Discipline Influence Score	Impact Factor	Total Citation Influence Measure
Am J Vet Res	1	3	*	*
J Am Vet Med Assoc	2	1	*	*
Vet Rec	3	2	*	*
Can J Comp Med	4	18	*	*
Science	5	*	9	4
Infect Immun	6	9	*	*
New Engl J Med	7	*	1	13
Brit Vet J	8	17	*	*
Res Vet Sci	9	6	*	*
Aust Vet J	10	5	*	*
Cornell Vet	11	16	*	*
J Immunol	12	14	13	6
Lab Invest	13	*	17	*
Avian Dis	14	8	*	*
Nature	15	11	6	3
J Comp Pathol	16	13	*	*
Immunol Rev	17	*	3	*
J Anim Sci	18	4	*	*
J Small Anim Pract	19	20	*	*
J Dairy Sci	20	10	*	*
Endocrinology	21	*	18	20
P Natl Acad Sci USA	22	*	8	2
J Biol Chem	23	*	15	1
J Exp Med	24	*	5	7
Biochem J	25	*	*	11
Cancer Res	26	*	*	18
Lancet	27	*	4	*
Thermiogenology	28	12	*	*
Am J Physiol	29	*	*	16
Ann Intern Med	30	*	10	*
J Cell Biol	31	*	7	17
J Reprod Fertil	32	7	*	*
Cancer	33	*	*	19
Cell	34	*	2	14
Eur J Immunol	35	*	16	*
J Clin Invest	36	*	11	10
Biochemistry-US	37	*	19	8
Biochem Biophys Acta	38	*	*	5
Deut Tierarztl Woch	39	15	*	*
Immunogenetics	40	*	20	*
J Mol Biol	41	*	12	*
Astrophys J	42	*	*	12
Berl Munch Tierarztl	43	19	*	*
Biochem Bioph Res Co	44	*	*	15
Brain Res	45	*	*	9
Nucleic Acids Res	46	*	14	*

* Indicates rank greater than 20.

Table 6.4
Spearman Rank-Correlation Coefficients for the Journals with High
Discipline Influence Scores, Impact Factor, Total Citation Influence
Measure, and Expert Evaluation

	Impact Factor	Total Citation Influence Measure	Discipline Influence Score
Total Citation Influence Measure	0.868*		
Discipline Influence Score	-0.545*	-0.434*	
Expert Evaluation	-0.201	-0.224	0.741*

*Significant at 0.01 level.

From each of the five journal lists ranked by the five different criteria, the top 20 journal titles were considered the most important by each selection method. Each of the set of 20 titles was compared with the 66 journals included in the recommended basic list. Table 6.5 (see page 94) shows the results of the comparison. The top 20 journals identified by the Discipline Influence Scores were all titles on the recommended basic list. A maximum of only ten titles in each of the other four lists was found on the recommended basic list.

Similarly, when the top 40 journal titles were compared, the list ranked by the Discipline Influence Score showed 38 titles from the recommended list. A maximum of only 20 titles from each of the other four lists was found in the list of recommended titles (Table 6.5, page 94).

Table 6.5
Number of Journals in the Top 20 and the Top 40 Journals Ranked
by Five Ranking Weights, and Selected by Recommended Basic Journal Lists

Journal Ranking Weights	# of Journal Titles also Selected by Recommended Lists	
	Top 20 Rankings	Top 40 Rankings
Article Counts	9 (45%)	17 (42.5%)
Citation Counts	10 (50%)	19 (47.5%)
Impact Factor	10 (50%)	18 (45.0%)
Total Citation Influence Measure	10 (50%)	20 (50.0%)
Discipline Influence Score	20 (100%)	38 (95.0%)

Conclusion

The objective of this study was to demonstrate that for a discipline-specific journal collection – in this case, veterinary medicine – an effective journal selection algorithm should identify two types of journals. The first consists of contributors to the subject content of the key journals in the discipline. These are often basic science journals and multidisciplinary medical journals with research emphasis. They are frequently cited titles. The second type publishes the literature of the discipline. Authors of papers in these journals are the professionals of the field. These journals frequently cite the publications in key journals of the discipline and other basic science journals. The proposed algorithm incorporates both cited and citing journals, which in this instance was used to generate a balanced journal list for veterinary medicine. This list consisted of 5 basic science journals, 78 medical journals, 20 agricultural journals, and 39 veterinary medical journals. The procedure was used with a journal scoring method, the Discipline Influence Score, to weight each journal in the list. The resulting ranked list of journals was shown to be a strong predictor of users' expressed preference for journals in relation to their professional work.

On the other hand, article counts, citation counts, impact factor, and total citation influence measure were unable to predict users' preferences for veterinary medical journals. Additionally, journals with high Discipline Influence Scores on this list also were selected independently by experts on their recommended journal lists.

Furthermore, this algorithm is able to accommodate any application-oriented discipline and to produce larger or smaller sets of journals as needed. Experience has also shown that this two-part algorithm is simple and easy to implement. The experiment also demonstrated that this technique appears to rank journals according to their usefulness as perceived by professionals.

REFERENCES

Bennion, B.C., and S. Karschamroon. 1984. "Multivariate Regression Models for Estimating Journal Usefulness in Physics." *Journal of Documentation*, 40(3):217-227.

Bernstein, L.M., E.R. Siegel, and C.M. Goldstein. 1980. "The Hepatitis Knowledge Base: A Prototype Information Transfer System." *Annals of Internal Medicine*, 93(1 pt2):169-181.

Boyce, B.R., and K. Primov. 1977. "Pao's Selection Method for Quality Papers and the Subsequent Use of Medical Literature." *Journal of Medical Education*, 52(12):1001-1002.

Boyd, T., D. Hull, K. MacNeil, J. Malamud, and D.C. Anderson. 1986. "Proposed Basic List of Veterinary Medical Serials, 2nd edition, 1981 with revision to April 1st, 1986." *The Serials Librarian*, 11(2):5-39.

Bradford, S.C. 1948. *Documentation*. London: Crosby Lockwood.

Brandon, A.N., and D.R. Hill. 1979. "Selected List of Books and Journals for the Small Medical Library." *Bulletin of the Medical Library Association*, 67(2):185-211.

Broadus, R.N. 1981. *Selecting Materials for Libraries*. New York: H.W. Wilson.

Chudamani, K.S. 1983. "Journal Acquisition — Cost Effectiveness of Models." *Information Processing and Management*, 19(5):307-311.

Curley, A., and D. Broderick. 1985. *Building Library Collections*. 6th edition. Metuchen, New Jersey: Scarecrow Press.

Drott, M.C. 1981. "Bradford's Law: Theory, Empiricism and the Gaps Between." *Library Trends*, 30(1):41-52.

Gardner, R.K. 1981. *Library Collections: Their Origin, Selection, and Development*. New York: McGraw-Hill.

Garfield, E. 1972. "Citation Analysis as a Tool in Journal Evaluation." *Science,* 178(4060):471-479.

Garfield, E. 1978. "Journal Citation Studies. 20. Agriculture Journals and the Agricultural Literature." *Essays of an Information Scientist.* Philadelphia: ISI Press, 2:272-278.

Garfield, E. 1982. "Journal Citation Studies. 35. Veterinary Journals: What They Cite and Vice Versa." *Current Contents*, 13:5-13.

Goffman, W., and M.L. Pao. 1980. "Retrieval of Biomedical Information for Emerging Interdisciplinary Problems." *Proceedings of the 4th International Congress on Medical Librarianship.* 39-50. Belgrade, Yugoslavia: GRO "M. Gembarovski" — Nova Gradiˇske.

Griffith, B.C., P.N. Servi, A.L. Anker, and M.C. Drott. 1979. "The Aging of Scientific Literature: A Citation Analysis." *Journal of Documentation*, 35(3):179-196.

He, C., and M.L. Pao. 1986. "A Discipline-Specific Journal Selection Algorithm." *Information Processing and Management*, 22(5):405-416.

Henley, A.L. 1978. "Organization and Compilation of a Basic List of Veterinary Medical Serials." *Journal of Veterinary Medical Education*, 5(3):136-138.

Hirst, G. 1978. "Discipline Impact Factors: A Method for Determining Core Journal Lists." *Journal of the American Society for Information Science*, 29(4):171-172.

Lawani, S.M., and A.E. Bayer. 1983. "Validity of Citation Criteria for Assessing the Influence of Scientific Publications: New Evidence with Peer Assessment." *Journal of the American Society for Information Science*, 34(1): 59-66.

Line, M.B., and A. Sandison. 1974. " 'Obsolescence' and Changes in the Use of Literature with Time." *Journal of Documentation*, 30(3):283-350.

McGrath, W.E. 1972. "The Significance of Books Used According to a Classified Profile of Academic Departments." *College and Research Libraries*, 33(3):212-219.

McGrath, W.E. 1978. "Relationships Between Hard/Soft, Pure/Applied, and Life/Nonlife Disciplines and Subject Book Use in a University Library." *Information Processing and Management*, 14(1):17-28.

Narin, F., G. Pinski, and H.H. Gee. 1976. "Structure of the Biomedical Literature." *Journal of the American Society for Information Science*, 27(1): 25-45.

Pan, E. 1978. "Journal Citation as a Predictor of Journal Usage in Libraries." *Collection Management*, 2(1):29-38.

Pao, M.L. 1975. "A Quality Filtering System for Biomedical Literature." *Journal of Medical Education*, 50(4):353-359.

Shaw, W.M., Jr. 1978. "A Practical Journal Usage Technique." *College and Research Libraries*, 39:479-484.

Virgo, J.A. 1977. "A Statistical Procedure for Evaluating the Importance of Scientific Papers." *Library Quarterly*, 47(4):415-430.

7

Information Representation

The sheer number of information sources is a major problem in retrieval. Retrieval problems for a small file are trivial. For example, the owner of a small collection of reprints knows the content of each publication. To retrieve a single item one needs only to leaf through the pile of reprints for the needed paper. One could even scan the entire collection in order to locate specific pieces of information.

Locating a single item in a large collection is a problem of a different magnitude. One needs to know either the exact location of the item or the general location of items which are on the same topic. A large array of aids has been designed to facilitate the retrieval of specific documents or groups of documents with common subjects. An index is by far the most common adjunct to any sizable collection of documents. Index cards serve as surrogates to the actual documents and may be easily arranged in various ways.

Information representation is that aspect of information retrieval in which the original file of documents is represented by a set of tags or surrogates such as abstracts or index terms. The concept of subject retrieval is also known as content representation. The physical forms of representation are organized in such a manner that they may be manipulated and searched to access more efficiently and effectively the content of the collection. The key concepts are *organization* of the information resources in order that *searching* can be facilitated. The aim of organization is not for the sake of organizing. Organization is for the express purpose of expediting information retrieval.

To illustrate with a case, consider a personnel file. Maintained in a filing cabinet, it is probably physically arranged in only one way, for example, alphabetically by employees' surnames. When the need for employees with one or two specific skills or in a particular department arises, use of this filing arrangement becomes awkward and time consuming. To facilitate retrieval, a department index and an index by skills can be created as additional indexes to the original file.

In document retrieval, most users seek information either by known-item searches or by subject searches. In a library card catalog, each physical document is represented by subject cards, author cards, and title cards with each card providing either a unique bibliographic description for known-item searches or a content representation for subject access. Since the majority of problems associated with retrieval are concerned with searching for materials on specific topics, this chapter will describe abstracting and indexing as the two major types of information representations. Book indexing, the mechanics of alphabetization, cross-indexing, forms of name, index entries, and formats of indexes are excluded since comprehensive treatment of these subjects are readily available (see Borko and Bernier, 1975, 1978; Collison, 1971). The focus here will concentrate on the underlying concepts of the major existing subject representation methods. The basis for several experimental automatic indexing methods will also be presented.

ABSTRACTS

Definitions

The American National Standards Institute (1979) defines an abstract as an abbreviated, accurate representation of the contents of a document, preferably prepared by its author for publication with it. In short, it is a concise condensation of the significant content of a document presenting its objectives, scope, and major findings. Its primary objective is to capture the essential content of the document thus saving the reader's time. Thus, instead of scanning the entire document, the reader may decide on its relevance by reading a short representation of it. An abstract assists the reader in determining whether there is a need to consult the full text in order to gain the needed information. An abstract also contains terms, called index terms, relating to the subject of the document. Thus, the abstract is often an integral part of a bibliographic record in an indexing system that enhances the retrievability of the original document.

Conciseness and *significance* are two key concepts in abstracting. Both are relative terms, subject to interpretation. Abstractors attempt to write in a clear, terse, accurate, and noncritical manner in a style similar to that of the original publication. Yet, different abstracts for the identical document may be written depending on the audience for whom the abstracts are intended. Abstracts from foreign journal articles generally contain more detailed information than those whose journals are more easily accessible. Most abstracting guidelines and published criteria suggest the inclusion of the objective of the document, the method used, the results, and the conclusion (Borko and Chatman, 1963; Weil, 1970; American National Standards Institute, 1979; Fidel, 1986a). These distinct components are not necessarily present in all papers. Discursive papers do not include methodology or results. In such cases, quantitative and qualitative information in the paper should be included. Since abstracting remains an art, many organizations train their abstractors in-house regardless of the experience gained in other work places. In all cases, an abstract should be a concise, accurate, comprehensive, and noncritical rendition of its original. It should also stand independent of the original document.

Functions of Abstracts

CURRENT AWARENESS

Because abstracts are short content representations of documents, they are useful for keeping abreast of fields of interest. Reading abstracts allows the reader to cover a much larger scope in a minimal amount of time. One may then concentrate on a smaller number of highly relevant documents for in-depth reading. Some studies have shown that many users read abstracts for specific information and they seldom reach for the original publications.

AVOIDANCE OF DUPLICATION OF EFFORT

Since abstracts permit the scanning of a much larger quantity of literature, there is less danger of overlooking duplicate research efforts conducted at other sites. In industry and business, duplicating a competitor's product can translate into a substantial loss of research and development dollars in terms of the man-months spent by professional and technical staff. The loss of time can also be translated into loss of ill-afforded market share. Duplication of academic research can cause serious embarrassment and loss of prestige.

ACCESS TO FOREIGN PUBLICATIONS

The difficulty in accessing foreign language materials may be a key reason for most individuals to ignore publications from non-English journals. In some fields, foreign publications comprise a significant segment of the literature. For them, abstracting foreign publications can be an important information service. Abstracts can bridge the language gap. Such abstracts are often longer, containing more details. They are intended for the most part to substitute for reading the original.

INFORMATION RETRIEVAL

In addition to the actual text of the abstract, the accompanying bibliographic citation is an indispensible part of the entire abstract. Citation accuracy is crucial so that the identification and location of the original document is insured. Other adjuncts to an abstract are the name index, the institution index, and index of references made. As an aid to information retrieval, abstracts have been used as an effective index enhancer. Particularly in an indexing system with a highly structured controlled vocabulary, words in the abstract field can be used to increase retrieval recall. In new and emerging topics, words in the abstracts are indispensible for searching purposes. In these cases, subject terms may not have been well established for the controlled vocabulary. Instead of searching with descriptors, natural language free-text searching of the abstracts can be rewarded with many more possible retrievals (Fidel, 1986a).

Types of Abstracts

Basically there are two types of abstracts, the *informative* abstract and the *indicative* abstract. The intended use of the original documents often determines the type of abstract written. The informative abstract acts as a substitute for the document. It is a miniature version of the document including the purpose, numerical data, methodologies, formula, conclusions, and recommendations. It is used most often for experimental work, and for specific research reports. It presents what has been done. Many abstracting services permit 100 to 500 words for each abstract. Writing informative abstracts for reviews and discursive papers on broader subjects is more difficult.

An indicative abstract describes what a document is about. It does not report on the actual findings. Therefore, it is well suited to state-of-the-art reviews, literary criticisms, lengthy texts, descriptive works, and general discussions of a topic. It tends to be shorter than an informative abstract, containing 50 to 100 words. It gives little detail and contains less content than the original document. In most cases, it can be written much faster and is less costly to produce. It is seldom used as a replacement for the original document. Ideally indicative abstracts give the reader ample information as to whether the original document should be read.

The type of abstract produced is often determined by its intended readers, the publication content, the journal availability, the language accessibility, and the cost of abstract production. Although for the most part, abstracts are noncritical, abstracts have been known to include a section of critical assessment if the subject warranted one.

The length of abstracts depends on the policy of the abstracting service and intended utility. Each service sets specific guidelines for their abstractors. Most abstracts are one-fifth to one-twentieth of the length of the original paper. Stylistic differences between abstracts of even the same paper can be great. Comparative examples may be found in Collison's text (Collison, 1971). The general approach is that each abstract must include only the content reported and steps taken by the author. The materials are expected to be accurate. Some specifics for writing good abstracts are universal. For example, the titles of the publication should not be repeated. Sentences should not start with superfluous words, such as, "The study is the result of ..." or "This paper is an attempt ..." or "The experiment has for its purpose ..." or "The author has succeeded in...." The reader is referred to Cremmins' text for further information on the characteristics of good abstracts, and abstracting practice (Cremmins, 1982).

INDEXES

Traditionally, the subject approach to document retrieval is solved by a two-step input process. First, each document is analyzed by an indexer according to its subject matter and is assigned to one or more concept classes. To facilitate manipulation of these classes, concepts are designated by index terms. Secondly, each document is represented by appropriate index terms which are assigned on the basis of their semantic similarities to the concept classes identified. This two-step process of content analysis and term selection is known as information representation. For all practical purposes, subject cataloging is a form of subject indexing. Subject headings and index terms reflecting the concepts are surrogates for the physical documents. Hence, instead of searching the large document file, a file of index terms may be arranged, rearranged, manipulated, and searched. As each index term is associated with unique document numbers, documents may be identified. Indexes are not restricted to indexes of subject terms. Index files of authors, titles, report numbers, chemical formulae, and social security numbers may provide other access points if they are useful for retrieval for the users. However, the greatest challenge in information representation is in the creation and maintenence of subject access to documents.

The traditional indexing method operates on the assumption that relevance exists between the chosen index terms and the document they represent. In human indexing, descriptors are subjectively chosen for their semantic similarities to the concept classes to which the document belongs. Document-representation activities today are dominated by this semantic approach to relevance. Similarly, to retrieve the document, the same dual process is at work: (a) the searcher identifies the concepts found in the query and (b) then proceeds to select index terms representing these concepts based on their semantic similarities. The same principle of relevance based on the semantic relationship between the chosen terms and query concepts applies. Thus a semantic approach to relevance dominates operating systems.

Definitions

The following are definitions of some commonly used terms in indexing (see Figure 7.1):

An *index term, descriptor,* or *keyword* is a word or a string of words denoting a concept and connoting a class. For example, the term *snow* definitely denotes the white flakes falling from above during winter days in the north. Yet it also connotes a variety of things. For some, it represents the Christmas season and skiing, and for others a time when families gather in front of the fireplace.

An *indexing language* is the total collection of index terms used in the system for indexing.

An *index* is a systematic guide to items contained in a collection or concepts derived from a collection. These items or concepts are represented by index terms in a known or searchable order. Therefore, the subject content of a collection may be revealed upon a closer examination of its index.

An *entry* in an index is the basic unit of the index. It provides a means of (1) identifying a physical item in a collection or a concept derived from the collection and (2) locating the item(s) or materials relating to the identified concept.

A *collection* (of items) denotes any body of materials indexed. It may consist of an entire library collection, a single text, a composite text authored by several individuals, a single journal with many papers, papers in a group of journals, or a set of some other form of recorded knowledge such as a tape of lectures or a file of maps.

An *item* in a collection denotes a unit of discourse in the collection. For example, an item in a collection may be a book in a library, an article in a journal collection in electronic form, a technical report in a database, or a musical score in a music collection.

Finally, *indexing* is the analytic process consisting of (1) the identification and selection of the concepts representing the document purpose and content, and (2) the representation of these concepts by terms acceptable to the retrieval system. Indexing is characterized by two distinct types of activities: *content analysis* and *term selection.*

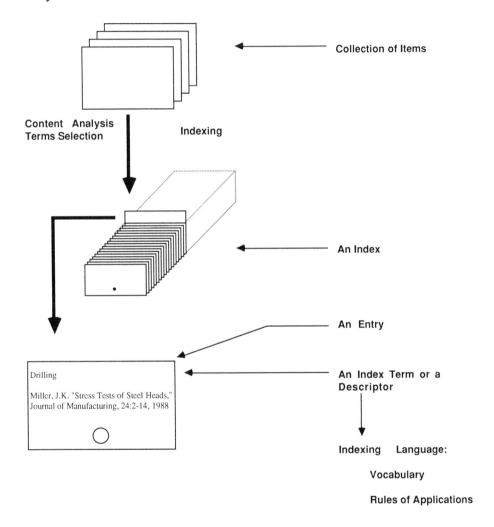

Fig. 7.1. Elements of indexing.

Limitations of Term Indexing

Unfortunately, despite the dominance of human indexing, very little is known about the intellectual task of indexing. Over the years, there have been numerous studies on various aspects of indexing. At one time, the quality of indexing was thought to be the dominant factor influencing the retrieval performance of information retrieval systems. Despite intensive investigation of how one indexes, very little insight has been gained as to how one transforms text content into index entries. In fact, indexing manuals often avoid the issue entirely (Unisist, 1975).

Although an understanding of the process of indexing is lacking, serious defects in this approach are well known. First, inter-indexer and intra-indexer inconsistencies are common in human indexing (Zunde and Dexter, 1969; Rolling, 1981). That is, for the same document, different indexers tend not to index with the same index terms. Intra-indexer consistency denotes the degree of match of index terms when the same document is indexed by the same individual. Over a period of time, the same indexer tends not to select the identical set of index terms to represent the same document. The root of the inconsistency is that richness of natural language allows the same ideas and topics to be expressed in many different ways. One cannot define precise relationships between concepts and their associated designators. A single topic may be expressed in different ways by different authors, indexers, abstractors, and searchers depending on the context and the vantage points from which these concepts are expressed. As a result, the terms which are used as designators for concepts from indexing and abstracting viewpoints are often different from those chosen by searchers and researchers as they attempt to locate documents containing such concepts. No indexer can anticipate all uses of a given document and all likely query terms relating to this document. Since operational retrieval systems are primarily based on a match between the terms used for searching and those found in the index, the incidence of nonmatch because of the use of different terms, even though they may connote similar concepts, is substantial (Blair, 1986). Saracevic and others have found that for the identical topic, different searchers retrieved different sets of citations reflecting the use of different search terms for the same concept (Saracevic and Kantor, 1988). Despite many years of research on natural language processing, Doszkocs' review stated that there seemed to be a virtual breach between research and application in information retrieval (Doszkocs, 1986).

Secondly, even if there is agreement on terms in representing topics, the existing indexing system is not able to indicate the degree of importance of a topic treated within the document. Since equal weight is given to all descriptors, once a concept is indexed, major and minor topics are undifferentiated in their representations. There are systems such as MEDLINE in which indexers can indicate if the descriptor represents a major or minor concept. Nevertheless, even though two categories are available in weight assignment, it can only be done on a subjective basis. There is a lack of consistency between indexers in their judgment. Furthermore, in analyzing the content of a document, not all ideas, topics, and concepts are selected to be indexed. Some concepts are central to the paper; some are mentioned in passing; some are noted for historical interest. The selection of ideas is a subjective matter. To compensate for errors, experienced searchers often review the titles of the list of retrieved items and delete those that are obviously of little value.

Index terms in online systems are also supplemented by keywords found in titles and abstracts. In recent years, many full-text retrieval systems have been developed in which no human indexer is needed. Each document is automatically indexed by every nontrivial word in the text. In other words, after deleting words such as *the, of, for,* and other connectives stored in a stop list, the other content-bearing words are left to represent the document. Such an automatic indexing system is based on the assumption that terms used in the text optimally represent the concepts in the document. The appeal is to eliminate the ineffective and inconsistent process of human indexing with its attendant high cost. Unfortunately, although it achieves consistency, free-text word indexing creates problems of synonyms and homographs. For example, a specific drug may be known by several names. To insure every search possibility, every synonymous term for a single entity must be posted. Homographs, such as *custom, seal, drill,* and *table,* are associated with different meanings depending on the context. *Seal* may be a sea animal; it may also denote a cementing agent. Using these search terms in natural language free-text searching would retrieve nonrelevant documents.

Furthermore, regardless of the importance of each text word, every word is tagged to the given document. In other words, each word is a representative of the document. Many nonrelevant documents may be expected in the indiscriminate use of full-text searching. Additionally, Blair and Maron (1985) have showed that from a large full-text database of 40,000 documents, an average of less than 20 percent of the documents relevant to any search were retrieved. Another aggravating factor is that broad comprehensive searching using the Boolean OR on several search terms of similar meaning quickly produces "output overload," that is, higher recall at the expense of disproportionately low precision. Thus, full-text systems have performed well only on small experimental databases. Much research must be conducted to improve systems recall.

Lastly, a significant time lag exists between the initial usage of a new term by the researchers and practitioners in a field and its eventual incorporation into the information system as an accepted commonly known key term (Goffman and Pao, 1980). Thus, poor retrieval can be expected for emerging and interdisciplinary subjects.

Post-coordination

There are several major approaches to indexing. Each represents an attempt to maintain a balance between providing specific and generic levels of description, and ease of application. The following section first presents the concept of post-coordinate indexing as applied originally in Uniterm indexing and edge-notched cards. The second includes a discussion of the types of vocabulary control and their role in retrieval. The chapter concludes with the basics of automatic indexing.

Traditional subject heading lists for the organization and retrieval of books are structured on a hierarchical basis. Basically, the world's knowledge is logically organized into a tree-like structure. The scheme usually consists of several major classes of knowledge, under which subclasses are formed.

Eventually, layers of subclasses are subsumed under these major classes until enough categories are formed to encompass every conceivable topic. Specific and narrow topics are defined. Labels incorporating specific qualifiers are assigned to each category. In essense, discrete subject categories with pre-coordinated headings are created such that papers written on each topic can be neatly fitted into these slots.

The assumptions underlying this approach are as follows. First, discrete classes of knowledge may be defined so that their contents do not overlap with each other. Secondly, the structure of the world's knowledge tends to remain stable and may be represented in a well-planned design. This is reflected by the static nature of the grand scheme in that once it is created and class labels assigned, changes are difficult. Lastly, this structural representation of human knowledge is assumed to represent a consensus view reflecting a common perspective on the world's knowledge.

The limitation of this approach is that artificially created boundaries for individual concepts can not keep pace with the dynamic growth and development of knowledge in a field. Pre-coordinate indexing schemes may be useful for the description of books. They are less satisfactory for in-depth subject indexing of journal publications and reports whose treatment of topics are more specific. Pre-coordinate subject classes are inherently more rigid and the resulting indexes that are specifically for scientific and technical subjects are difficult to update and revise.

UNITERM INDEXING

When World War II ended, many scientists turned their attentions to the study of science and technology. Strong research support was available from the government and industries. Specializations became the norm. Simultanously, advances were made in many interdisciplinary fronts. Developments in both specialization and interdisciplinarity of sciences were accompanied by large volumes of publications. There was a great awareness that research results were critical to finding solutions and applications in industries, businesses, and the military. The effective retrieval of information assumed great importance.

In the early 1950s, Mortimer Taube proposed a new way of organizing and retrieving information by the principle of post-coordination, also known as coordinate indexing. This new indexing method was based on the notion of *Uniterms*. Taube discovered that in a pre-coordinate index many individual terms were posted in many different entries. If single terms, each representative of a component concept, were used to index different facets of each document, searching a more specific concept could be accomplished by the Boolean combination of two or more terms. In most cases, the component concepts designated by single words were larger in scope. They were combined into a phrase or a single entry to describe the narrower concept. An identical term could be repeatedly posted in the index in different entries. Taube proposed that instead of coordinating two or more terms into an entry representing narrow specific concepts at the time of indexing, the coordination of terms, and thus, concepts, could be done at the time of retrieval. Combining the appropriate component concept terms, the searcher would formulate a Boolean function for searching. Boolean logic formed the basis of the concept of post-coordination in retrieval.

Furthermore, the size of the entire index was greatly reduced since each unique term only appears once in the index. This approach allowed for maximum search manipulation. Concept coordination at the time of retrieval shifted the responsibility to specify and to coordinate concepts from the indexer to the searcher (see Lancaster, 1972, for a fuller description).

Taube found in a list of 50,000 subject headings, there were only 3,000 unique terms used in various combinations. In a technical report collection consisting of 200 items, 205 unique terms were used to index the first 50 reports, an additional 80 terms were needed to index an additional 50 documents, and the next 50 documents required only an increment of 62 new terms (see Figure 7.2). That is to say, the number of unique terms levels off as the number of documents indexed increases. In terms of the number of documents posted under each individual term, Taube also found that although there were only a few terms assigned to a large number of documents, the remaining terms were posted to only a few documents.

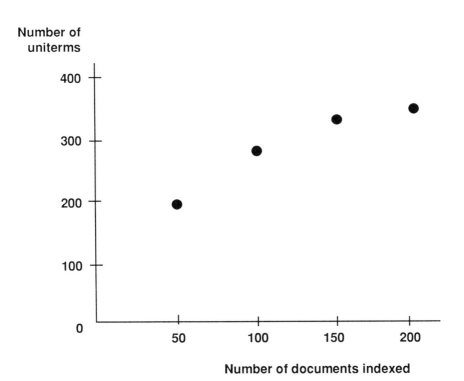

Fig. 7.2. Relationship between number of Uniterms and number of documents indexed.

Post-coordination starts with the analysis and indexing of a document by its component facets. A number of these concepts are coordinated in the search statement in order to retrieve the document. The concept of post-coordinate indexing may be formalized by the following:

1. A subject may be described by a finite set of subject terms, represented by

$$T_1, T_2, T_3, T_4, \ldots T_n.$$

2. A document may be reduced to a number of basic concepts each expressible by single terms, thus enabling their description by a subset of the large set $(T_1, T_2, T_3, \ldots, T_n)$ as

Document 1	Document 2	Document 3	Document 4
T_1	T_1	T_4	T_1
T_3	T_4	T_7	T_3
T_5	T_7	T_8	T_9
T_{10}			
.	.	.	.
.	.	.	.

3. A question may also be analyzed and described by a subset of the entire subject term set.

4. Retrieval may be conducted by the following logical operations:

(a). All documents indexed by T_m

T_m

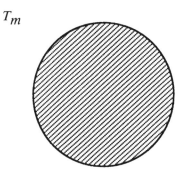

(b). All documents dealing with both the concepts represented by T_m and T_n, i.e.,

T_m AND T_n

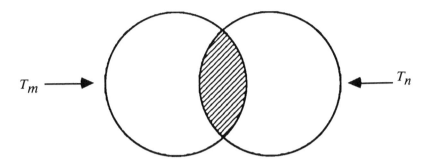

(c). All documents dealing with either one of the concepts represented by T_m or T_n, i.e.,

T_m OR T_n

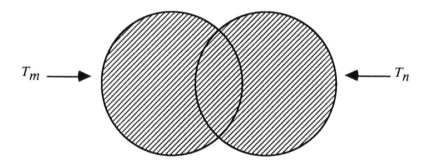

(d). All documents dealing strictly with the concept represented by T_m, and suppressing those items which also deal with the concept represented by T_n, i.e.,

T_m AND NOT T_n

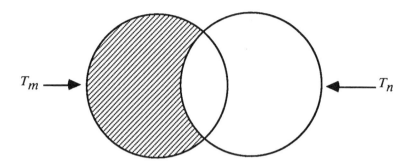

In Uniterm indexing, different facets of the document content are analyzed and each individual facet is identified with a single index term. In Taube's original design, each Uniterm is represented on a separate card with the subject term serving as a label. On each card, documents represented by the given Uniterm are indicated by their unique document identification numbers. To search for documents which are represented by the coordination of two Uniterms, the two appropriate Uniterm cards are pulled. Identification numbers appearing in both cards are noted and the associated documents are located. Actually, special cards are used. Figure 7.3 shows that document numbers are arranged by their last digits in the appropriate columns. This is done to facilitate visual matching of document numbers. To coordinate two Uniterm concepts, document identification numbers appearing on both cards are noted. For example, Figure 7.4 shows four Uniterm cards. Each card represents a single concept, such as *schools, training, students,* and *library.* If documents on *library students* are needed, one may check the last two cards. Comparing the last digits, one finds that documents 374, and 37 contain this compound concept.

Initially, single descriptive terms were selected directly from the text. In technical publications such as quantum mechanics and inorganic chemistry, technical terms are relatively easy to identify. Compound names and chemical elements were fairly standardized. Taube saw no need to establish a list of authorized terms. There was no need to set up any rules for citation order since only single words were used. Citation order is the principle by which certain types of words were to appear first in order to facilitate filing and searching of the manual card system. No rule was needed for punctuation or subheadings since none were used. As a result, the processing of indexing was quite simple, and it was done expeditiously.

WOOD									
001	002	003	004	005	006	007	008	009	000

Fig. 7.3. Sample Uniterm card.

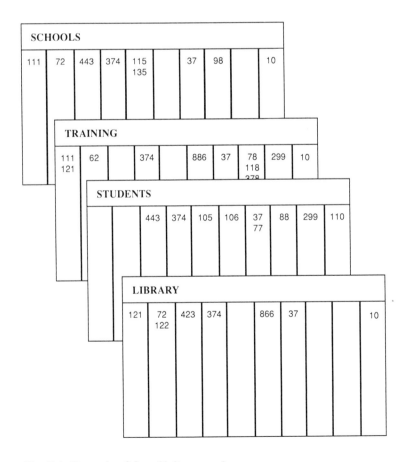

Fig. 7.4. Example of four Uniterm cards.

The Uniterm indexing scheme is based on the following assumptions:

1. The terms found in the document are those most expressive of the document content since they are the author's own original words.

2. Without having interpretation of the author's own words by an indexer acting as an intermediary, indexing is more consistent and the selection of terms more objective.

3. Each content term is used directly as a class label for a class of documents.

4. Retrieval is more effective if the searcher is able to analyze the topic sought into its component concepts.

5. Since the manipulation is based on Boolean logic, the speed of retrieval is greatly increased if computers are employed for processing.

Soon after the implementation of Uniterms in manual systems, problems surfaced. The most serious was the assumption that text words appropriate for indexing were also appropriate for searching. Except for technical terms found in the natural, physical, and biological sciences, most individuals had different ways in expressing a given idea. In searching for a topic, the searcher may not select the same words used by the author. In order to search for all documents on the topic, all synonymous terms must be used. Since there is no authority list of terms, it was difficult to identify all related terms. Synonyms tend to scatter similar documents into different locations. In a manual card file, it is impossible to scan all near-synonyms and related terms.

The second major problem was false coordination. Suppose the desired topic was "washing machine." As in the previous example, the cards on "washing" and on "machines" would be pulled for comparison. A number of documents would be retrieved. Yet this particular combination did not exclude topics such as "machine washing." One or more of the retrieved documents would possibly have dealt with a totally different concept. Even in technical subjects such as atomic physics, or cryogenics, spurious relations between terms could arise from indiscriminate coordinations. False coordination problems are more serious in the humanities and social sciences.

In summary, there are strengths as well as weaknesses in post-coordinate indexing systems. In Uniterm indexing in particular, there is no limit to the number of Uniterms used. As a collection is being indexed, the addition of new Uniterms tends to increase rapidly. However, the number of new terms soon levels off and stabilizes. The cost associated with the original manual Uniterm system is relatively low. Today, the Uniterm system as such is not commonly used, but most automated indexes are based on the same indexing principle. A file of records is first indexed manually or automatically. A subject index is represented by an inverted file similar to an Uniterm index. As a result, many commercial database management systems may be used to implement a Uniterm index. The intellectual process of indexing is fairly straight forward and easy to apply. Only single subject terms need to be selected with no regard to cross-referencing or authority list maintenance. For specialized subject areas limited in scope, it is ideal in that many Uniterms may be assigned to each document allowing for in-depth indexing.

Because of the major problems of false coordination, bound terms were introduced. A bound term specifies that a given word is always associated with another word for a specific concept. The pairing of words are pre-coordinated as if they are part of a whole. One may find "machine washing" and "washing machine" as different bound terms consisting of the two identical Uniterms. Bound terms are a form of pre-coordinated subject headings. Their purpose is to create terms denoting more specific concepts. In this sense, there appears to be a rediscovery of the use of subject headings through partial pre-coordination in the post-coordination schemes. At the time, "judicious-precoordination" was soon introduced to reduce the amount of manual manipulation and false drops. Finally, decisions were made to reduce different variant forms of the same word to a single root. For example, *weld, welding, welders, welded, welds,* and *weldability* were reduced to the root form *weld.* For manual searching, generic searches became more effective when these various word forms were brought together.

EDGE-NOTCHED CARDS

Post-coordination was first applied in Uniterm indexing using an inverted file structure as discussed in Chapter 8. Edge-notched cards represented a different implementation of the concept of post-coordination. Traditionally, each publication was usually represented by a unit record in the card catalog. These were known as item cards. In other words, each card represented a single physical item. The file structure of this index or catalog was based on the publications or items themselves. Even though other cards, such as added entry cards, could be made for the same publication, their contents were derived from the basic unit record. The edge-notched card system was based on the item card concept. Although it is not often used in practice today, the item card concept is important in the understanding of information representation. Its underlying principle was distinct from that used in the Uniterm indexing system. Uniterm indexing utilized the unit records in a different way. A single term representing a concept or a feature of the document was posted on a card. In a manual system, an actual card was used as a unit record. These were known as feature cards or term cards. The difference between an item card and a term card was that the former represented the physical object and the latter, a concept. The organization of the item cards mimicked the collection, whereas the term cards file actually turned the idea of a document collection upside down. Instead of constructing a miniature representation of the actual file, the file was represented by the file content which in turn was labelled by a set of content-bearing terms. This type of index was called an inverted index. It is also sometimes known as a feature card index. Obviously the references to "cards" was not restricted to physical cards. More often they were represented by "unit records" in electronic files and should be understood as such.

Historically, Calvin Mooers has been credited with inventing the Zatocards, the first edge-notched card system. It was an attempt to access needed information in a timely fashion. In dealing with publications with concentrated information such as internal technical reports, Mooers was concerned with the retrieval of the information content of documents, and not merely the physical documents themselves. He designed a new system in which these materials were represented by a limited number of concepts. His major aim was the rapid retrieval of information in documents in a specialized technical subject domain. He coined the term information retrieval. For a collection of approximately 20,000 documents, 250-350 specially chosen terms, or descriptors, were used to represent their corresponding concept classes. He called them *descriptors* because they were carefully selected for the subjects covered by the collection. Each descriptor was considered a label for a class of subject content, and it did not necessarily reflect the dictionary meaning of the term. Each could consist of a phrase or a single English word. Yet each was carefully defined and acted as a code for the designated class of objects or concepts. By limiting a subject field to a small number of concepts, indexers and searchers both had an improved chance of matching terms with concepts.

Specially made cards were used. Holes were punched on the peripheries of each card (see Figure 7.5). On the card, the bibliographic description of the document was recorded, so that each card was a complete representation of the document for which it was a surrogate. Often each document was carefully abstracted. The abstract together with the bibliographic information was recorded on the edge-notched card. Each type of information or each field was allotted a number of holes so that information on the specific field could be

Fig. 7.5. Edge-notched card.

coded. For example, Figure 7.6 shows that ten holes could be assigned to code the last two digits of the date of publication by the use of a pyramid code. The example shows the date as 49. A number of coding schemes existed. Some were efficient in terms of the number of holes required, whereas others were less ambiguous in the data coded. A suitable one could be selected for coding textual data as well as numeric data. Descriptors chosen to represent the given document could be coded on the holes on the edge of the card.

In designing an indexing system for a collection using edge-notched cards, the indexing procedure could be summarized as follows: The descriptors must be selected to represent the topics of the file of documents. Each descriptor must be carefully defined in an authority list. Since this file serves as an authority for the use of descriptors, both indexers and searchers must refer to it. A coding system is then chosen for coding each field of data. The code for each descriptor must be recorded in a second authority list. As new documents are added to the system, the bibliographic description of each document, as well as the location symbol, is recorded onto an edge-notched card. The document is then indexed by assigning one or more descriptors to it. The codes for the chosen descriptors are identified and notched onto the card. The collection of cards need not be alphabetized or kept in any order.

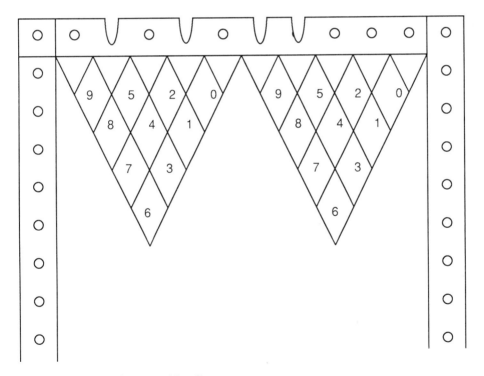

Fig. 7.6. Example of a pyramid coding.

In searching for documents on a specific topic, the most appropriate descriptors with their codes must be identified. At the appropriate positions of the holes, the entire stack of cards may be needled. Those cards dropping from the needles would be those indexed with the appropriate descriptors.

Obviously, the principle on which the edge-notched card system is based is the same as the Uniterm system. They are only represented differently, one by the feature card and one by item cards. For both, retrieval is based on Boolean logic in that if a given topic is analyzed as a combination of two concepts, a coordination of the two appropriate index terms representing the two concepts must be performed. If either concept is desired, a Boolean OR is used. A Boolean AND used on both concepts would produce a narrower concept which is the intersection of two concepts. Since the order of the two concepts is not specified, false coordination is also a problem for the edge-notched card system. Indeed, those cards dropped by the needle which are not relevant to the query are known as false drops.

This manual system was popular because only one file was needed. Each card contained all the information for the document. Since some specially made 8 x 11 cards were large enough to record the abstract of the paper, needed information was directly available through searching without referring to the original file of documents. The cost of such a system was and is today modest. Best of all, there is low maintenance in that the cards in the collection need no special arrangement. However, there are unavoidable problems. First, since retrieval is conducted on the code representing the descriptors, the coding scheme is crucial in minimizing false drops. Simple codes tend to be ambiguous, and elaborate ones require many more holes on the card. There is also a limit to the number of allowable descriptors since there is a maximum number of holes on the card. Lastly, although only one file is needed, an authority record must be kept for the descriptors for their definitions and scope, and their associated assigned codes.

Although both Uniterm and edge-notched systems have been largely replaced by electronic systems, the principle of post-coordination is still being used in all operating retrieval systems. Soon after the proposal of the Uniterm indexing system, the indiscriminate scattering of related terms became unwieldy. The need for some term control was evident. Mooers advocated "judicious precoordination" which is a form of vocabulary control used for a small number of bound descriptors. These early pioneers in information retrieval found the totally uncontrolled use of natural language in manual systems to be impractical.

VOCABULARY CONTROL

The term *vocabulary control* is defined as a limited set of authorized terms to be used in indexing documents as well as in searching those documents in a given information system. The total set of terms forms an indexing language (see Figure 7.1). In some vocabularies, the use of these terms is often specified in conjunction with a set of rules. In others, no formal syntactic rules are needed for application.

According to Lancaster (1986), a controlled vocabulary is used to achieve two objectives:

1. To insure, as far as possible, the consistent representation of the subject matter of documents at the time of indexing and at the time of searching

2. To facilitate the conduct of searches in the system, by bringing together, in some way, the most closely related terms with respect to their meanings.

To achieve these objectives, several mechanisms are used. First, the vocabulary is controlled by choosing a preferred term from among a group of terms with similar meanings. The indexer and the searcher are directed to the preferred term by *use* or *see* references. Thus, a *see* reference is made to control the use of synonyms, near-synonyms, and quasi-synonyms. A term is chosen because it is the one most often used by users of the system, or in the opinion of the systems designer, the most appropriate term for the concept. Secondly, the controlled vocabulary clarifies the use of homographs which are candidates for potential false drops. They are words with different meanings spelled exactly the same way. For example, *pitch* may be related to music in the acoustical context. It may also be used in the context of baseball games or in the arena of aeronautics. Specific scope notes are used to distinguish the use of each homograph in its proper context so as to avoid a false drop.

The third control is to group together terms associated with related concepts. Two different devices are used. First, hierarchically related terms are explicitly linked. At a glance, the system user is able to compare and select the most appropriate term for the concept in question. For example, among the list of terms, *optical equipment, binoculars, electron microscopes, periscopes, stroboscopes,* and *infrared binoculars*, one is aided in the choice of the most appropriate term to represent the given concept in the document or the query. Secondly, terms representing the concept of *cooling*, such as *refrigeration, air-conditioning,* and *cooling systems* are alphabetically scattered. They are related in concept. By linking them to each other, through notations of *related terms* or *see also* references, the searcher is reminded to use the most appropriate one for searching. For example, for a broad search on *cooling*, all the related terms may be linked in a Boolean OR. The purpose is to suggest to the indexer the most appropriate terms representative of the document. For the searcher, related terms suggest other terms otherwise not thought of at the time of the system's use. It is also done in the case of antonyms. For example, in the search of *cooling* systems, the suggestion of *heating* systems may produce appropriate documents.

Vocabulary control is an aid to indexing in that it helps to suggest and to prescribe the most appropriate terms for the indexer. It provides standardization for the selection of index terms, for the usage of terms, and for the interpretation of the scope of the terms used. In using such a vocabulary, one is able to discriminate between similar terms representing similar ideas. As a result, terms most descriptive of the concept may be chosen. In providing scope notes to the authorized terms, it reduces inconsistency among indexers in selecting terms for a given concept resulting in better inter-indexer consistency. It helps to maintain higher consistency level for the same individual indexer over time. The vocabulary establishes a record of authoritative decision regarding term usage and the accepted spelling used by the system. It also resolves problems with synonyms and homographs. Lastly, a good controlled vocabulary helps the indexer in comprehension of the subject matter by suggesting and providing leads to the most precise, accurate, and appropriate index terms. In so doing, it helps to extend the subject knowledge of the indexer.

With regard to searching, vocabulary control facilitates the location of index terms to which the appropriate classes of documents belong. A good controlled vocabulary displays the relationships among terms. Thus, a term is placed in its semantic context with other related terms. Clarification of terms and their associated concepts is provided for the searcher in terms of the proper terms for searching. Finally, for the searcher, the vocabulary could give clues for better search formulations for the retrieval of maximum number of relevant documents. For example, if a high percentage of relevant documents is needed for a given topic, the vocabulary could lead the searcher to all the related terms as well as all broader and narrower terms associated with the topic for a generic search.

Types of Vocabularies

There are two types of controlled vocabularies, those used in pre-coordinate indexing and those for post-coordinate indexing (Lancaster, 1972). Most library classification schemes are pre-coordinate vocabularies in that the form of each entry is designed with respect to logical categories of knowledge. Indexers must first analyze the document content and fit the documents into the predetermined knowledge classes. Entries are arranged according to the lead terms which are specified in the vocabulary. At the time of searching, the exact same entry must be identified in order to retrieve the documents assigned to it.

Vocabularies for post-coordinate indexing are basically synthetic. All terms in the vocabulary serve as lead terms so that search statements are formulated by the coordination of several terms. The searcher analyzes the sought topic into its component concepts, identifies their corresponding index terms, and then synthesizes them by coordinating the terms into a search statement representing the desired topic.

Consider vocabulary control in several types of indexing. The original Uniterm system does not formally have an indexing language since no authorized term list is used. This is in direct contrast to controlled vocabulary. When an unlimited number of terms are used for indexing and for searching, uncontrolled vocabulary is in effect. In other words, any word in the natural language may be a member of the unlimited set. In such cases, documents are indexed by the natural language, and the system is said to allow for free-text searching. Natural language consists of an unlimited vocabulary with virtually no rules for application.

Since a totally uncontrolled use of terms in a manual system with no capability of searching by word stems is chaotic, the introduction of term lists enables some degree of control. A term list is an alphabetical list of terms including those lead terms not used in indexing or searching. Yet, provision for entries for these nonauthorized terms with cross-references could lead the user to preferred terms. For specialized subjects, a term list of approximately 500 descriptors can be a low-cost term compression device which does not require much maintenance. Most back-of-the-book indexes are term lists.

Moving one step toward more control, the subject heading lists used in library cataloging are truly controlled vocabularies. They are lists of predetermined authorized terms with elaborate syntactic rules for application. The subject headings cover the universe of knowledge. Although they contain a large number of categories, they are inadequate to distinguish between subtopics within a given field of knowledge, such as chemistry, mathematics, plastics, and so forth.

Of the various types of controlled vocabularies, the oldest exists in the form of classification schemes. Classification is the grouping of like entities according to selected attributes and rules. Classifications are designed to organize things so that they serve some specified purpose. For example, books are classified by their content. Classification schemes for books are often built from a logical arrangement of the universe of knowledge. They attempt to be comprehensive, inclusive, consistent, flexible and expandable enough to accommodate and to anticipate change. Since books are written on every conceivable subject, the concept categories chosen to classify books must be general. These concepts are enumerated and arranged such that hierarchical and collateral relationships are made explicit. Usually an alphabetical index of all entries is compiled as a key to the classification scheme.

Library classification schemes are in general too broad for effective categorization and retrieval for information retrieval work outside of the general library. Special libraries and information centers organize files of materials on a wide range of subtopics within a specific subject field. Retrieval on narrow aspects is needed. Over the years, schemes similar to the concepts used in classifications have developed particularly for scientific subjects. Although the basic function remains, these new vocabulary-control devices are more structured. They are known as thesauri.

Thesauri

A thesaurus is a controlled vocabulary of semantically and generically related terms covering a specific area of knowledge. Designed specifically for concept coordination, it is a terminological control device which translates both the natural language used in documents by indexers, and topics sought by searchers into a mutually precise language. The key difference between a subject heading list and a thesaurus is that (1) it is not designed for the world's knowledge but for a well-defined area of knowledge, and (2) it must display hierarchical and associated relationships among terms as well as provide definitions for the scope of terms. There are explicitly three types of term relationships. They are *synonymous, hierarchical,* and *associated.* An example is shown in Figure 7.7 (see page 120).

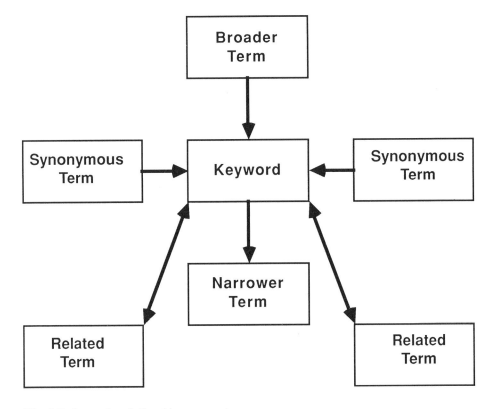

Fig. 7.7. Semantic relationships among terms.

EVOLUTION OF THE THESAURUS FOR INFORMATION RETRIEVAL

The early development of thesauri has been described in Vickery's (1960) paper. Briefly, the term *thesaurus* has always been associated with Roget. However, as a tool for information retrieval, the information retrieval thesaurus is meant to be a guide for input as well as output in a post-coordinate retrieval system providing terminological control. The term used in this context was coined and first used in print in 1957 by Hans Peter Luhn of IBM. The first thesaurus for the purpose of information retrieval was developed and constructed by the DuPont Company for indexing documents in chemical engineering and chemistry in 1959. At the same time, progress was being made in another thesaurus at the Armed Services Technical Information Agency (ASTIA), which is the former name for the Defense Documentation Center. The *Thesaurus of ASTIA Descriptors* was published one year later and became the first widely used thesaurus for science and engineering. In this work, many pre-coordinated terms are introduced similar to the descriptors Mooers has advocated. A revision in 1962 attested to its utility and formed the basis for the NASA Thesaurus. The *Chemical Engineering Thesaurus* was completed by the American Institute of

Chemical Engineers. This work was based largely on the first effort done at the DuPont Company, which was used by the American Institute of Chemical Engineers to index their journals.

Since then, many thesauri have been developed for information retrieval. They covered a wide spectrum of fields of knowledge. Most thesauri are constructed for scientific and technological subjects. Among the major works is included the special redesign of the Medical Subject Headings (MeSH) by the National Library of Medicine for use in the post-coordinate computer-based system MEDLARS. It resulted in a second edition of MeSH in 1963. This elaborate subject heading list is continuously updated and maintained. It is still used for both MEDLINE, the largest online database for biomedical sciences and its printed counterpart, *Index Medicus.*

The other landmark work in thesauri is the *Thesaurus of Engineering Terms* by the Engineering Joint Council (EJC) first published in 1964. Work on the thesaurus began in 1962. It quickly became one of the most influential works in the field. Enormous gains in the knowledge of the construction and use of thesauri were made. Many national professional engineering organizations joined forces with NASA and the Department of Defense in the making of this thesaurus. A committee structure was elaborately organized. One hundred thirty-one expert members were grouped into 10 subcommittees. Eighteen organizations submitted term lists for consideration for the indexing vocabulary. Of the 119,000 terms, only 87,500 were unique terms. Of these, 74,602 appeared only in one list, and 13,948 appeared in two or more lists. A total of 130 man-weeks were spent in reviewing the collected pool of terms. At the end, 10,515 unique terms were chosen. At that time, it was the most carefully compiled thesaurus with input solely from a large number of subject experts.

Amazingly, within five years, Project LEX was launched to produce a completely different version, entitled *Thesaurus of Engineering and Scientific Terms* in 1967. This was a joint effort pooling the Department of Defense with an even larger segment of engineering-professional societies. Approximately 300 individuals participated in some capacity between 1965 and 1967. Many were assigned to various subject committees. Twenty-three man-years were spent before the completion of the project. Three hundred thirty-three lists of terms were reviewed. Authority lists, dictionaries, glossaries, and lists from data banks were all represented. Of these, 145 lists were used, and terms were input into a computer for ease of manipulation. Rigid criteria were used in term selection. A total of 145,000 separate terms were entered on magnetic tapes for merging. Eliminating the duplicates, 23,364 unique terms were generated. Eventually, through panel discussions within the subject committees, 17,810 scientific or technological terms were chosen. They were also selected with a view toward retrieval requirements. In order to facilitate the use of the thesaurus, 5,554 USE references were made so that these terms could lead the searcher to the appropriate preferred terms. Including all cross-references, lead-in terms, and the descriptors themselves, there were a total of 162,657 line entries. Several different indexes were included to permit different types of access. A permuted index of compound terms, a subject category index, and a hierarchical index were among the enrichments included. Even so the EJC thesaurus itself has been found to provide a coverage of science and technology that is too broad to be of real practical value as a retrieval device. On the other hand, this monumental effort to redesign the engineering thesaurus led to a work which has been the foundation for many specialized thesauri. The EJC thesaurus became the framework on which many other mini-thesauri were built. The experience gained in this project was consolidated into useful guidelines and conventions for thesaurus construction. These were subsequently reflected in the standard issued by the American Standards Institute (1980).

THESAURUS CONSTRUCTION

Just as a thesaurus is defined as a controlled vocabulary of terms covering a specific area of knowledge, the need for a thesaurus for a subject domain must first be established. Since one of the most important considerations of a thesaurus is its constant need for update and revision, strong financial and management support in its creation and its maintenance must be secured before undertaking its construction. A detailed discussion of thesaurus construction is beyond the scope of this text. The reader is referred to texts by Aitchison and Gilchrist (1987), Soergel (1974), and Townley and Gee (1981) on this subject. However, an outline of the key processes and concerns follows.

Term generation. Terms are collected from as many relevant sources as possible. Specialized dictionaries, glossaries, index terms found in indexing services and back-of-the-book indexes of textbooks, and subject bibliographies are potential sources. One may also start the initial list from a subset of pertinent headings from a thesaurus with broader coverage, such as the EJC thesaurus. Another valuable source is from opinion given by subject experts.

Term consolidation. The function of term consolidation is to provide adequate access to the subject by the inclusion of most terms used by users and to balance this global access with a restricted list of authorized terms that are necessary to represent the topics in the subject. A simple merging is the first attempt to eliminate duplicate terms found in more than one list. The second consolidation process should be the linking of synonymous terms and near-synonyms. These could be trade names, names reflecting popular usage, or superceded names. The decision to select the preferred term among similar terms should be weighed by its accepted usage, its use frequency, and other factors which could promote the retrieval of documents. This can then be followed by a choice of the word stem from words with different endings and a preferred spelling from its variant forms. Certain bound terms may be used.

This process should result in two types of terms, namely, descriptors or the authorized term set and entry terms or terms leading to the appropriate descriptors. The latter are also known as lead-ins. In a printed index, both types of terms are arranged in a single alphabetical file. Under the lead-in entries, the searcher will be directed to the preferred term. Often there are scope notes accompanying the descriptors for clarification of the coverage of each term.

Categorization of terms by subjects. After the core group of descriptors has been selected to represent the subject domain, they are logically categorized into subgroups according to content. The aim is to link terms within each group for easy retrieval. Similarly, certain terms from different groups should also be connected. For example, *German shepherds* being a term in the subject group of *animals* might also be linked to the *drug control* group.

There are several ways to categorize terms. Individual subject experts could be consulted. Compromised consensus may also be sought by committees of experts on different topical subareas. Although expert consultation is subjective, it does reflect the opinion of a group of informed users. Different facets of each term may be analyzed and factor analysis may be conducted. Another approach is to take a representative group of documents from the subject domain and to perform a statistical analysis of the terms used.

Hierarchical ordering of descriptors. There are two different types of semantic relationships to be specified in the chosen descriptors of a thesaurus. The first is that of the hierarchical relationship. If descriptor *A* is inclusive of descriptor *B*, under *B*, *A* would be listed as the *BT* or "broader term" for *B*. Conversely, under *A, B* would be listed as *NT* or narrower term of *A*. The obvious function of the explicit relationship is for generic searches. The user can easily find more general headings, and hierarchically narrower descriptors with either genus-species or a part-whole relations. An easy test for hierarchical relationship is: "*B* would always be *A*." For example, *poodles* are always *dogs*, and *Dallas* is always a part of *Texas.*

Collateral and associative linkage of descriptors. The second type of semantic relationship is more difficult to specify. The purpose in retrieval is to display explicitly terms that are related in their viewpoints, perspectives, treatments, or in similar useful ways. In the above example, the terms *dogs* and *pets* should be linked. However, they do not stand in hierarchical relation to one another. One cannot assert that dogs are always pets. This particular relation is an associative one rather than a hierarchical one. It is denoted by posting *pets* as *RT* on a related term under *dogs* and vice versa. However, no one single criterion exists to test the validity of this relationship since there are many types of relations which qualify as associative relations including those of antonyms. The selection of them depends on the perception of the thesaurus maker in terms of their relevance to the subject.

Enrichment of entry terms. To facilitate ease of access to the thesaurus for the searcher in locating preferred descriptors, a rich entry vocabulary is mandatory. Its purpose is to include a large number of terms under which the user might look. These are known as lead-ins whose role is to direct the searcher quickly to the preferred term used by the system.

Format and display of the entries. Visually, display and format of the thesaurus contribute to the ease of use of the thesaurus. It should be easy to distinguish between the descriptors and the lead-ins. The various types of semantic relationship should also be clearly displayed. Examples in Figures 7.8 and 7.9 (see page 124) show the entry for "Case Studies" from a 1987 online ERIC thesaurus and the corresponding entry from the 1987 ERIC-printed thesaurus respectively.

```
E CASE STUDIES


Ref   Items  RT  Index-term
E1      1        CASE REVIEW SYSTEMS
E2      1        CASE STATEMENTS 4
E3    8128    9  *CASE STUDIES (DETAILED ANALYSES, USUALLY FOCUSING ON A
                  PAR...)
E4      6        CASE STUDIES (EDUCATION)
E5      0     1  CASE STUDIES (EDUCATION) (1966 1980)
E6      1        CASE STUDIES (LEGAL)
E7      3        CASE STUDIES IN SCIENCE EDUCATION
E8      1        CASE STUDY APPROACH
E9      2        CASE SURVEY METHOD
E10     1        CASE WESTERN RESERVE SCHOOL OF MEDICINE
E11    40        CASE WESTERN RESERVE UNIVERSITY OH
E12     2        CASE WESTERN RESERVE UNIVERSITY SCHOOL OF MEDI

        Enter P or E for more

?E E3


Ref   Items  Type RT  Index-term
R1    8128         9  *CASE STUDIES (DETAILED ANALYSES, USUALLY FOCUSING ON A
                       PAR...)
R2       0    U    1  CASE STUDIES (EDUCATION) (1966 1980)
R3     206    N    5  CROSS SECTIONAL STUDIES
R4     223    N   10  FACILITY CASE STUDIES
R5    4435    N    8  LONGITUDINAL STUDIES
R6   15694    B   61  EVALUATION METHODS
R7  158643    B   82  RESEARCH
R8     216    R   10  CASE RECORDS
R9   24791    R   39  COUNSELING
R10    203    R   10  QUALITATIVE RESEARCH
```

Fig. 7.8. Printout of a page from the ERIC online thesaurus.

CASE STUDIES   Apr. 1970
CIJE: 3346   RIE: 4223   GC: 810
SN   Detailed analyses, usually focusing on a
     particular problem of an individual,
     group, or organization (note: do not
     confuse with "medical case histories" --
     as of oct81. use as a minor descriptor
     for examples of this kind of research --
     use as a major descriptor only as the
     subject of a document)
UF   Case Studies (Education) (1966 1980)
NT   Cross Sectional Studies
     Facility Case Studies
     Longitudinal Studies
BT   Evaluation Methods
     Research
RT   Case Records
     Counseling
     Qualitative Research

Case Studies (Education) (1966 1980)
USE   CASE STUDIES

Fig. 7.9. Page from the ERIC printed thesaurus. James E. Houston, ed. *Thesaurus of ERIC Descriptors*, 11th ed. (Phoenix, Arizona: The Oryx Press, 1987), 30. Used by permission of The Oryx Press, 2214 North Central at Encanto, Phoenix, AZ 85004-1483. Copyright © 1986.

FACTORS INFLUENCING THE MAINTENANCE OF A THESAURUS

As stated earlier, the creation of a thesaurus is only the first step. To be an effective vocabulary control device, the thesaurus must be constantly kept up-to-date. Several major factors could necessitate changes in the thesaurus. First, the introduction of new topics necessitates additions of new descriptors. For example, *digital sound recordings* and *compact discs* are new terms introduced only in recent years. Secondly, obsolescence of old terms conversely means that the elimination of obsolete descriptors must also be accommodated. Third, allowance must be made for the subdivision of existing subject headings into more specific headings. In science and technology, specialization creates finer divisions of subjects. For example, microprocessing is a specialization within computer engineering; and bioengineering or bioethics are newly combined areas. Fourth, changes in the meaning of existing descriptors must be considered. For example, sound recordings in the 1950s was the only type of popular audio medium. Today, distinctions must be made between *monoral, stereophonic, digital*, and others. Lastly, provisions for the addition and deletion of hierarchical or associative relations must be allowed for when the subject warrants such changes.

Factors Affecting Systems Performance

In this section, indexing and indexing languages are examined in terms of those characteristics which could affect the retrieval performance of the system. Systems performance is often expressed in terms of recall and precision. It is important to select an indexing vocabulary which is more likely to produce the degree of recall and precision desired. Both of these commonly known performance measures have evolved from intensive retrieval testing in the past. The prevailing hypothesis in the 1960s was that indexing languages held the key to retrieval performance. Researchers experimented extensively with various indexing languages and several factors in indexing. Several factors in indexing and indexing language were found to exert substantial influences on retrieval. Three important concepts were *specificity, exhaustivity,* and *density of indexing.* Specificity was and is a characteristic of the indexing language. Both exhaustivity and depth of indexing are determined by indexing policy decisions. Each concept is linked with the recall and precision of the indexing language used.

SPECIFICITY

Specificity of indexing describes the types of preferred terms included in the indexing language. It is a measure of the degree of precision with which the subjects or topics of the documents may be represented by the indexing language. A high level of specificity denotes a high degree of precision with which index terms are used in describing concepts in documents. For example, if the subject of the document relates to expert systems, and if the index term *expert systems* is an allowable descriptor, there is a precise matching of the concept and the term. On the other hand, a lack of specificity is indicated if the only index term which is closest to the concept is *artificial intelligence*. This term is not specific since expert systems are but one form of the application of artificial intelligence.

The vocabulary with a high level of specificity would appear to contain many more terms than one with low specificity. Many more specific terms would be needed to describe a more general concept allowing for specificity. A larger vocabulary size intuitively implies high specificity. In truth, it is not a necessary condition for high specificity in an indexing language. In a large vocabulary, higher specificity could have been applied unevenly to certain areas of the subject while neglecting others. To achieve specificity, it is more appropriate to provide the types of specific terms appropriate for the subject at hand and those warranted by the document content.

In terms of retrieval performance, precision is the percentage of relevant documents contained in the retrieved set. With highly specific index terms, each retrieval set tends to contain highly relevant documents. That is, the precision of retrieval system increases. Conversely, with a less specific index language, each index term would cover a larger topical domain, not all of which terms are related to the specific area needed. The retrieved set would be larger, and more nonrelevant or marginally relevant documents would be included. Precision of the system suffers. At the same time, as many more documents of less relevance are retrieved, some of these documents may contain information of pertinence to the topic sought. Consider the previous example of the needed topic *expert systems*. Under *artificial intelligence*, relevant information on cognitive science that has important implications for the building of expert systems may be found. Specificity of the indexing language is the single most important factor affecting search precision.

Obviously, specificity of an index language or thesaurus is determined when the vocabulary is constructed. Once the choice of the vocabulary is determined for the retrieval system, little can be done to change the specificity of the language. Therefore, to begin an indexing project, the choice of an indexing language with the desired level of specificity is an important consideration. It is a challenge to determine exactly how specific the vocabulary needs to be. For most individuals who come to indexing projects after a vocabulary has been in use for some time, there is no easy way to remedy an indexing language with low specificity without a major overhaul and retrospective indexing.

A related issue is the important implication associated with the maintenance of a controlled vocabulary. As the subject area develops, the systems manager must be vigilant in adding new index terms, in updating and revising the scope of existing terms, and in deleting obsolete terms. There is no precise procedure for the adjustment needed to assure coverage of specific subject domains and expansion into other areas. Ideally, a continuous evaluation program should be an integral part of the maintenance program. The constant monitoring of the controlled vocabulary is one of the major contributors of effective retrieval.

EXHAUSTIVITY

Exhaustivity of indexing refers to the degree of indexing coverage of the topics found in the document file. It is a measure of the extent to which all distinct subjects or topics discussed in a given document are analyzed, recognized, and indexed in the indexing operation. In any single publication, the document often deals with more than one concept or theme. Naturally some are given more emphasis and are more central to the document. It is the task of the indexer to ferret out the concepts and to decide which of the ones referred to should be indexed. An exhaustive indexing process represents an attempt to index all concepts. It is primarily the decision of management to limit the number of concepts to be indexed.

The major factor in support of selective indexing of topics is the high cost associated with exhaustive indexing or indexing all concepts found in a document. A decision to index a maximum of thirty concepts as opposed to a maximum of five concepts per document in a printed index translates into an increase of from two to four times as much printing, amount of paper used, postage costs, and time and effort of the indexers employed. Consequently, the degree of exhaustivity is a practical consideration made by management as a matter of policy.

Indexing exhaustiveness is also a major consideration in terms of recall and precision. Each index term serves as a tag for a theme or concept in the document. If a term is assigned to a document, it is also an information representation for the paper. If every facet of a paper were indexed and as many as 30 index terms were used to represent the paper, then a search with any one of the index terms would be able to retrieve the paper. Clearly with indexing exhaustivity, a high probability exists that most of the relevant papers as represented by the index term would be retrieved. Exhaustive indexing does insure high recall.

Obviously the treatment of the topic as reflected by the index term in some of the retrieved documents may be less important to the document. Some may even be highly peripheral. If only highly relevant documents on that topic are needed, use of a particular term as a search term would retrieve many papers with only minor mention of the sought topic. High recall from exhaustive indexing often results at the expense of scanning many marginally relevant documents.

Generally, the degree of indexing exhaustivity is proportional to the number of index terms assigned per document. However, depending on the type of publications indexed, it is not a necessary condition. A paper may deal with two or three concepts so that exhaustive indexing could only produce a few index terms for the paper. Suppose a paper presents five different concepts. It is conceivable to index exhaustively different aspects of three of the five themes with many terms and ignore the other two. In cases of this kind, the number of index terms assigned is not an accurate indicator of the degree of indexing exhaustivity. Therefore, it may be misleading to measure indexing exhaustivity by the average number of terms assigned per document.

DENSITY OF INDEXING

Often the phrase *density of indexing* is used interchangably with indexing exhaustivity. It is a measure of the average number of index terms selected to represent each document. In the previous section, a cautionary note was given on equating the depth of indexing or the average number of index terms used per document with indexing exhaustivity. If there are only two simple concepts discussed in a given paper, assigning twenty terms would not be more exhaustive than using two appropriate terms to cover the document's content. Obviously, it is difficult to check the degree of exhaustivity among a group of indexers or to monitor the same indexer over a period of time. It is even harder to produce a quantitative measure for the degree of indexing exhaustivity. In lieu of indexing exhaustivity, a more pragmatic measure has been devised. Density of indexing is purely an estimate of exhaustivity. It is believed that although they are not equivalent, experienced indexers can achieve a desired degree of exhaustivity given an upper limit of the number of index terms allowed. Studies have shown that an average of 70 to 80 percent of the total relevant documents in the file can be retrieved if ten terms are assigned for each document (see Figure 7.10). On the other hand, a diminishing return is noted in experiments in which the indexer is asked to assign many more terms. A much greater effort is required to retrieve the last 10 percent of the remaining relevant documents in the file. By assigning an additional 40 to 50 terms per document, 90 percent recall may be achieved. Therefore, a much greater amount of effort must be expended to improve the recall to 90 percent. Figure 7.11 also shows that most terms are assigned within the first 10 minutes. By requiring many more terms from the indexer, a substantially lowered cost effectiveness is evident.

Lancaster provides a summary for the important requirements found in a controlled vocabulary for information retrieval. He states that the vocabulary should have both *literary warrant* and *users warrant*. The concept of *literary warrant* simply means that if enough publications on this subject are known to exist, appropriate index terms derived from the literature should be added to retrieve these documents. Similarly, terms are *users warrant* if they are likely to be employed by users in requests for information. Yet it is uneconomical to develop language more specific than warranted by the literature or by the systems users. The vocabulary must only be sufficiently specific to allow searchers to achieve the desired levels of precision. The use of pre-coordination should be allowed so that excessive false coordination can be avoided. The vocabulary should also provide adequate control of synonyms and homographs. Finally, the hierarchical and cross-reference structure should assist both the indexer and searcher in the selection of appropriate terms.

Recall

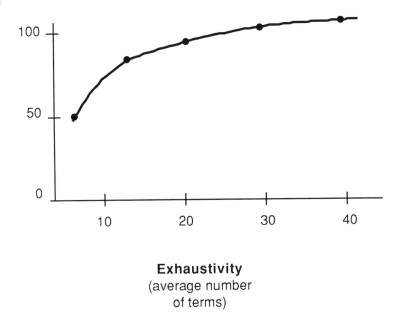

Exhaustivity
(average number
of terms)

Fig. 7.10. Recall versus density of indexing.

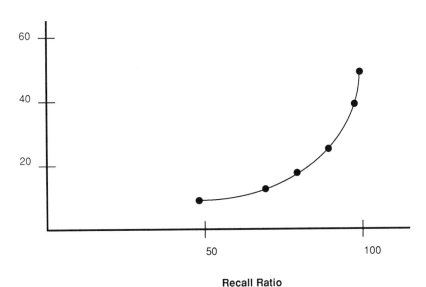

Fig. 7.11. Recall versus indexing effort.

Auxiliary Online Devices

WORD TRUNCATION

Since bibliographic files have been made available online, several retrieval aids shown to be powerful in improving recall and precision have made enormous impact on retrieval capabilities. The first is the truncation capability, which allows the searching of a term by its word stem, regardless of its prefixes or suffixes. Particularly in systems with uncontrolled vocabulary, a search by a word stem such as *weld-* collects all words starting with this character string with various endings. Naturally, one must be aware that homographs or words with identical spellings having different meanings could not be discriminated. Also, the same word stem may be used in an entirely different context. The MEDLINE database also allows for an even more powerful broadening device known as *exploding*. It permits the retrieval of documents related to a specified subject class by all classes at hierarchically narrower levels. In a well-structured vocabulary, such as the Medical Subject Heading List, this device is capable of automatically accessing a large number of subheadings, thereby retrieving a large number of related documents.

PROXIMITY SEARCHING

Fortunately, online systems also offer another device to improve the precision of these broad searches. Word proximity searching permits the request for a word to appear with another word. Additionally, these two words may appear within a specified number of other words. This is indeed a powerful feature of database management systems. Therefore, if *serv-* were to appear within two words of *custom-*, one could retrieve documents on *customer's service, serving of customers, service to customers,* or *customized service.*

TERM WEIGHTING

Some systems also distinguish between terms denoting major concepts from those labelled as minor concepts. When documents are indexed, the indexer could select a number of the index terms assigned to the document and tag them as those representing the document's major points. After the database is compiled, the computerized retrieval system is able to segregate documents indexed with the same term from those with an added tag. This term weighting device is an effective tool for higher precision searches. These are the most common aids that help to influence the recall and precision of retrieval.

AUTOMATIC INDEXING

Indexing has been discussed as an activity involving two separate steps, namely, the content analysis of the document to be indexed and the selection of terms as labels for the document. Both require intellectual effort on the part of the indexer thus making indexing an expensive and time-consuming operation. Over the last three decades, various attempts have been made to reduce one or both of these steps to algorithmic procedures. Any indexing method automating at least one or both steps is considered automatic indexing. The following section presents different automated methods, from the simple KWIC (Keywords in Context) indexing to the complex multi-valued probabilistic indexing.

Concordance Types

Examples of simple automated indexes are KWIC and its variant KWOC (Keywords Out of Context). The underlying premise is that title words are sufficiently indicative of the information content of a document, and that the individual words presented within the context of the title help to define its true meaning. Every nontrivial word is a potential subject access point to the document. A stop list or a negative dictionary of trivial words is kept so that words such as *the, of, to,* and *from* may be eliminated from consideration. Each content-bearing word together with the document title is listed in the alphabetical sequence of the index to be displayed and highlighted. As a result, the same title is listed in many locations of the alphabetical sequence. This type of indexing requires no intellectual content analysis. Since every content-bearing word acts as a label for the document, no term selection is needed. KWIC indexes are inexpensive and easy to produce. KWIC indexes of current publications have been useful as effective current awareness vehicles, but they are of limited use since title words often do not reflect all the concepts covered. They are also unsuitable for generic searches.

It is not difficult to extend this concept to the use of all content-bearing words in the entire text as index terms for the document. With many more texts available in machine-readable form, free-text indexing/searching is becoming more common. Again, no content analysis or term selection is necessary. There are no human errors except those that occurred during typing. No vocabulary needs to be maintained.

The family of legal databases, known as LEXIS, is searchable by the uncontrolled vocabulary of the full text. These large databases can be overwhelming for the novice searcher since retrieval can produce large citation sets. This lack of precision is the major limitation of free-text searching. The most common remedy is in the form of the combined use of truncation and word proximity. Finally, since retrieval is largely dependent on the exact match of the search term with that found in the text, a high level of typographical error in the database can substantially reduce recall.

Citation Indexing

Few concepts can boast of changing an entire way of approaching and solving problems in any field. In the last few decades, citation indexing has come to be considered a revolutionary concept in information retrieval. With the appearance of the *Science Citation Index*, the Institute for Scientific Information has introduced a new tool for subject search and retrieval. Two other citation indexes are also available: the *Social Science Citation Index* and *Arts and Humanities Citation Index*. Citation indexing is wholly independent of linguistic representation and subjective content interpretation. Unlike the semantic approach, documents are represented by other documents, namely, through their references and citations. Since most papers are cited for their subject relatedness, a strong case can be made that subject relevance exists between citing and cited papers. That cited references can be considered content identifiers which reflect the document content avoids the subjective assignment of index terms by indexers. Experimental results have provided convincing evidence that papers with high frequencies of citations correlate positively with subject experts' evaluation of the importance of the works (Virgo, 1977; Lawani and Bayer, 1983). Traditionally, librarians have always suggested references in relevant papers as possible useful materials. They have also used descriptors from a known relevant paper to recycle the initial search. This citation retrieval strategy appears to be based on a *pragmatic approach* to relevance which is different from the traditional *semantic approach* to subject retrieval.

Operationally, every bibliographic reference contained in a document acts as an access point for those documents in which it appeared. It avoids the entire unpredictable process of subject analysis by humans. One can assume that labels have been precisely chosen by the author in the form of full bibliographic citations. The citation index has been designed primarily as a retrieval device to circumvent some of the linguistic, terminological, and discipline-oriented problems of subject indexes. Yet little is known about the underlying relevance between citing and cited works. That they are topically related allows for a practical way to retrieve similar documents.

Although most papers are cited to substantiate, to refute, and to augment content in the citing papers, Smith (1981) and Garfield (1979) have noted several problems of citations with obvious implications for their retrieval effectiveness. In terms of retrieval, the primary concern is the degree of relevance between citing and cited papers. Aside from the obvious misuses and abuses, such as honorific citations and excessive self-citations, there appears to be a wide variety of reasons for citing a specific document. Papers are cited for their background information, for the use of a specific procedure or apparatus, or for their data set used. Clearly, all cited references are not equal in their degree of relevance to the citing paper. Citing a theoretical work to support an experimental design is substantially different from citing a reference of historical interest to the research problem. Various attempts have been made to isolate those citations which are considered more relevant to the source paper. Practical solutions have yet to be found.

One obvious disadvantage of citation retrieval is that a search topic must be represented by a published relevant document. If the requestor could not identify a document relevant to the topic sought, one could not find other citing documents. Thus, searching by citation is impossible.

Refinements in the Use of Citations

Citation retrieval can be made operational in a number of ways. In addition to using direct citation links, Kessler (1963) and Small (1973) have suggested refinements in the form of coreferenced documents and cocited papers, respectively. Thus, bibliographic couplings, cocitations, and references/citations can be expressed as measures of relevance. As early as the 1960s Kessler showed that papers that shared a large number of common bibliographic references were more likely to be closely related than those that did not. He called this measure by coreferences, bibliographic coupling. Papers that were cocited a large number of times had a higher probability of being closely related in terms of their subject content. Small named these cocitations. In a recent research project, Goffman and his associates showed that traditional subject searching failed miserably in an emerging interdisciplinary subject (Goffman and Pao, 1980; Kochtanek, 1982). Yet by using a single relevant paper on the subject of iron deficiencies in child development, a group of relevant papers was retrieved by the citation relationship. The retrieval was based on using both citing and cited papers. A recent paper is handicapped, since it has not had the opportunity to be cited by as many papers as an older one. Thus, potentially fewer retrievals would be triggered. On the other hand, although an old paper could have more chance to be cited, it does not have as many relevant papers to cite from. Using citing and cited papers compensates for the time lag needed for papers to be cited. Goffman's experiment showed that this citation approach was effective in generating relevant papers in an emerging, cross-disciplinary topic in which traditional term approach to subject retrieval had failed.

Finally, it was surprising to find from various studies that there is little overlap in the retrieved sets when using different document representation as retrieval keys. Katzer and his colleagues (1982) used seven different types of document representation such as descriptors, text words in titles, abstracts, text themselves, and the like; and each type seemed to retrieve different items. The results from Pao and and from McCain also showed that citation searching and term searching produced largely different sets of documents (Pao and Worthen, 1989; McCain, 1989).

In summary, little is known about the process of indexing. Indexing results vary widely between different indexers and in the works of the same indexer over a period of time. Different term-based document representations such as index terms, title words, words in the abstract and in the full text, as well as citation-based representations, appear to retrieve different documents. Such results are alarming with respect to retrieval. At the moment, although there are databases on almost every conceivable topic, and term-based representations could probably produce some documents, there is also great uncertainty in the retrieval results. In spite the amount of work performed in testing indexing languages in the last three decades, there is still much research to be done in information representation.

Indexing Based on
Statistical Principles

Hans Peter Luhn (1957) proposed that indexing should be based on "literary warrant." Relevant topics, terms, and the relationships among them on a given subject should be derived from analyzing a representative sample of documents on that subject. The simplest method was to count the number of times unique words occurred in a given text (Swanson, 1960). Create a list in which words appear in descending order of frequencies. The word frequencies are normalized in percentage values. The value associated with each word is compared with its usage in standard texts as published in word lists such as the corpus produced by Kucera and Francis (1967), or *The American Heritage Words Frequency Book* (Carroll, Davies, and Richman, 1971). If the relative frequency of each word type exceeded that found in normal usage, that word would be chosen as an index term for the text.

Another technique was to take the top 5 percent of the words frequently occurring in the word list. By eliminating articles, prepositions, conjunctions, and other noncontent words listed in a stop list, a list of index terms for the text could be identified. Another modified automatic indexing method was to select only content-bearing words which appeared at least twice within the same paragraph (Salton, 1970; 1986).

These methods are based purely on the statistical nature of how words are used. In any special context, content-bearing words which are of particular relevance to the document tend to be overrepresented. As a field of study, the statistical study of the characteristics of natural languages is known as computational linguistics. Indeed, George Zipf (1949) formulated two laws which have often been noted in automatic indexing. In his general observation of the way humans tend to conserve energy, he asserted that in a given text, the use of the high frequency words follows a predictable formula. His first law of high frequency words states that if the words of any text are arranged in order so that the most frequently used word is first and has rank *one*, the second most frequently used word comes second and has rank *two*, and so on, then

$$r \times f = c \qquad\qquad (1)$$

where r is the rank; f is the number of times the given word is used in the text; and c is the constant for the given text. An example illustrating this formulation is shown in Table 7.1. Note that the figures in the third column tend to fall within the range 91 to 161.

Table 7.1
Ranked List of High Frequency Words in the Article "A Law of
Occurrences for Words of Low Frequency," by A.D. Booth

Rank (r)	Frequency (f)	rf	Words
1	91(1)	91	the
2	70(1)	140	of
3	36(1)	108	is
4	30(1)	120	and
5	28(2)	140	that
	28	140	to
6	24(1)	144	in
7	23(1)	161	a
8	20(1)	160	for
9	16(1)	144	law
10	15(1)	150	by
11	14(3)	154	word
	14	154	words
	14	154	it
12	13(1)	156	which
13	11(1)	143	frequency
14	10(4)	140	Zipf's
	10	140	text
	10	140	this
	10	140	general
.	.	.	.
.	.	.	.
.	.	.	.
.	.	.	.

Zipf went on to present his second law of low frequency words. It states that the ratio of the number of words occurring only once to words occurring n number of times is a predictable ratio represented by the following formula:

$$I_1/I_n = (4n^2 - 1)/3 \qquad (2)$$

Where I_1 is the number of words appearing once in the text, I_n is the number of words appearing n times. This law has been modified by Mandelbrot and Booth (Booth, 1967). Their revised version of the second law appears to be a better predictor. The revised version is:

$$I_1/I_n = n(n + 1)/2 \qquad (3)$$

where I_1 is the number of different words occurring once in the text; I_n is the number of words occurring n number of times in the text; and n is the frequency of occurrence (or f in the first law). Table 7.2 shows Booth's data obtained from four sample texts, indicated by WRU1, WRU2, WRU3, and Eldridge, with the addition of a text written by Booth himself. Here, if one actually counted the words that occurred only once and divided that number by the number of words that occurred twice, one would obtain those ratios under "Observed Values." Under "Computed Values," the predicted ratio using Zipf's second law and Booth's revised version were computed for comparison. For example, in the WRU1 text, the ratio $I_1/I_4 = 9.66$ is derived from the actual counts of words which occurred once and those which occurred four times. The calculated ratio using both Booth's and Zipf's formulations are 10 and 21 respectively. Clearly, except for the WRU2 text, all the observed ratios matched results computed from Booth's revised formula much more closely than those computed from Zipf's formula.

Table 7.2
Low Frequency Word Counts of Five Texts

Observed Values					Computed Values	
Texts					Booth Revision $n(n+1)/2$	Zipf Second Law $(4n^2-1)/3$
WRU1	WRU2	WRU3	Eldridge	Booth		
I_1 541	710	887	2976	256		
I_1/I_1 1.00	1.00	1.00	1.00	1.00	1	1
I_1/I_2 3.56	3.13	3.25	2.76	2.46	3	5
I_1/I_3 5.76	7.80	5.87	5.77	5.82	6	11.67
I_1/I_4 9.66	17.32	9.86	10.12	11.6	10	21
I_1/I_5 15.03	22.19	14.31	14.04	14.22	15	33

*I_1 = # of words which occur once in the text.

I_2 = # of words which occur twice in the text.

I_3 = # of words which occur three times in the text.

I_4 = # of words which occur four times in the text.

I_5 = # of words which occur five times in the text.

How are these two laws related to automatic indexing? In the early 1960s, William Goffman (Pao, 1978) observed that since these two laws apply to any text, they characterize the two extreme ends of the same distribution. He hypothesized that words appearing at the transition between the high and low frequency words could be content-bearing words which may be most descriptive of the content of the text. Thus, these could be used as appropriate index terms for the document. He went on to identify the exact demarcation between the two types of words. In examining Booth's revised second law in Equation (3), he noted that the denominator of the observed ratio on the left hand side of the equation represented the number of words which occurred n number of times. For words in the low frequency region, I_n was usually greater than one. Yet as one followed the distribution up towards the high frequency region of the distribution, the value of I_n gradually approached unity. That is, for those words which were used frequently in a text, it was less likely that any author would use two words the exact same number of times within the same text. If that were the case, as I_n approaches unity, the equation could be rewritten as:

$$I_1/I_n = n\,(n+1)/2$$

$$I_1/1 = n(n+1)/2$$

$$2\,I_1 = n^2 + n$$

$$n^2 + n - 2I_1 = 0$$

Solving the quadratic equation for the value of n,

$$n = (-1 \pm \sqrt{1 + 8\,I_1})/2$$

Since n is the number of times a given word is expected to occur, it must have a positive value. Thus, the value of n from the transition formula is:

$$n = (-1 + \sqrt{1 + 8\,I_1})/2 \qquad (4)$$

Goffman named the n value the transition point between high and low frequencies. Operationally, he proposed that once the transition point was found, the same number of words above the transition point as below it should be collected. Eliminating trivial words by a stop list, the remaining content-bearing words would be indicative of the document content.

To illustrate, the number of times each unique word occurred in two papers written by Booth were counted. The subject of the first paper was a proposed revision of Zipf's second law (Booth, 1967). The word distribution lists are shown in Table 7.1 (page 135). There were a total of 188 words which occurred once in the text. Substituting this value in Equation (4), the transition point was computed to be approximately 19. That is, the transition from high frequency to low frequency occurred at the point which each word appeared approximately 19 times. Or,

$$n = (-1 + \sqrt{1 + 8(188)})/2$$

$$= 19$$

In Table 7.1, $n = 19$ occurs between the words *for* and *law*. As a practical strategy for selecting index terms, the number of words above and below the transition point or a total of 18 words were chosen. Eliminating prepositions, articles, and others, this method identified the content-bearing words for this article as *law, word, words, frequency, Zipf's*, and *text*. This list gave a rough indication of the article's content.

The subject of Booth's second paper was a proposed new way of filing and shelving books based on the frequency of use of the books in the collection (Booth, 1969). Counting the number of words in this article, there were 256 words which occurred once. The transition point was computed as approximately 22. Table 7.3 shows that there were two words, *library* and *which* that each occurred 22 times. Since they occupied the 15th and 16th ranks, a total of 32 words were collected for inspection. The group of content words were *access, frequency, library, collection, books, distance, most, shown, book, shelf, stack, analysis*, and *use*. The list contained several words with identical word stems. For indexing purposes, they would be consolidated by a vocabulary control device. Nevertheless, by using the statistical property of written texts, an automatic procedure could possibly be used to extract words as a first step toward automatic indexing. Finally, Salton has experimented extensively with both statistical and syntactic automatic text analyses. His SMART Project is the largest retrieval testing system with the longest history. Readers are referred to several of his key papers and books listed at the end of this chapter (Salton, 1971; 1975; Salton, Yang, and Yu, 1975; Salton, Wu, and Yu, 1981; Salton and McGill, 1983).

Probabilistic Indexing

All of the indexing methods discussed rely on a two-valued retrieval logic, namely, that each document in the file is either relevant or not relevant; thus, retrieved or not retrieved. Index terms or tags are selected to represent a given document. Once they are entered into the retrieval system, they are identified as the index terms by which documents are retrieved. With respect to any document, a given index term is either a representation or not a representation. There are only two values available. Such retrieval systems cannot accommodate the notion that an index term may be partially indicative of the content of a given document. For example, not all the medical subject headings assigned to the article from the MEDLINE database shown in Figure 7.12 (page 140) under the field label MH are equally relevant to the content of the article.

Table 7.3
Ranked List of High Frequency Words in the Article "On the
Geometry of Libraries," by A.D. Booth

Rank (r)	Frequency (f)	rf	Words
1	218(1)	218	the
2	120(1)	240	of
3	105(1)	315	is
4	70(1)	280	in
5	65(1)	325	to
6	64(1)	384	that
7	58(1)	406	and
8	53(1)	424	a
9	46(1)	414	be
10	39(1)	390	this
11	35(1)	385	for
12	33(1)	396	it
13	26(1)	338	access
14	23(1)	322	frequency
15	22(2)	330	library
	22	330	which
16	19(4)	304	collection
	19	304	books
	19	304	by
	19	304	are
17	17(1)	289	has
18	16(3)	288	distance
	16	288	most
	16	288	so
19	15(2)	285	shown
	15	285	book
20	14(3)	280	shelf
	14	280	stack
	14	280	from
21	13(4)	273	analysis
	13	273	use
	13	273	can
	13	273	as
.	.	.	.
.	.	.	.
.	.	.	.
.	.	.	.

```
PROG:

1
UI   - 85022618
AU   - Pepe G ; Holtrop M ; Gadaleta G ; Kroon AM ; Cantatore P ;
       Gallerani R ; De Benedetto C ; Quagliariello C ; Sbis:a E ;
       Saccone C
TI   - Non-random patterns of nucleotide substitutions and codon
       strategy in the mammalian mitochondrial genes coding for
       identified and unidentified reading frames.
LA   - Eng
MH   - Amino Acid Sequence ; Animal ; Base Sequence ; Cattle ; *Codon ;
       Comparative Study ; Cytochrome Oxidase/*GENETICS ; *DNA,
       Mitochondrial ; Human ; Mice ; Multienzyme Complexes/*GENETICS ;
       Phosphotransferases, ATP/*GENETICS ; Rats ; Rats, Inbred Strains
       ; *RNA, Messenger ; Species Specificity ; Support, Non-U.S. Gov't
DA   - 841102
DP   - 1983 Apr
IS   - 0158-5231
TA   - Biochem Int
PG   - 553-63
SB   - M
ZN   - Z1.338
IP   - 4
VI   - 6
JC   - 9Y9
AA   - Author
RN   - EC 1.9.3.1 (Cytochrome Oxidase) ; EC 2.7. (Phosphotransferases,
       ATP) ; EC 2.7.4.- (ATP synthetase)
EM   - 8501
AB   - The base sequence of large part of the mitochondrial DNA of
       Wistar rats is presented. The sequence is compared with those of
       other mammalian mitochondrial DNAs. The nucleotide and amino acid
       homologies, codon strategy, nature and patterns of substitutions
       are reported. It results a very high amount of silent
       substitutions and, in short divergence time, a predominance of
       transitions on transversions. In both types of substitutions a
       strong bias in avoiding the use of the G in the third codon
       position is observed.
SO   - Biochem Int 1983 Apr;6(4):553-63
```

Fig. 7.12. Printout of a bibliographic record from MEDLINE.

In formulating a request, searchers must intuitively weigh the likelihood of the chosen term against the desired topic. In choosing a term, one must take the chance that major or minor treatment of the topic represented by the term would have an equal opportunity of being selected.

Maron and Kuhns (1960; Maron, 1979) proposed a probabilistic approach to both indexing and searching. The rationale for a probabilistic retrieval system was accompanied by a demonstration of an indexing method. Since then several methods to implement indexing systems that could accommodate gradation of term weights have been proposed. Several have been tested in experimental settings.

The suggestions made by Maron and Kuhns (1960) consist of the following: upon receipt of a query, the retrieval system assigns a relevance number to each document in the file. This number expresses the probability that the document will satisfy the given query. Thus, the retrieved set from the file consists of a ranked list of documents associated with nonzero relevance numbers. These relevance numbers may be derived from the common key terms between the query and each document. If the query is presented in the form of a bibliographic citation, Kessler's bibliographic coupling technique can be utilized to compute the probability of relevance between the query and each document (Kessler, 1963). That is, if the patron wants papers similar to a given key paper, the number of references cited in both the query document and each document in the file may be used to compute the relevance number. Cocitation data can also be used to generate relevance numbers (Small, 1973).

The interdependence of documents in the file can also be expressed by a similar method. Instead of comparing each query with each document, probabilistic indexing extracts an approximation of the degree of relatedness between every other pair of documents in the file (Doyle, 1961). In so doing, a probability value is attached to each document with respect to all other documents in the search file. This probability value between two documents is known as similarity measure, or associative measure. Ideally, documents could then be topographically displayed showing their interrelationship with respect to their subject matter. A direct implementation of this notion was suggested by Goffman in his proposal of an indirect method of searching. A detailed description of the search method is presented in Chapter 9.

As far as the indexing is concerned, several automatic methods are possible. First, the relatedness between any two documents may be obtained by comparing the words found in the two texts. One may assume that the more terms they share with each other, the more closely related they are in subject content. Secondly, one also examines the relative number of references shared by the two documents. Presumably, documents with similar contents also share many of the same bibliographic citations. Thirdly, instead of using common references, the proportion of more recent papers which cite the two documents can also be used to generate a similarity measure.

The advantage of a document file represented by similarity measures is that with respect to each query, the relevance of every document is expressed in a probability value. A list of all documents is ranked according to these probability values. Depending on the degree of relevance required, the user can determine the desired cutoff point on the list. This represents a flexible system of retrieval. For more detailed discussion on probabilistic indexing and retrieval, the reader is encouraged to consult works by Salton and McGill (1983) and Sparck Jones (1981).

However, for each document in a search file of n documents, $n(n - 1)$ similarity measures must be computed. If each computation of a similarity measure is considered an indexing decision, the number of indexing decisions for a collection of reasonable size can be staggering.

In summary, access to the intellectual content of recorded information resources has been shown to be a major concern for information retrieval. Likewise, information representation has been demonstrated to be a well-researched area of study in information retrieval. Yet the complex nature of language upon which all indexing and abstracting are based has defied full understanding. The concept of relevance has eluded precise definition and representation. Much more work in natural language processing remains.

REFERENCES

Aitchison, J., and A. Gilchrist. 1987. *Thesaurus Construction – A Practical Manual.* 2nd edition. London: Aslib.

American National Standards Institute. 1979. *American National Standard for Writing Abstracts. ANSI Z39-14-1979.* New York: American National Standards Institute.

American National Standards Institute. 1980. *Guidelines for Thesaurus: Structure, Construction & Use.* New York: American National Standards Institute.

Blair, D.C. 1986. "Indeterminacy in the Subject Access to Documents." *Information Processing and Management*, 22(3):229-242.

Blair, D.C., and M.E. Maron. 1985. "An Evaluation of Retrieval Effectiveness for a Full-Text Document-Retrieval System." *Communications of the Association for Computing Machinery*, 28(3):289-299.

Booth, A.D. 1967. "A 'Law' of Occurrences for Words of Low Frequency." *Information and Control*, 10(4):386-393.

Booth, A.D. 1969. "On the Geometry of Libraries." *Journal of Documentation*, 25(1):28-40.

Borko, H., and C.L. Bernier. 1975. *Abstracting Concepts and Methods.* New York: Academic Press.

Borko, H., and C.L. Bernier. 1978. *Indexing Concepts and Methods.* New York: Academic Press.

Borko, H., and S. Chatman. 1963. "33 Criteria for Acceptable Abstracts: A Survey of Abstractors' Instructions." *American Documentation*, 14(2): 364-376.

Carroll, J.B., P. Davies, and B. Richman. 1971. *The American Heritage Words Frequency Book.* New York: American Heritage Publishing Co.

Collison, R.L. 1971. *Abstracts and Abstracting Services.* Santa Barbara, California: American Bibliographical Center-Clio Press.

Cremmins, E.T. 1982. *The Art of Abstracting.* Philadelphia, Pennsylvania: ISI Press.

Doszkocs, T.E. 1986. "Natural Language Processing in Information Retrieval." *Journal of the American Society for Information Science*, 37(4):191-196.

Doyle, L. 1963. "Semantic Roadmaps for Literature Searches." *Journal of the Association for Computing Machinery*, 8(4):553-578.

Fidel, R. 1986a. "The Probable Effect of Abstracting Guidelines on Retrieval Performance of Free-text Searching." *Information Processing and Management*, 22(4):309-316.

Fidel, R. 1986b. "Writing Abstracts for Free-text Searching." *Journal of Documentation*, 42(1):11-21.

Garfield, E. 1979. *Citation Indexing—Its Theory and Application in Science, Technology, and Humanities.* New York: John Wiley & Sons.

Goffman, W., and M.L. Pao. 1980. "Retrieval of Biomedical Information for Emerging Interdisciplinary Problems." *Proceedings of the 4th International Congress on Medical Librarianship*, 39-50. Belgrade, Yugoslavia: GRO "M. Gembarovski"—Nova Gradiˇska.

Katzer, J., M.J. McGill, J.A. Tessier, W. Frakes, and P. DasGupta. 1982. "A Study of the Overlap Among Document Representation," *Information Technology: Research and Development*, 1(4):261-274.

Kessler, M.M. 1963. "Bibliographic Coupling Between Scientific Papers." *American Documentation*, 14(1):10-25.

Kochtanek, T.R. 1982. "Bibliographic Compilation Using Reference and Citation Links." *Information Processing and Management*, 18(1):33-39.

Kucera, H., and W.N. Francis. 1967. *Computational Analysis of Present-Day American English.* Providence: Brown University Press.

Lancaster, F.W. 1972. *Vocabulary Control for Information Retrieval.* Washington, D.C.: Information Resources Press.

Lancaster, F.W. 1986. *Vocabulary Control for Information Retrieval.* 2nd edition. Arlington, Virginia: Information Resources Press.

Lawani, S.M., and A.E. Bayer. 1983. "Validity of Citation Criteria for Assessing the Influence of Scientific Publications: New Evidence with Peer Assessment." *Journal of the American Society for Information Science*, 34(1): 59-66.

Luhn, H.P. 1957. "A Statistical Approach to Mechanized Encoding and Searching of Literary Information." *IBM Journal of Research and Development*, 1(4):309-317.

Maron, M.E. 1979. "Depth of Indexing." *Journal of the American Society for Information Science*, 30(4):224-228.

Maron, M.E., and J.L. Kuhns. 1960. "On Relevance, Probabilistic Indexing, and Information Retrieval." *Journal of the Association of Computing Machinery*, 7(3):216-244.

McCain, K.W. 1989. "Descriptor and Citation Retrieval in the Medical Behavioral Sciences Literature: Retrieval Overlaps and Novelty Distribution." *Journal of the American Society for Information Science*. In press.

Pao, M.L. 1978. "Automatic Text Analysis Based on Transition Phenomena of Word Occurrences." *Journal of the American Society for Information Science*, 29(3):121-124.

Pao, M.L., and D.B. Worthen. 1989. "Retrieval Effectiveness by Semantic and Citation Searching." *Journal of the American Society for Information Science*. In press.

Rolling, L. 1981. "Indexing Consistency: Quality and Efficiency." *Information Processing and Management*, 17(2):69-76.

Salton, G. 1970. "Automatic Text Analysis." *Science*, 168(3929):335-343.

Salton, G., ed. 1971. *The SMART Retrieval System: Experiments in Automatic Document Processing*. Englewood Cliffs, New Jersey: Prentice Hall.

Salton, G. 1975. *Dynamic Information and Library Processing*. Englewood Cliffs, New Jersey: Prentice Hall.

Salton, G. 1986. "Another Look at Automatic Text Retrieval Systems." *Communications of the Association for Computing Machinery*, 29(7):648-656.

Salton, G., and M.J. McGill. 1983. *Introduction to Modern Information Retrieval*. New York: McGraw-Hill.

Salton, G., W.H. Wu, and C.T. Yu. 1981. "The Measurement of Term Importance in Automatic Indexing." *Journal of the American Society for Information Science*, 32(3):175-186.

Salton, G., C.S. Yang, and C.T. Yu. 1975. "A Theory of Term Importance in Automatic Text Analysis." *Journal of the American Society for Information Science*, 26(1):33-44.

Saracevic, T., and P. Kantor. 1988. "A Study of Information Seeking and Retrieving: III. Searchers, Searches, and Overlaps." *Journal of the American Society for Information Science*, 39(3):197-216.

Small, H. 1973. "Co-citation in the Scientific Literature: A New Measure of the Relationship Between Two Documents." *Journal of the American Society for Information Science*, 24(4):265-269.

Smith, L.C. 1981. "Citation Analysis." *Library Trends*, 30(1):83-106.

Soergel, D. 1974. *Indexing Languages and Thesauri: Construction and Maintenance*. Los Angeles, California: Melville Publishing Company.

Sparck Jones, K., ed. 1981. *Information Retrieval Experiment*. London: Butterworths.

Swanson, D.R. 1960. "Searching Natural Language Text by Computer." *Science*, 132(3434):1099-1104.

Townley, H., and R. Gee. 1980. *Thesaurus-Making: Grow Your Own Word Stock*. Lexington, Massachusetts: D.C. Heath Company.

Unisist. United Nations Educational, Scientific and Cultural Organization. 1975. *Indexing Principles*. Paris: Unesco.

Vickery, B.C. 1960. "Thesaurus—A New Word in Documentation." *Journal of Documentation*, 16(4):181-189.

Virgo, J.A. 1977. "A Statistical Procedure for Evaluating the Importance of Scientific Papers." *Library Quarterly*, 47(4):415-430.

Weil, B. 1970. "Standards for Writing Abstracts." *Journal of the American Society for Information Science*, 21(5):351-357.

Zipf, G.K. 1949. *Human Behaviour and the Principle of Least Effort*. Cambridge, Massachusetts: Addison-Wesley.

Zunde, P., and M.E. Dexter. 1969. "Indexing Consistency and Quality." *American Documentation*, 20(3):259-267.

8

File
Organization

File organization or file design refers to the complete specification of the types of information to be stored in the file. This includes the amount of data to be stored in each record, the record structure, the relationship between different data elements, where the file is to be stored, and how the records are to be stored and accessed.

Physical, structural, and logical aspects of file organization are three issues of particular importance to electronic files. First, physical aspects are concerned with the physical media or materials on which the information is actually recorded and stored, and the computers with which data is manipulated. The chosen hardware places rigid constraints on the processing of the file. Unique features of each medium restrict and often dictate the mode of access and the efficiency of maintenance of the file. Key features of storage media are discussed in connection with the file structure.

Secondly, file structure governs the organization of data elements and records. For the file designer, a logical file structure is the single most important consideration. This chapter concentrates on the different file structures and organizations available. The understanding of file structure is as important for the searcher as it is for the file designer, since knowledge of the structure of record and file can facilitate the quality and speed of retrieval.

Finally, the logical aspects of the file are concerned with the underlying search logic which provides the search mechanism. In operating systems, Boolean logic is the basis of all search strategies, and it is implemented on many commercially available computer programs for file management. Chapter 9 is devoted to search strategies.

HIERARCHY OF
DATA CONTENTS OF FILES

File organization refers to the logical way a collection of items is arranged physically in the storage medium to facilitate processing and searching. The most familiar file organization is an alphabetically ordered linear sequence of items. An example is the telephone directory. The entries are arranged in an alphabetical sequence according to last names. If the name of an individual or a company is

146

known, the arrangement is simple and convenient to use. However, the telephone book is found to be inadequate by itself, and is usually supplemented by the Yellow Pages. This book often contains much of the same information found in the main telephone book, with a major difference. Instead of an alphabetical arrangement of names, these same entries are now arranged according to their associated businesses and professions. Without knowing the name of any dentist, one is able to find all dentists listed in the telephone book. The file organization of the Yellow Pages offers a subject approach which is very different from that in the main telephone book, even though each entry may contain essentially the same information. Files are not limited to data records in printed forms, such as card files or file drawers. The term *database* is used to denote a collection of data records in any electronic media. The electronic equivalent of the magazine *Business Week* and the journal *Harvard Business Review* are both databases.

Before discussing the different file organizations used in information retrieval systems, it is useful to consider files and their general structure. The content of a file is structured hierarchically. Therefore, in order to fully understand the relationship of data in files, each level in the hierarchy should be examined.

A file is made up of a group of records. An individual record contains a number of fields each of which may be consolidated to be considered as a component unit within the record. A field consists of one or more data elements. Each element contains words which in turn are composed of characters. Finally, a character is built up from bytes of information. The component parts of a record should be planned carefully before designing a file since they are the basic building blocks. In document retrieval systems, each record represents a document. The type of data and the record content should be carefully selected according to the anticipated use of the file. Such decisions by the file designer ultimately have an effect on whether the record can be manipulated and retrieved. The efficiency with which records are retrieved is affected by how the records are arranged and the record structure of the file. Understanding record structures and file design are also essential for the effective use of thousands of already existing databases.

File

A file is a collection of data records which share some common characteristics. For example, the common attribute of all data records found in a telephone directory of Albany, New York, is that the listed individuals and businesses must have their addresses within the greater Albany area. On a broader level, a collection of books or journal articles dealing with a specific topic may be considered a file. Items in a library collection share a common ownership. A file can display multiple attributes. Thus, materials in the Hoover Library deal with Americana, in addition to being owned by Stanford University. Other attributes can be, for example, a pre-1750 printing date. On a smaller scale, the entire run of the journal *Harvard Business Review* is also a file. Each record is a journal article in either printed or electronic form. In all cases, each record represents a physical object: a book, a journal, a musical score, and the like. The common characteristic of the records in a bibliographic file is usually a specific topic or subject area such as physics or chemistry.

There are machine-readable files or databases on almost every conceivable subject. Electronic files are produced by database producers. Many are made available directly by the producers themselves, and others are bought or leased by online search vendors; these latter files are searchable online by subscribers of these search services. Examples of database producers are the American Psychological Association which produces PSYCINFO, and the Institute for Scientific Information which produces SCISEARCH. Others such as the National Library of Medicine and Mead Data Central are the producers of MEDLINE and LEXIS, respectively. They also provide search services for these and a number of other databases. They are both producers and search vendors. Several hundreds of online databases are maintained and made searchable online by the two largest online search services, DIALOG and BRS. Finally, information utilities which provide extensive bibliographic services to libraries also maintain massive databases. Two outstanding examples are RLIN (Research Libraries Information Network) and OCLC (Online Computer Library Center, Inc.). They provide search capability as well as many library functions.

Databases are often compiled on a specific topic such as agriculture, or on a problem area such as water pollution. Each collection of records is most likely to be stored, processed, and searched as a single unit. Upon specification of search criteria, records from the database may be retrieved. In many ways, a file or a database is itself an information retrieval system since items are collected, stored, and organized so that they may be retrieved again at a later date. Selection policy has to be established for the types of documentary materials to be included in the database. Bibliographic records must be created for the documents and each document must be indexed. The content and format of a typical record must be determined. Since the collection of records must be organized and stored as a file to be of value, in designing a file, all important functions of an information retrieval system should be considered together with the file's intended purpose.

Record

If a file is an aggregation of records, then a record is the basic unit within a file. An entry in a telephone directory is a record. It simply contains the name of an individual or a business organization, the associated address, and telephone number. A record in a personnel file contains the employee's social security number, the date of employment, the name of a contact person in case of emergency, and other personal data. Each and every book in a given library is a record. Each journal title in the Harlan Hatcher Graduate Library of the University of Michigan is a record. Each article in the magazine *Science* is a record if the entire run of the journal is considered a database. Likewise, each entry in the card catalog, the electronic online catalog, or a bibliographic database is also a record. Therefore, what constitutes a record depends on the basic design of the file.

However, in document retrieval systems, a record often refers to a bibliographic record which is a bibliographic description of the actual document itself. That is, a bibliographic record may contain the author(s) of the document, document title, title of the publishing journal, volume and issue numbers, inclusive pages, its date of publication, and the index terms assigned to the specific publication. In most of the commercially available databases, a record consists of a bibliographic record which contains two parts, a bibliographic description uniquely identifying the journal article or the report, and a topical representation consisting of a set of index terms describing the subject content of the document. For a file in printed form such as the library catalog, each catalog card is a record representing a book. For an online catalog file, the same book is represented by an online bibliographic entry. Increasingly, individual bibliographic records may contain the full text of a document. Although a few years ago LEXIS, a file of legal materials, was the only major full-text database, data files of full text articles are being produced in large numbers. For example, each record of the electronic version of the *Harvard Business Review* contains a bibliographic description as well as the entire text of each paper.

The content of a bibliographic record consists of a collection of related data items, which are processed and retrieved together as a single unit. In other words, a record is a group of data items indicating the attributes of the document. Each data item is a field of the record. Records are the basic building blocks of files.

Field

A field is a logical unit of information within a record. Each field contains a specific type of information or an attribute. For example, name, address, and telephone number are the three fields commonly found in an entry in a telephone directory. Fields in a personnel record may include the employee's name, social security number, and spouse's name, and so on. In a bibliographic record, fields for other types of information are also included. Since information on the author(s) is essential for identification and retrieval, an author field is set aside to contain the given names and surnames. Other fields can include the document title, journal title, volume number, corporate source, and/or abstract of the document for which the record is made.

Record design must start with decisions about the type of information or fields which will be needed for each record for this file. Are affiliated institutional names of the authors needed? Is it necessary to include coauthors? Should the date of publication include the month? Although almost all types of information may be of some use at some future time, in general the basic principle is to include only those fields with a reasonable amount of anticipated use. Adequate planning and consultation with potential users are essential. The simple reason is that with each added field, the file size increases accordingly. A larger file requires considerably more data input, storage capacity, and access time. Electronic storage of files of immense size can be costly. Large files also require longer access time in searching, and in updating with new data. Adding a single line of text to an average citation in a major printed index such as *Index Medicus* would result in a substantial increase in the number of pages in its annual index. In turn, it would increase the cost of postage as well as for shelf space in each library. Although storage for electronic files is trivial in comparison, access time for large files can be substantial. Access time is defined as the time required to locate information stored at a known memory location. An increase in processing time for an average transaction can become costly and intolerable.

The data items in a typical record fall into several logical groups. Each group forms a field in the record. Based on the analysis of the data items, format specifications of the record can be drawn up for the record design. There are several parts of a record structure. Figure 8.1 shows an example. First, each field is identified by the assignment of a name. A field name distinguishes one field from another. It also serves as a convenient field label or prompt during data input. The example shows four fields with their respective field names. The field name is to be distinguished from its data or value. Thus, *Adams* is the data value for the name field of the first record. *File Management* is the data value for the title field of the second record.

Field name:				
	name	title	year	descriptor
Data type:	c	c	n	c
Field size:	14	35	4	20
Field values:				
	Adams	Pascal Programming	1987	Pascal Programming
	Dates	File Management	1984	file organization,
	Krohn	C Programming	1981	computer programming
	Martin	Data Structure	1986	software development

Fig. 8.1. Sample of a linear file.

Next, the type of data to be included in each field must be decided. It is possible to have alphabetic, numeric, or special character data. Data type specification may be used by the search program to check the accuracy of data input. Once a data type is defined for a field, the input module of the search program can detect errors if other types are used. For example, if the year field is declared as a numeric field, and if *Pascal* is typed into the year field, an error message will be issued. In the case of numeric data, data storage is usually more efficient and mathematical manipulations are possible.

Lastly, the size of each field is usually specified. The name field in the example has been allotted 14 characters and the total characters reserved for each record is 73. This is a requirement for many file storage and retrieval programs which are used to store, maintain, organize, and search the file.

Knowledge of the fields in a record is essential for the formulation of effective search statements. One cannot reasonably search a file without knowing the available fields and the types of data contained in each field. Such knowledge about the record constitutes the specifications of the record structure.

Even after the decision is made on the numbers and types of fields for each record, at least three other crucial factors must be considered in file design. They are (1) searchable fields and printable fields, (2) field lengths, and (3) repeatable fields. All three are of concern to both file designers and users in that they not only impart useful information but affect the use of the file.

SEARCHABLE AND PRINTABLE FIELDS

Data values in a field may be used to uniquely identify a record. Such a field is known as a key field. For example, social security numbers are often used as unique identifications for personnel records. One's social security number is unique, whereas one's personal name is not. A name such as John Anderson is not unique. Thus, the field assigned to contain social security numbers is a key field. Key fields are important because they may be used directly and efficiently in searching. Unfortunately, there are very few key fields in bibliographic records. Often the accession number assigned by the database producer serves as the only available key field, but the data value in the accession number field is useless for the information searcher. No one remembers a record by its accession number. The usefulness of an OCLC number, a unique number assigned by Online Computer Library Center, is also limited. Other key fields are ISBN (International Standard Book Numbers) numbers and library call numbers. They are equally limited in their use as search keys. However, unique identification may be established indirectly by the data contained in more than one field. For example, one is likely to identify a citation given the author's name together with two or more content words in the article title. Thus, inverted files or indices must be created for both the author and title fields so that these fields are made searchable. The creation and maintenance of inverted files require substantial additional memory and processing.

Since not all fields are used by searchers, searchable fields are predetermined at the time of the file design. The data value is indexed. Non-searchable fields contain data value as part of the record and they are only accessible when the record is printed. For example, the field containing information on the country of publication or the date when the record was entered into the database are often not searchable. However, they may be printed as part of the output of the entire record.

FIELD LENGTHS

The second problem is the number of characters within the record reserved for each field. For hard-copy printed records, the determination of field length is not necessary since searching is normally done manually. In browsing through a library catalog, most users scan a record and visually decide where one field ends and another field begins. The use of proper nouns and punctuations helps to delineate fields.

For electronic files, searching must be performed by a search program. Most commercially available computer programs for file management such as RBase and DBase III are known as relational databases. They are based on the concept of fixed field length. That is, the number of fields is predetermined and the position of each field relative to the beginning of the record is fixed. For the computer-search program to operate properly and efficiently, the format specification of the records in the file is first transmitted to the program. The program then anticipates the way the data are stored, and interprets according to the instructions concerning the data format. Since each record occupies a fixed number of characters, the program can locate the beginning of each record as well as the beginning of any field of any record in this file. For example, data in Figure 8.2 is readily interpreted as: the first field for author names occupies 14 characters, the second field starts at the 15th character and occupies 21 characters, the third at the 36th character, and so on.

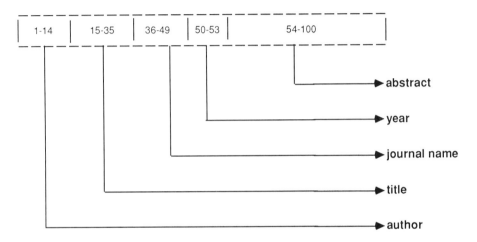

Fig. 8.2. Sample fixed field length record structure.

As far as the efficiency of the program is concerned, fixed field length files can be processed rapidly since the search program can quickly locate the needed data from a known memory address. For certain types of data, such as a field for the year of publication, which always occupies four characters, a fixed field is optimal.

The problems of using fixed field records are found in many text fields. Once information about the fixed length of the name field is known to the program, no matter how long or how short the actual author name is, 14 character spaces must be reserved. If the name is *Adam, Joe*, five spaces are left unused and must be padded with blanks. Whereas, if the name is *Beethoven, Ludwig von*, the name would be truncated to *Beethoven, Lud*. The estimation of optimal length for each field is often difficult. As a result, reserving enough characters for an occasional long name means that the file size is inflated by a large number of blanks padded at the end of most names.

There are computer programs for searching based on variable field length specially designed for bibliographic files. They are less common and the design is more elaborate. Whether variable or fixed field length is to be used must be decided before the file is built. As a result, for the individual responsible for building a file, the appropriate search program must be selected based on such decisions as search capabilities, ease of use, cost, the availability of programs, and support. As for searching the online databases of the major online search services, there need be no concern at all about fixed or variable field length. These powerful programs are preprogrammed to accommodate variable field length.

REPEATABLE FIELDS

Another concern in building a bibliographic file is the availability of repeatable groups in the computer program used for searching. A repeatable field is one in which the number of data elements may vary from one record to another. Figure 8.3 shows that the number of descriptors in the descriptor field is different depending on the record. Such a varying set of entries of the same type of data in the same field in each record is referred to as repeatable field. With this feature, any given entry is directly searchable.

Field name				
	name	title	year	descriptor
Field values:				
	Adams	Pascal Programming	1987	Pascal Programming
	Dates	File Management	1984	file organization, database management system DBMS
	Krohn	C Programming	1981	software development structure programming programming
	Martin	Data Structure	1986	software development programming

Fig. 8.3. Sample of a repeatable field.

In bibliographic records, the author field and the descriptor field require a varying number of entries. File processing of business files tends to use one data element for every category of information. For example, a personnel record may contain the employee's name, his social security number, his address, his home telephone number, his office extension, his department name, and his spouse's name. For this same individual, it is impossible to have two social security numbers or two addresses. Even in the case where two telephone numbers are available, it is relatively unimportant to list both numbers. Information in a bibliographic record is different. Many documents are authored by more than one individuals. Moreover, each document may be indexed by many index terms.

All relational database management systems do not allow repeatable fields. Unfortunately, the commonly available file management computer programs such as DBase III are designed without this feature. It is unsatisfactory to use such systems for bibliographic files. Consider the situation in which only one field is assigned for the assigned index terms of articles. If all 35 descriptors of a given article are listed in the field, searching by a known index term would involve the sequential examination of all index terms in the descriptor field of all records in order to match the specific term. Worse still, the searching of two specified index terms within the same record would necessitate first identifying a subset of records with the first search term. Then those records with the first term would have to be reexamined to verify if the second term was present. This is an extremely clumsy sequential scanning operation which requires very inefficient use of computer processing.

For the present, to build a bibliographic file, one must choose an appropriate application program best suited to one's needs. There are programs which are specially designed for bibliographic files, such as PRO-CITE from Personal Bibliographic Softwares, ISI's SCI-MATE, Cuadra Associates' STAR, INMAGIC, and others. General purpose, hierarchical database management systems such as Revelation can provide both variable field length and repeatable fields.

Careful planning of the record structure is essential for a file design which will meet the requirements of the users and the computer system used. A thorough understanding of the record structure is crucial for the effective retrieval of information from the file.

FILE ORGANIZATION

Sequential File

File organization is simply the way records in the file are arranged. In generic terms, a collection of books, a complete file of films, or a library of sound recordings are files. Libraries must shelve or store the physical records as individual books or journal issues and volumes. For those files of publications in printed form, physical organization is restricted to a linear sequence on the shelves. This file organization of the physical documents traditionally must be designed both for storage and for retrieval. It is supplemented by other logical indexes.

For electronic files, knowledge of the sequence of records in the file is analogous to the format information about the fields in a record. However, knowledge of the physical location of records in the computer memory is not helpful in searching. Obviously space and storage requirements are different for printed and electronic files, but their basic functions of storage and retrieval are the same. Records may be physically arranged in one way, and logically arranged in another. It is the logical structure of the file which is important for file design and for effective and efficient retrieval.

The following is an illustration. Suppose the books in a library are known to be arranged according to the order in which they were purchased. Each book is assigned a sequential accession number as it is processed. To access record number 100, it is necessary to go through the first 99 records. Table 8.1 shows a simplified version of a portion of a bibliographic file. If one is seeking a book dealing with a given topic described by a term, $T4$, this sequence is of little value to the searcher. One must scan every record to find those with the specified value $T4$ in the descriptor field. This is the essence of the simplest file organization. The individual records follow one another in a fixed order. It is referred to as a linear or a sequential file. One must examine the entire file to locate a specific record.

Table 8.1
Sample of a Linear File

Document Number	Terms					
0001	T3	T4	T6	T12	T15	
0002	T1	T3	T4	T7	T9	T13
0003	T5	T12	T15			
0004	T11	T12	T15	T16		
0005	T2	T3	T5	T7	T8	T12	T15
0006	T1	T4	T5			
0007	T3	T5	T6	T7	T13	
0008	T1	T2	T7	T9	T12	T13
0009	T4	T6				

The linear file organization is used for a number of purposes. An example is shown in a manual system of the sound recording collection of a radio station. Recordings can be arranged on the shelves according to the Schwann catalog numbers. By looking up the desired compositions under their composers in the Schwann catalog, their associated Schwann numbers may be identified. With the Schwann number, specific recordings can then be located quickly on the shelves. Therefore, the linear physical arrangement of recordings can be efficient for retrieval and storage if a good index is available.

Despite the fact that locating a specific data value such as *T4* in the above example requires the searching of every record of the file, the sequential searching of records in a small electronic file is fast. It is with large files that search speed slows down considerably. It is intolerable to scan a large file even at electronic speed. Therefore, a key field, which can directly locate any given item, is essential. If a specific accession number is known, the physical address of the record is also known instantanously. Retrieval is extremely rapid. In a fixed field record structure, when the record length (*ln*) is known, the address of the *n*th record is also known as the (*ln* x *n*) memory location. Processing is uncomplicated, even though it is not particularly efficient. For infrequently searched large archival files, the magnetic tape which is a sequential-storage medium, is a relatively inexpensive substitute. The other type of use of linear file organization is the searching of many items in a single pass. In other words, a number of requests are frequently processed together. For example, for the updating of customers bank transactions at the end of a day, a single pass could result in finding all the accounts processed for the day. This mode of file organization can also be effective for the archival storage of large files. New records are merely attached to the end of the file without regard to file updating or maintenance. The location address of each item may be manipulated from the accession number. The linear file is also useful as an arrangement for the master file of a collection. After the identification of the addresses of the needed items by an inverted file, a single pass through the master file is able to produce and to print the content of the retrieved records.

Most sequential files are ordered by the data value of a specific field found to be useful for searching. Typically, records are sorted into a logical order by the values in the name field which contains the first author of each paper. The sort key is useful for searching by names. Unfortunately, most bibliographic searching is not commonly performed by a single known key field. Generally, a combination of several keys is needed to identify potentially useful items. Moreover, the addition of new records and revisions made to the file necessitates a resorting and re-recording of the entire file. A large amount of data must be moved to insert a new record in its proper place. For the computer, the sorting of records is a complex, inefficient process usually involving many swappings and file maintenance is difficult.

Inverted File

Most files are supplemented by inverted files which are indexes to the main file. These provide an efficient means for searching. An inverted file consists of an ordered list of data values in a key field, such as index terms. Associated with each index term are document identifications which have been assigned to the appropriate terms. Therefore, each index term in the inverted list of index terms is associated with the relevant document numbers which are also indicators to their memory locations. Once the appropriate index term is accessed, relevant document numbers can be retrieved that, in turn, lead to their appropriate record content. Table 8.2 shows an inverted file of descriptors formed on the basis of the original sequential file in Table 8.1. Here, terms in the descriptor field are arranged alphabetically. With each term, the document numbers assigned to each

Table 8.2
Sample of an Inverted File

Terms	Document Numbers				
T1	0002	0006	0008		
T2	0005	0008			
T3	0001	0002	0005	0007	
T4	0001	0002	0006	0009	
T5	0003	0005	0006	0007	
T6	0001	0007	0009		
T7	0002	0005	0007	0008	
T8	0005				
T9	0002	0008			
T10					
T11	0004				
T12	0001	0003	0004	0005	0008
T13	0002	0007	0008		
T14					
T15	0001	0003	0004	0005	
T16	0004				

term are listed by their location symbols. Given any descriptor, one is able to retrieve the associated documents by their addresses. An inverted file serves as an index to the linear master file in much the same way as the Yellow Pages is an index to the main telephone directory.

Since the key field is usually used for the arrangement of the linear file, the inverted file is often based on fields other than a key field. Obviously, inverted files may be compiled for data values in as many fields as needed. The operating retrieval systems at the large search services consist of master files containing the full record content. Inverted files for every field of the record are usually created for rapid search capability. The purpose of this file organization is to facilitate the rapid retrieval of any nontrivial data elements in any searchable field. In addition to a sequential list of the full record of each document in the database, an inverted file is made for author names, for content words found in the titles, for journal titles, for index terms, for related terms in the thesaurus, for citations found in the documents, and for the classification numbers assigned to the documents. Once the document numbers are identified as the result of a search, they are used to locate the full records in the master document file. The full record or any of its fields may be printed out. Indeed, it is possible to build a giant inverted file using elements from all fields found in the record. This allows every data element to be available for direct searching. For example, in the Basic Index of the databases maintained by DIALOG Search Services, data elements in four fields, that is, title, abstract, descriptor, and identifier, are merged into one single, super-inverted index.

Even in the citation indexes produced by the Institute of Scientific Information, the file organization is based essentially on the inverted file principle. There are two basic files: the Source Index, and the Citation Index. The Source Index contains the full bibliographic description of every paper indexed. It is arranged alphabetically by the senior authors. The Citation Index is a file arranged by the names of authors of papers cited by the source articles in the Source Index. It acts as an inverted file to the Source Index. The record structure of the source documents consists of the usual fields, that is, author, title, journal, and so on. The Citation Index inverts the file by the data elements found in the cited references. To search the Citation Index, a standard format is used. A typical entry contains the name of the cited author with the volume number, page numbers, and the year of publication, as follows:

Kochen M, 1987, V38, N3, P206

An inverted file provides rapid access in retrieval. In this file organization, the index table rather than the entire record is searched. Only identified items from the master file are examined. All commercially available information retrieval systems are based on the concept of the inverted file. The principle of the inverted file is particularly suited for use with Boolean search logic which has found easy application on the digital computer. The major disadvantage, however, is that a large dictionary or directory is necessary. The values of the data elements in the system together with all the addresses of all the locations of these data values must be stored and maintained. A large overhead of internal memory is needed for maintaining the data and for internal processing. Each addition of new records and any changes in existing records require an updating of the data in the dictionary. A large amount of memory space is needed for extensive processing. For this reason, most instructional manuals of file management programs caution that a fairly large memory is required for use of the software. Furthermore, there is a noticeable time interval needed to create an index file for a medium-size file on most database management programs. With the cost of memory decreasing at a rapid rate, this limitation is becoming less critical. Improvement in the processing speed of many file management programs is expected in many updated versions of the popular programs.

In summary, two basic type of files are needed for the majority of document retrieval systems. A master file contains the original file of documents. Since each bibliographic record serves as a surrogate for the physical document, this collection of records is referred to as the master file. For storage purposes, the records are arranged in a linear sequence in the order in which the documents have been acquired or they are arranged by arbitrarily assigned numbers such as accession numbers. To organize the collection, each document is represented by its complete bibliographic representation which identifies the document and/or its physical location. In many systems, data values from each field of the master record structure are made into an inverted file. Under each data value, the appropriate document identifiers are posted. Thus, a number of inverted files are created for the master file so that they may be used for searching. For example, many databases in the DIALOG search service are accompanied by an author index, a journal index, a language index, etc. The subject content of the document is then analyzed and is represented by a set of appropriate index terms. These terms also form an inverted file for subject access. The master record file is enhanced for searching by several inverted files.

List Chain

A third type of file structure organizes records in sequential order, eliminating the need to sort the records and physically place them in the new order. This is accomplished by the use of pointers and linked lists, which are common devices employed in data structure by programmers. Basically, only one copy of the master record is needed. However, these records may be arranged logically by different data elements in searchable fields. To illustrate the linked list concept, suppose a group of account records is physically arranged according to dates of transactions. In the first list, the objective is to arrange this file by the contract numbers. For each account, a record is created in which an additional field is reserved for a pointer. The pointer contains the address, which, in turn, contains the record of the next contract record in that sequence:

| Records | | | Pointers | Pointers |
Company Name	Contract #	Addresses	(by CN#)	(by name)
Xerox	CN2	100	3	0
IBM	CN5	50	0	3
Sony	CN3	3	75	75
Digital	CN1	15	100	50
Unisys	CN4	75	50	100

Under the column "Pointers by CN#," "Digital" with CN1 refers to the address location 100, which is the memory location of the record for "Xerox" which has been assigned CN2. The pointer field by CN# for Xerox points to the memory address 3 where the record for "Sony" resides. And Sony has been assigned CN3. Searching this particular list enables the searcher to retrieve records by specification of contract names. In fact, another list of these records sequentially arranged by another data element such as the company name, can easily be created by the addition of another pointer field which would point to the address containing the record of the next alphabetical name. Any number of lists can be created to support different orders of the records. In addition to forward pointers, another set may be used to point backward, allowing the file to be read in reverse order.

File Based on a
Self-optimizing Principle

A file organization based on a self-organizing principle was proposed by Booth (1969) in the 1960s. This novel approach is based on the simple notion that a file could be arranged according to the frequency of use of its items. He states that a collection of documents can be arranged physically according to any numeric sequence. A system is designed to track the current address of each document and to display the information on an output device. As requests are received, individual documents are retrieved from their locations to be loaned to patrons. Then, as each document is returned, instead of returning it to its original location, it can simply be placed at the head of the file which is the nearest location for easy retrieval. Every other document would then be pushed down one position towards the rear of the file. The new locations of all items in the file would consequently be updated in the system, so that as the next request for any document was received, it could be located with the updated information in the display system. Suppose 10 percent of the documents are requested and taken out frequently. Each time they are returned, they are placed at the head of the file. At any time they would always be near the beginning of the file. On the other hand, items that are never used would naturally be pushed down and relegated to the back of the file. Those that are occasionally taken out would find themselves in the middle of the linear sequence. After a period of time, the positions of the documents would effectively reflect the frequency of use of the documents themselves. One could envision a completely automated document retrieval system in which the actual documents could be retrieved by mechanical means driven by the information stored in a computer controlled system. A system based on this self-optimizing principle could facilitate a mechanical retrieval system.

Clustered File

In the last twenty years, increasing research efforts have been given to yet another experimental file organization. Maron and Kuhns (1960) first proposed an approach to retrieval based on a probabilistic principle of relevance between queries and documents which would allow for their partial matching. Subsequently, many investigators have experimented with this probabilistic approach (Van Rijsbergen, 1976; Croft, 1977; Van Rijsbergen, 1979) Goffman (1969) suggested "an indirect method" for organization and searching. He demonstrated this cluster-based file in an experiment. His retrieval output was lists of documents ranked according to their probable relevance to the query. In his experimental automated information retrieval system, SMART, Salton (1971; Salton and McGill, 1983) conducted extensive experiments using a similar approach to file organization producing ranked lists of retrieved documents.

Basically, records in a file are organized by the degree of subject similarity between every other pair of documents. The distance between any pair of documents is expressed by an associative measure. This measure reflects the degree of subject relatedness between the two papers. A subject expert or an indexer could judge the level of subject relationship between every pair of documents in the collection and assign the appropriate similarity measure. Other researchers suggest that the value of the associative measure may be computed by various similarity features, such as the percentage of their common index terms or the proportion of common title words shared between every pair of documents. These values may be arranged on an n by n matrix where n is the total number of documents in the file. The value in each cell A_{ij} contains the associative measure reflecting the subject distance between document i and document j.

The search strategy of this file is based on a new file structure. On the specification of the level of required similarity, the total file may be partitioned into groups of documents. At the specification of a high critical associative measure, the file may be partitioned into a larger number of smaller document groups. That is, within each document group, the documents are highly relevant to each other. At the specification of a low critical value, a smaller number of larger document groups may be obtained. Each document group contains many more documents which may be more or less related to each other. Within each group, documents may be ranked according to their similarity measures. In theory, upon the submission of a query, the system could directly identify a subset of documents which has the potential of supplying relevant documents to the query. Depending on the user's requirements, a greater degree of flexibility is allowed than in a straight Boolean matching. For example, in requesting documents which are highly relevant to topic x, a high critical associative value of 0.90 can be specified. The resulting partition of the file will probably result in very few groups of documents with only a few members in each while the rest of the documents in the file will form groups of single membership. Unfortunately, the cluster file organization requires a large memory and powerful processing capabilities that are not economically feasible at the present time.

DATABASE MANAGEMENT SYSTEMS

A database management system (DBMS) is a complex computer program designed to store, organize, and retrieve files of records. There are basically three types of designs, namely, relational, network, and hierarchical. Examples of relational database systems are INGRES, and many of the DBMS used on microcomputers. IDMS (Integrated Database Management System) which runs on an IBM mainframe is a powerful network database management system. Examples of hierarchical database management systems are IMS (Information Management System) which also operates on the IBM mainframe and Revelation for the microcomputer.

As has been pointed out earlier, knowledge of the record structure of the file to be searched is important for effective search formulations. Information on file organization is crucial for the file designer. In today's environment, the preparation of inhouse files usually no longer includes the choice of the type of file organization. The reason is that it is expensive and ineffective to write a customized computer program to execute the desired functions. The market is flooded with programs which could be adapted for local applications. Many of them are commonly available in organizations. Others are relatively inexpensive to acquire. Most of them have adequate characteristics for the creation, storage, indexing, sorting, merging, and searching of records. There are two basic types of computer programs for the maintenance and retrieval of files. They are the simple file managers, and those more elaborate database management systems.

Historically, files have been designed to match a specific application. A student academic record file at the university contains all the data needed to keep track of students' academic standings. A student housing file holds only those fields needed to support housing distribution. A file manager is a software product which allows the creation of a file of records, its maintenance, and the retrieval of records according to specified search criteria. One can easily design a file on a file manager for the purpose of keeping track of students' academic records, and one for their housing needs. However, this customization limits the usefulness of each file and creates redundancy in data. As a result, they are difficult to maintain, revise and update. A simple name change necessitates many file updates. Accurate data are hard to maintain. An example of a simple file manager available in the public domain is PC File. Other commonly available filers are PFS:File and Filebase.

Database management systems are other types of software tools designed to manage and maintain file resources. The basic concept of DBMS is that it is a program independent of any application. It can operate on several data files and link data needed in certain fields to process and output needed information. For example, in the above example, each student might be assigned a master record containing key personal data. A number of pointers are created to point to other records including his academic record, and housing record. There are hundreds of these programs ranging from those used on microcomputers such as DBase III,

RBase, INMAGIC, SCI-MATE, and PRO-CITE to ones such as BASIS, INGRES, STAR, SYSTEM-1022, and SPIRE which are used on mainframes and minicomputers.

Most DBMS include an input module to allow for the input of data. Typically, the module requires a complete specification of the format of the record. The design of the record should precede the actual specification and should be conducted with some knowledge of the available functions of the software package. The number of fields, and the type of data in each field must be indicated. The complexity and the use of these modules varies. Searching is usually incorporated in a separate module. The search mechanism used varies greatly from program to program. The most powerful systems allow for the use of nested Boolean operators. Other features include such conveniences as truncations and adjacency searches. Still others not only create and maintain index tables for the inverted files, but provide alphabetical listings of each data value such as names or index terms as well as the number of documents associated with each. One of the most important and difficult features is the sorting capability. The speed with which a sorting procedure is performed may be ascertained from reviews of the products. Another common module is the output-report-writing facility. Finally the cost of the program is an important consideration.

Since at the moment, data input is still a primarily manual operation, significant cost is associated with it in terms of time and effort. The prospect of re-entering an entire data file is daunting. One should be aware that once the data of the file is input, there is strong pressure to use the system. Unfortunately, problems regarding the use of a specific DBMS are only discovered after the system is installed. Adequate investigation of a suitable DBMS should be conducted. Each DBMS should be carefully evaluated, based on its strengths and weaknesses, before the final decision. One might even contemplate the testing of the system with a sample data set. Other considerations should include the ease of use and the quality of the accompanying documentation and supporting service. Reviews of these software products may be found in many computer journals.

In this chapter, the basic unit record in a file has been discussed in the context of retrieval. Sequential and inverted files, the two most commonly used file organizations, have been presented, together with several experimental approaches to file organization.

REFERENCES

Belkin, N.J., and W.B. Croft. 1987. "Retrieval Techniques." *Annual Review of Information Science and Technology.* Edited by Martha E. Williams. Vol. 22, 109-145. White Plains, New York: American Society for Information Science, 1987.

Booth, A.D. 1969. "On the Geometry of Libraries." *Journal of Documentation*, 25(1):28-40.

Croft, W.B. 1977. "Clustering Large Files of Documents Using the Single Link Method." *Journal of the American Society for Information Science*, 28(6): 341-344.

Goffman, W. 1968. "An Indirect Method of Information Retrieval." *Information Storage and Retrieval*, 4(4):361-373.

Maron, M.E., and J.L. Kuhns. 1960. "On Relevance, Probabilistic Indexing, and Information Retrieval." *Journal of the Association of Computing Machinery*, 7(3):216-244.

Salton, G. 1971. "Cluster Search Strategies and the Optimization of Retrieval Effectiveness." *The SMART Retrieval System: Experiments in Automatic Document Processing*. Englewood Cliffs, New Jersey: Prentice Hall.

Salton, G., and M.J. McGill. 1983. *Introduction to Modern Information Retrieval*. New York: McGraw-Hill.

Van Rijsbergen, C.J. 1976. "File Organization in Library Automation and Information Retrieval." *Journal of Documentation*, 32(4):294-317.

Van Rijsbergen, C.J. 1979. *Information Retrieval*. 2nd edition. London: Butterworths.

9

Question Analysis
and Search Strategy

The previous chapters on information retrieval systems have focused on how document files are built. Principles of selection are based on relevance and quality. After documents are chosen, records are made for each item. The contents of each document are eventually extracted, indexed, and represented. This aggregate of information on the document collection is arranged, stored, and organized so that it is suitable for searching in a chosen search system. Up to this point, the functions of selection and organization are directly initiated and controlled by the system in preparation for the actual searching. However important they are in producing and maintaining an effective system with a quality document file, these functions are internal to the system. They are largely invisible to the users of the retrieval system. Yet, a document retrieval system must be judged by the success of its retrievals. This means that items resulting from searching the file must satisfy queries directed to the system. In the words of Cochrane (1981), online bibliogaphic searching begins with the requestor and ends with that person using or not using the information obtained. Therefore, the previous four chapters represent only half of the total retrieval process as depicted in the schema in Figure 9.1 (see page 166). They deal with how the system is organized to prepare for searching.

RETRIEVAL TRANSACTIONS

The other half of the total retrieval process may be typified by the following scenario. A patron with a need for information on topic x suspects that the desired information may be contained in one or more documents. He or she goes to a document retrieval system and seeks the help of an information searcher. At this point, the patron then expresses this need verbally. An exchange takes place during which the searcher clarifies and confirms what the patron wants. Often subject terms are solicited from the patron. The searcher transforms the articulated need into a query. The content contained in the query is analyzed into component concepts which may be represented by separate groups of subject

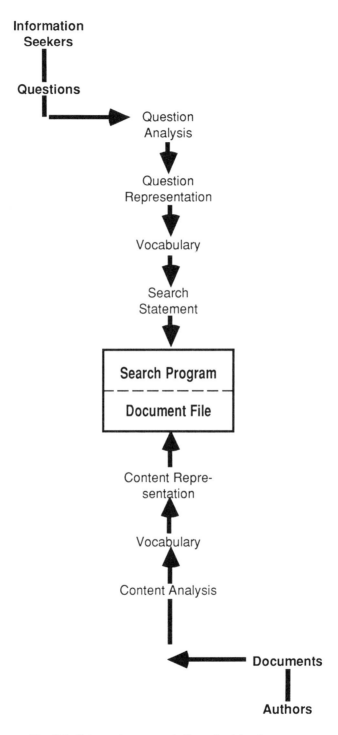

Fig. 9.1. Schematic representation of retrieval process.

terms. These terms may or may not be those acceptable to the document retrieval system. Utilizing search aids such as thesauri and term lists, those subject terms are translated into searchable key terms. If the searcher chooses to utilize an online bibliographic service, an appropriate search statement is formulated. At this point, once the search statement is entered online, the actual search itself is taken over by the online system. As far as the searcher is concerned, the computer search process is algorithmic and straightforward. Depending on the particular system used, the computer within which the search program and the database reside executes precisely those instructions submitted by the searcher. The output is delivered. Utilizing the user's relevance feedback, the search may be refined before the final delivery of search results.

The steps taken in the above retrieval transaction may be summarized as follows:

1. Patron initiates contact with the system.

2. Patron verbalizes the question.

3. Searcher analyzes the question.

4. Verbal exchange and clarification of the question occurs between the searcher and the patron.

5. Final expression of the question based on the consolidation and understanding of concepts is derived.

6. Searcher enumerates searchable concepts.

7. Search aids translate search concepts into the indexing language of the system.

8. Search statement is formulated.

9. File is searched.

10. Search output is evaluated.

11. Output is disseminated.

These steps are typical of a retrieval transaction regardless of how the document file is constructed. From the standpoint of the system, wide variations are introduced before the execution of the search at Step 9. In particular, Step 4 is highly unpredictable depending on the individual searcher and the patron. Steps 1 to 8 may be viewed as an elaboration of the first half of Figure 9.1 in that the aim is to formulate a search statement which reflects the true needs of the patron. Thus, the transformation of verbalized needs and queries is similar to the analysis and indexing of document content. On the one hand, the indexer must identify the subject concepts in each document, and select the appropriate terms to represent those document concepts that have been identified. On the other hand, the searcher must analyze and identify the content of each query and thus, choose systems terms representative of each query submitted to the system. Both the indexer and the searcher perform similar dual functions, that is, to crystallize the concepts embedded in the expressions in a document and in a query, and convert them into the system's vocabulary.

Additionally, a new dimension is called for in question analysis. In reexamining Figure 9.1, a document retrieval system could not control how documents are produced nor whether authors include the intended subject content. By and large, the system's operation starts with the arrival of an available body of literature. It is inherently understood that if no material exists on a topic, no retrieval can result, no matter how effectively the system operates. Likewise, the searcher's task cannot simply begin with the submitted question. Results of many investigations have shown that questions submitted to document retrieval systems often do not reflect the true needs of the requestor. Since retrieval is based on a matching process between a given query and each document in the file, the query is central to the success of the retrieval transaction. The searcher must probe, prod, interpret, interpolate, and help the patron in expressing his or her information needs. Indeed, the searcher also serves the role of the information giver in that during the exchange the patron has the opportunity to understand what is needed for a searchable query.

An overwhelming number of other variables are also present which have a major influence on this complex process of human interaction and problem solving. They are difficult if not impossible to control. For example, the urgency of the use of the information sought, the extent of the users previous knowledge of the topic, the communication skills of the two individuals, the motivation of the questioner, and the familiarity with and expectation of the search program exert major influence on the effectiveness of negotiation. Question asking and question handling both involve a complexity of linguistic, psychological, cognitive, sociological, educational, political, and economic aspects.

This chapter is devoted to two major phases occurring before the actual search. The first phase is known as question analysis which requires the participation of the patron. The second, known as search strategy, is largely performed by the searcher with the aid of various search tools. Yet question analysis is necessary for the formulation of a search. The process of negotiation is often iterated so that the initial formulations are modified and refined by information extracted from verbal exchanges between the patron and the searcher.

QUESTION ANALYSIS

Question analysis is the study of the process of human information seeking behavior. It is involved with the dynamic understanding of the needs of the information seeker, the psychology of establishing effective interpersonal relationships, the technique of question asking, and the logical formulation of a searchable request for information. This complex area of study includes the principles and practice of question negotiation drawing specifically upon the content of a number of disciplines including those of communication and the skills and psychology of problem solving. Question analysis is further divided into two stages. The first is understanding the process of internalizing of an information problem by the requestor, which eventually presents itself as a request for information. The second may be characterized by a form of clarification consisting of a series of exchanges between the user and searcher concerning the request. The aim is to inform the requestor about the system's capabilities, and to draw accurate information from the requestor in order to clarify the question. It is with such information that the searcher will be able to formulate a search statement which is the system's representation of the query.

From Information Problem to Question

Figure 9.2 (see page 170) is a model proposed by Rees and Saracevic (1963) in the early 1960s describing the information-seeking process. It gives special emphasis to the evolutionary character of an information problem as it progresses to its final state of an information request. Two distinct phases are noted. The first, question asking, involves both the requestor and the searcher. The second, question answering, is conducted by the searcher based on information obtained from the requestor. Ultimately, question answering depends on the success of question asking. The model also distinguishes between *relevance* and *pertinence* in that the former is the property resulting in a match between the information needs as expressed by the actual question and the retrieved set. The latter is a match between the retrieval and the true information problem. This property is nebulous.

The model in Figure 9.2 makes distinctions among *information problem, information need, question*, and *request*. Taylor (1962) among others has noted that the final request submitted to the system often bears little resemblance to the various initial forms of the same question. What should have been asked and what are actually posed as questions are very different. The initial verbalized form often does not coincide with what the individual thinks he or she needs, nor does it agree with what is actually wanted.

Saracevic (1983) identifies five basic elements in an information-seeking situation. They are (1) problem, (2) internal knowledge state, (3) intent, (4) question, and (5) request. The complex nature of the information seeker is characterized by Saracevic as a person who

- is confronted with a problem without a clear resolution at hand

- has a given state of knowledge about that problem

- intends to use information in one way or another in the process of treating the problem by altering his/her state of knowledge

- has formulated a question about the problem or some aspect thereof

- has submitted a request to a retrieval system for answers to the question

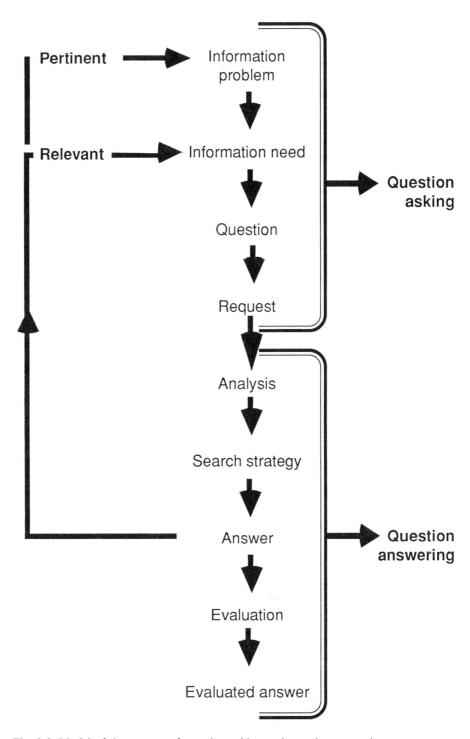

Fig. 9.2. Model of the process of question asking and question answering.

Taylor (1968) had categorized four levels of question formulation: (1) the actual level of unexpressed need for information which is the visceral need, (2) the conscious need which exists as a description within the brain, (3) the formalized need which is represented by a formal statement, and (4) the compromised need which is the request actually presented to the information system. Both Saracevic (1983) and Taylor (1968) recognize the complex nature of the formulation of questions in the mind of the requestor as well as in the search formation in the mind of the searcher. There is a transformation in the patron's state of uncertainty. The verbal interchange about the request between the searcher and the patron also affects the knowledge state of both individuals during and after the exchange. What is certain is that what actually takes place between two individuals is not adequately understood. In this chapter, each element required for question asking in the model in Figure 9.2 is examined.

INFORMATION PROBLEM

An information problem provides the context within which requests are made. Information problems arise when there is a gap in one's knowledge about something in the world. The problem area is often ill defined, and uncertainty is felt. For any individual, there are many areas in which this condition holds; not all require resolution. If and when the problem assumes a proportion of importance in one's mind, and there is a growing need to alter the state of uncertainty to some goal state, the problem then surfaces in one's conscious level. At this point, the information problem has proceeded to the level of information need. This specific motivation produces the need which eventually ends up in a question or even a set of questions posed to the information system. Information systems are concerned with information problems that are fueled by a set of goal-oriented behaviors often generated in the course of one's daily life.

INFORMATION NEED

Although information problems are often encountered, one is not always motivated to search for the solution. Certainly, many information problems do not proceed to the stage of solution seeking. In the life of an individual, many specific information problems are encountered but not all require resolution by answers. For example, few people know the molecular structure of the AIDS virus, and even fewer would ever want to know. Therefore, the existence of an information problem does not necessarily translate into an information need. Information need originates from a desire to know. It is the presence of motivation which propels the problem into need. Belkin, Oddy, and Brooks (1982a; 1982b) have examined information problem statements as being true representatives of questions. These were conscientious descriptions of the problem area which formed the basis of questions. In the present vocabulary, each of these statements is a statement of information need.

QUESTION

A question is a more concrete concept than either an information problem or an information need. It consists of a statement which requires an answer. It is a verbalization in oral or written form of an information need. In reality, a stated question does not always represent the true information problem. Although it is an information-seeking expression, the question may be broader than the problem, or it may be narrower, or it may be only peripherally related to the problem.

Why are questions poor representations of true information problems? The reasons are many. First of all, people are not always willing to verbalize a question and its underlying motivation in search for information. Secondly, not everyone is able to articulate a query in precise terms that express the information need. Furthermore, since words are only substitutes for thoughts, it is not uncommon to lose the exact concept in the translation of thought to words. Paradoxically, when the information need is great, pressure and tension render it more difficult to formulate a clear question representing the need. Thirdly, certain concepts may have become so familiar that one tends to refer to special terminology and jargons which are not the most effective tools for expressing precise concepts to others who are not intimately familiar with the subject. To bypass the need to verbalize information needs, Selective Dissemination of Information (SDI) services have proved to be enormously successful in meeting information needs of users without explicit requests from the user. SDI services are customized information services providing information to patrons on a continuous basis. This is done by the careful construction of user information profiles reflecting users' needs. Lastly, vanity can prevent the accurate expression of information needs. For example, a person who is not too knowledgeable about American football may be too embarrassed to ask what a *rooky* or an *end zone* is. Instead, the actual question, "Can you tell me something about football?" may be asked. An individual who wants to know about Apollo II may only ask about the "American space program."

It is important to note that as far as the system is concerned, a verbalized question is the starting point of a retrieval transaction. At this point, the searcher is charged with the responsibility of helping to produce documents which satisfy the patron's information need.

REQUEST

Although the terms *question* and *request* are used interchangeably in the present context, a request is the question submitted to a retrieval system for searching. The distinction is made because although the request may be identical with the question, they are not necessarily the same. A request is often formulated following the process of question negotiation between the user and the systems representative. The searcher, mindful of how the system is to be utilized, prods, suggests, focuses, and sometimes broadens the question into a form acceptable to the information system. Modifications in terms of scope and emphasis are made to the question so that the actual request received by the system is searchable.

There are many types of requests. As early as 1936, Carter (1936) wrote about the analysis of the structure and types of questions and requests. Since queries are linguistic devices, meaning and language comprehension are important considerations. Saracevic (1983) classifies requests by the following criteria: the subject domain, the clarity of expression, the specificity of the query, the complexity of the concept embedded, as well as linguistic classes. At present, it is not known whether there are differences in retrievals resulting from searching these different types of questions.

In conclusion, several steps in question asking can be found. Before the user ever comes to the information system, the information problem must be crystallized into a conscious need for information. In other words, the information problem must be felt as a need in the conscious mind, and in turn be materialized into a question. Before a question is formed, there is very little the system can do to help in providing better focus. The system is unable to intervene at these cognitive stages of the transformation of information problems into information needs. On the other hand, if the user is made aware that engaging in a process of negotiation with a searcher can clarify and focus the information need, the transition to a better formed and more realistic question may take less time and effort. Conversely, the question negotiation process may also hasten the realization that certain types of questions have little probability of resulting in any useful retrieval. Therefore, familiarity with the system may bring realistic expectation as well as improved service. For the time being, investigators have mainly examined factors affecting question clarification from the viewpoint of the system.

From Question to Request

The second stage of question clarification involves the interplay between the patron and the searcher. Although the aim is to seek amplification and clarification, Hitchingham (1979) and others found that information giving appeared to be a primary activity by both the searcher and the user. In particular, the searcher plays a key role in giving helpful suggestions. Appropriate information on the capabilities, cost, systems mechanics, and limitations of the system can greatly affect retrieval results.

From the searcher's point of view, information extracted from a negotiation process should consist of two types: factual, concrete requirements, and those relating to the resolution of the knowledge gap which motivated the query. The searcher can derive great value from a precise knowledge of why a question is posed, under what conditions it is proposed, and the use for which the derived information is intended. Specific requirements include

1. *Known item versus subject search.* It is helpful to know whether a search for information is on some subject area or on a specifically known bibliographic item. A known item search often starts with partial identification of the author's name or some title words, whereas a subject search usually requires more in-depth concept coordination, clarification, and identification.

2. *Subject.* The general topic area must be clearly established from the outset. Since questions may be ambiguous, depending on the context in which certain terms are used, the verification of what one assumes to be correct may go a long way towards question clarification. For example, a question on pollution may be related to health concerns, or to governmental regulation concerns, or to legal concerns. Effective question clarification requires the immediate establishment of the central focus. All subsequent exchanges between the searcher and the client depend on it. Additionally, this information is needed for the identification of the relevant database(s) to be searched.

3. *Time, language, and document type.* Often clients particularly interested in scientific and technological topics specify that only papers published in recent years are of use. Others may require articles written only in English. In knowing that an exhaustive search is desired, different document types may also be needed. If technical reports, patents, regulatory publications, dissertations, audiovisual materials, monographs, and journal publications are desired, searching of many databases may be necessary. The searcher may wish to probe for specific information necessary for searching specific relevant databases such as the *Comprehensive Dissertation Index.* With the appropriate information, specifications of years, languages, and document types are easily accommodated on most online bibliographic database search systems.

4. *Scope of the search.* Depending on the eventual use to be made of the documents retrieved, the user can specify the extent of the search. Requesting a search to prepare for the writing of a state-of-the-art review for a scholarly journal may require at least a near-exhaustive search within a specified time interval. Finding a few recent papers to prepare for a talk to a group of high school students probably requires a quick and dirty search of a few articles. Yet, often the motivation to initiate a search is not as distinct as the two previous examples.

Another clue may be simply the amount of material desired. The length of time the user has to devote to examining retrieved documents is in direct proportion to the amount of material requested. A comprehensive search on a topic is quite different from one which aims to retrieve only a few relevant documents. Most likely, a broad-based search is associated with many more marginally relevant documents. The searcher must determine whether there is the time and willingness to sift through a larger retrieved set, and if higher online cost is acceptable. This type of information can greatly benefit the searcher. If a high recall is desired, an extensive list of subject terms and partially related terms would be solicited during question negotiation. The interviewer would probably seek information on the desired topic in the context of other related topics in an attempt to better understand the broader perspective as well as the more specific aspects of the topic.

Since question analysis and question handling are largely dependent on the knowledge state of individuals and their social interaction abilities, there are many variables which are hard if not impossible to control. Yet, they have a major influence on the success of the negotiation process. For example, the effectiveness of the interaction between the patron and the searcher may be influenced by the urgency of use of the information sought, the context of the user's previous knowledge of the topic, the personalities of these two individuals, their verbal skills, their familiarity with the search system, the motivation of the questioner, the systems vocabulary, and by the patron's experience of prior retrieval. Different searchers who interviewed the same patron have been found to retrieve different sets of documents for the identical question.

Obviously, since a system's performance is found to vary widely depending on the precision with which the query is understood and explicitly expressed, the negotiation process should be carefully studied. Due to its complex nature and the difficulty encountered in controlling variables, it is not surprising to find only modest results from research in this area to date.

SEARCH STRATEGY

Bates (1979a, 1979b) distinguished the differences between search strategy as an area of study and search strategy as a plan for a search. As a field of study, it is the study of the theory, principles, and practice of making and using search strategies and search tactics. Thus, it also includes the more specific meaning of search strategy which is the design of a search plan. As part of the retrieval process, search strategy is the process by which a file is searched in order to identify documents relevant to the needs of the system's user. These documents are retrieved according to a given set of criteria set by the requestor.

A search plan begins with an articulated request and ends with a document set. Different search systems offer different types of search capabilities and also impose different limitations. Even databases are designed in a number of ways such that search capabilities are not uniform. As a result, a search strategy must take into account the specific search system to be used and the database to be searched. At the present time, all operating search systems are unified by the same underlying Boolean search logic. A rudimentary knowledge of Boolean algebra and its applications to information retrieval is essential in search formulation. Although Boolean logic is powerful in its application in computers and elegant in its simplicity, severe limits are set by its use. Various retrieval testings have shown less than optimal results. To overcome the basic flaw of Boolean logic in retrieval, an entirely different approach has been proposed. Retrieval based on the probabilistic principle could provide a dramatic improvement. In this section, the basis for both Boolean and probabilistic search logic are presented.

Boolean Search Strategy

BOOLEAN ALGEBRA

The underlying search logic for all operating retrieval systems is based on a single theoretical foundation, Boolean logic. The Boolean model has played a profound role in the development of online database search programs and database management systems that are the software programs used for the construction and maintenance of files. All commercially available databases are structured to be used with Boolean logic. An elementary discussion of set operations which have applications in information searching follows.

Boolean algebra is a branch of mathematics first developed by George Boole, an English mathematician, around 1850. Because it was developed from the study of logic, it is also known as Boolean logic. It is closely related to the fields of sets and probability. Various other names such as the algebra of sets, algebra of classes, propositional calculus, and calculus of sets, have also been associated with it. Actually an entire class of Boolean algebras was developed from formal logic and deals with the algebraic manipulation of sets of elements rather than of numbers. Set theory is a more general name for the branch of mathematics which deals with the properties of sets. Since set operations are involved in operating retrieval systems, both Boolean algebra and set theory are of the same form and thus are said to be isomorphic. That is, a one-to-one relationship exists between these different algebras in mapping one set of elements into the other while preserving the original relationship of the elements. However, all operating document retrieval systems are based on only a few elementary operations and a limited number of fundamental notions of Boolean algebra. These are discussed in the remaining sections of the chapter. Some basic definitions in set theory and some set operations useful for information retrieval are examined.

BASIC DEFINITIONS

The notion of a *set* or *class* is undefined and is used intuitively to refer to a collection of entities with certain common characteristics. For example, individuals registered for the course Math 401 at the University of Kentucky in the fall of 1987 constitute a set.

1. If A is a set and the element x is a member of A, this relation may be expressed as

    $$x \in A$$

2. Conversely, if x is not a member of A, then

    $$x \notin A$$

3. If set A has n finite number of elements, it may be enumerated as

    $$A = \{ x_1, x_2, x_3, \ldots x_n \}$$

4. When two sets, A and B, have the identical elements, they are said to be equal, or

    $$A = B$$

5. Given two sets, A and B, if all the elements in B are also elements in A, B is said to be a subset of A, or

    $$B \subset A$$

    In other words, A contains B. It is also true that every set is a subset of itself.

6. When $B \subset A$ and $B = A$, B is said to be a *proper subset* of A.

7. The empty set or the *null set* is a set with no elements, and it is represented as

    $$A = \emptyset$$

    It follows that the null set is a subset of every set.

8. Any given set A is referenced with respect to a *universal set*, although sometimes, it may be implicitly stated. In other words, A is contained in a universal set. Thus, one is able to refer to a complement set of set A consisting of members who are not members of set A.

It is important to note that a set can be specified by explicitly displaying the elements contained in it. Another way of specifying a set is by a distinguishing property that all elements of the set have in common. If $P(x)$ is a property of objects x, then the set may be represented by:

$$\{x \mid P(x)\}$$

This notation stands for the set of all objects x which have the property $P(x)$. For example, if x are whole numbers, and the specified property is "it is not divisible by any other number into another whole number except itself," then $\{x \mid x \text{ is a prime}\}$. In other words, $\{x \mid P(x)\}$ consists of the set of numbers:

$$\{1, 3, 5, 7, 11, 13, 17, \ldots\}$$

In this specific case in which an infinite number of prime numbers exists, it is impossible to list all members in the set.

In summary, there are essentially two different ways of specifying a set: by listing all the members of the set, or by specifying some common property shared by the entire membership of the set. In retrieval, it is the latter approach that is used.

SET OPERATIONS

In mathematics, operators are the connectives used to act upon operands. Familiar operators operate on two operands. For example, in arithmetic, all real numbers are operands. Multiplication is an example of an operator which connects two real numbers, that is, 10 x 2 = 20. In set theory, there are three distinct operators, one of which is a unary operator which operates on only one operand. These operators satisfy many basic algebraic laws. Some basic operations are presented.

1. The *union* of two given sets, *A* and *B*, produces a set which contains all members in either *A* or in *B*. The operator for union is indicated as U.

   If $\qquad A = \{a,\ b,\ c\ \}$

   $\qquad\qquad B = \{\ a,\ c,\ d,\ e,\ f\ \}$

   then $\qquad A \ U\ B = \{a,\ b,\ c,\ d,\ e,\ f\ \}$

   In other words, by eliminating the duplicate members in the two sets, all unique elements in the merged set are members of the union set.

2. The *intersection* of two given sets, *A* and *B*, produces a set which contains all members in *A* that also appear in *B*. The operator for intersection is indicated as ∩ .

   If $\qquad A = \{a,\ b,\ c\ \}$

   $\qquad\qquad B = \{a,\ c,\ d,\ e,\ f\ \}$

   then $\qquad A \ ∩\ B = \{a,\ c\ \}$

   In other words, duplicate members found in the two separate sets constitute members of the intersection set.

3. The complement set of set *A* with respect to some universal set *C* consists of all members in the universal set *C* that are not members of set *A*. The unary operator *complementation* is indicated as − .

   If *C* is the universal set,

   $\qquad\qquad C = \{a,\ b,\ c,\ d,\ e,\ f,\ g,\ h\ \}$

   and $\qquad A = \{a,\ b,\ c\ \}$

   then, $\qquad \overline{A} = \{d,\ e,\ f,\ g,\ h\ \}$

4. The rule of precedence dictates that intersection is applied before union, and complementation is applied before intersection. Thus,

   a. $(A \cup B \cap C)$ is equivalent to $(A \cup (B \cap C))$
      both of which are different from $((A \cup B) \cap C)$

   b. $(A \cap B \cup \overline{D} \cap E)$ is equivalent to
      $((A \cap B) \cup ((\overline{D}) \cap E))$

As in the case of algebra, the proper use of the rules of nesting and parentheses clearly establishes the precedence of each operation and thus greatly clarifies the operations.

Since Boolean algebra and set theory are isomorphic, the two sets of notations for these three operators are often used interchangeably in information retrieval. The Boolean OR operates on two sets to form a *Union* set. The Boolean AND operates on two sets to form an *Intersection* set. The Boolean NOT is a unary operator to form a *Complement* set. To further complicate matters, there is a natural correspondence between the three propositional functions disjunction, conjunction, and negation in propositional logic to the operations of union, intersection, and complementation in set theory. The following table shows the equivalent terms and notations used.

Propositional Logic		Set Theory		Boolean
prepositions	p, q	sets	A, B	A, B
disjunction	$\vee$	union	$\cup$	OR
conjunction	$\wedge$	intersection	$\cap$	AND
negation	$\frown$	complement	$-$	NOT

Lastly, as in other branches of mathematics, values are derived from algebraic manipulations. In Boolean algebra, as in classical logic, there are only two allowable values, namely, true or false. Boolean algebra is known as a two-valued logic in that an element either belongs to or does not belong to the resultant set according to the condition specified.

VENN DIAGRAMS

The English logician John Venn devised a method for illustrating various combinations of sets. These visualizations have come to be known as *Venn diagrams*. Venn diagrams are identical to symbolic representations of sets. Traditionally, the universal set is denoted by a rectangle. Subsets of the universal set are represented by circles inside the rectangle. For convenience, the universal set is often omitted in these illustrations. The following illustrates the use of Venn diagrams in the representation of several Boolean expressions:

1. (*A* OR *B*)

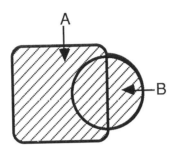

2. (*A* AND *B*)

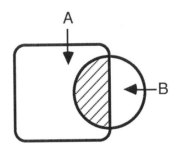

3. (*A* AND NOT *B*)

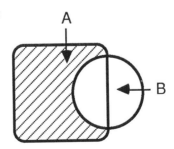

4. ((A OR B) AND C)

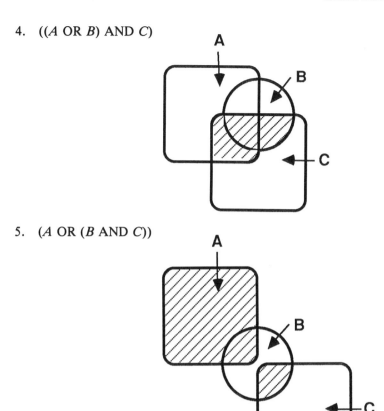

5. (A OR (B AND C))

A note of caution is offered. Although a Venn diagram is a handy device to show the relation between sets, there may be many different Venn diagrams appropriate for each Boolean expression. In the light of information retrieval, each set represents a set of documents indexed by the same index term. Hence the size of each set varies according to the file it actually represents. Since the number of documents sharing two index terms also varies, the size of the overlap between two sets is different in different situations. In Example 5, it is possible for set B to represent documents on acoustics, set C on printing, and set A on music. In a given collection, sets B and C may have no overlap, that is, no document deals with both acoustics and printing. Since (B AND C) is a null set, the intersection of a null set with set A results in the single set A. The following Venn diagram different from the previous ones, represents (A OR (B AND C)) in this particular condition of the file:

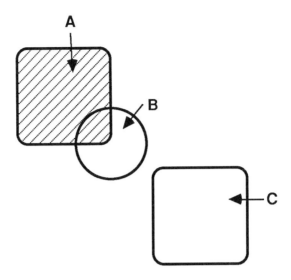

On the other hand, if *A* happens to be a subset of *C*, the same expression may be represented by another Venn diagram:

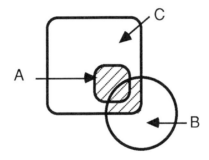

Many different Venn diagrams may be drawn to represent a single Boolean expression.

APPLICATIONS IN INFORMATION RETRIEVAL

Boolean algebra provides the ideal logical structure for files organized as inverted files. As documents are indexed by terms, sets of documents are being formed. For example, the term-document matrix in Table 9.1 shows that five sets (indicated by the five columns) are formed by these five index terms. The set represented by Term *A* consists of documents *a, b, d*, etc. The inverted index file conveniently partitions the document file into sets. Each set is associated with a term. Since each document may be indexed by more than one term, this logical structure also accommodates overlapping sets as well as disjoint sets. If each term is considered a label for the document set it represents, these sets may be manipulated by the rules of operation of Boolean algebra.

Table 9.1
Term-Document Matrix

	Term A	Term B	Term C	Term D	Term E
Document a	x		x		
Document b	x	x		x	
Document c			x	x	
Document d	x				x

The operator AND tends to narrow the scope of the search. For example, if set *A* consists of documents indexed under the phrase *excessive drinking*, and set *B* contains documents indexed with the term *accidents*, documents which deal with the phrase *accidents associated with excessive drinking* are those at the intersection of *A* and *B*. In Table 9.1 since only document *b* is indexed under both Term *A* and Term *B*, it is the only document retrieved. It is obtained by an intersection between sets *A* and *B*, as

(*A* AND *B*)

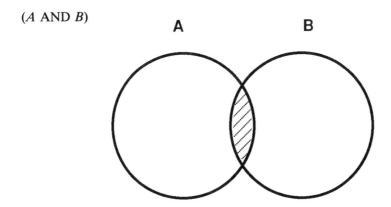

On the other hand, the OR operator allows the searcher to expand on the concept by retrieving documents indexed with several semantically similar terms. If one wishes all the documents on *accidents* in general as well as on *excessive drinking*, the union of the two sets is in order, as

(*A* OR *B*)

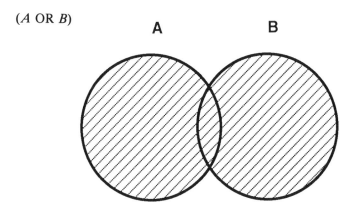

Another example is

DOCUMENTS ON THE IMPACT OF REAGAN'S NEW TAX BILL ON HIS FARM POLICY AND ON THE NATIONAL DEFICIT.

To manipulate the resulting set from the inverted file, assume that each index term is represented by a symbol. It follows that there is a set associated with each symbol.

Let P be Ronald Reagan
  Q be tax bill
  R be farm policy
  S be national deficit

To formulate a Boolean statement which represents the concept specified in the query, an analysis can be conducted. The query asks for Reagan's tax bill as a unit, which may be expressed as (P AND Q). The second part of the query is on the impact of the bill on either his farm policy or on the national deficit, which may be expressed as (R OR S). Combining these two expressions, the result is

(P AND Q) AND (R OR S)

A second example is illustrated by the following request:

IDENTIFY ALL DOCUMENTS ON AUTOMATIC SEAT BELTS AND AIR BAGS ON CASUALTY RATES.

Assuming that *automatic seat belts, air bags, casualty*, and *death* are terms found in the control vocabulary, an appropriate Boolean expression for the query is

(AUTOMATIC SEAT BELTS OR AIR BAGS) AND (CASUALTY OR DEATH)

Search statements consisting of a combination of sets joined by Boolean operators are known as Boolean expressions. The inverted file structure is ideal for the application of Boolean algebra as its search mechanism in that each term indexed in the inverted file forms a set.

Caution should be directed to the use of the negation operator, NOT. Although it is used as a device to focus more specifically on a facet, it may also exclude desired documents. In the earlier example on Reagan's tax bill, if the question is rephrased as

DOCUMENTS ON THE IMPACT OF REAGAN'S NEW TAX BILL ON THE NATIONAL DEFICIT, BUT I DO NOT NEED DOCUMENTS WHICH SPECIFICALLY DEAL WITH THE IMPACT ON HIS FARM POLICY.

Using the same symbols for the sets, the Boolean expression excluding documents dealing with farm policy is:

(P AND Q AND S) NOT R

The danger here is that documents which deal with Reagan's tax bill on both farm policy and the national deficit would also be excluded in the above expression even though the Boolean expression appears to retain only those dealing with the national deficit. The reason is due to the rule of precedence in the application of these operators. Negation is applied before either intersection or union.

KEYWORD ELABORATION

The searcher begins the formulation of the search statement with a request which has been clarified by question analysis conducted with the client. Using a number of search tactics and idea tactics as suggested by Bates, the searcher first identifies the most likely databases to be searched. The query content is then usually analyzed into identifiable facets. These may be thought of as subtopics, different approaches, or varying aspects related to the main concept. Since most search statements are Boolean expressions of terms, for each of these facets, a group of semantically related terms or keywords may be identified.

How does the searcher find these keywords? During the question interview, often with the help of the requestor, the query content may be decomposed into several subareas. The client may suggest useful terms which express different aspects of the query. Each subtopic should be identified and listed on the search form (see Figure 9.3). Since related terms for each aspect may be useful in broadening or narrowing the scope of the search, as many related terms as possible should be found.

Although the users can provide relevant search terms, these may not be the terms directly searchable in the database. They may be synonymous terms. In order to translate the user's terms into the system's terms, the thesaurus used by the database is consulted.

SEARCH FORM

Date Requested_____Date Run_____Date Mailed_____

Name_____Status-Member_____
                                          instit_____
                                          faculty_____
Department/Address_____student_____
                                          other_____
_____phone_____

Subject of inquery - Please define question fully, including
terms and synonyms under which mateiral may be indexed. Please
use sentences so that the searcher may see the relationships
between them.

YRS TO BE COVERED:_____
LANGUAGE: English_____; English Abstract_____; Other (specify)
OTHER PARAMETERS: dissertation_____; technical report_____;
                  other_____

RELEVANT CITATIONS:(Published within the current three years, if
possible)

_____

_____

****
FORMULATION: (do not write in this area)

Fig. 9.3. A sample search form.

   The thesaurus is a linear representation of a semantic net, because it shows
the semantic linkage of any subject term within the given subject domain. Three
types of relationships are indicated, namely, synonymous, hierarchical, and
lateral. The first is obviously a controlling device allowing only authorized terms
to be used for searching in that specific database. The other two types of
relationships may be visually displayed as in Figure 9.4. The complex linkage of

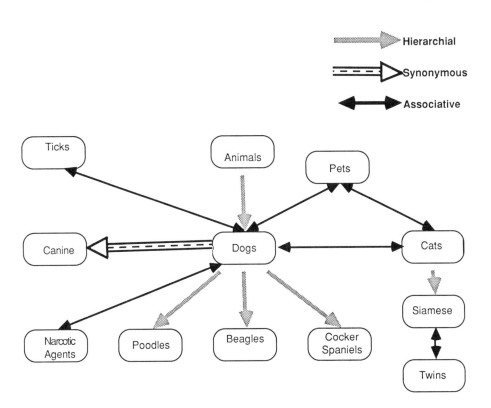

Fig. 9.4. A semantic network.

concepts denoted by terms is referred to as a semantic net in the literature. The term *dogs* is a narrower term for *animals*. It is a broader term for poodles, beagles, and other types of dogs. The hierarchical relationship is indicated by grey lines. Terms such as *cats, pets,* and *narcotic agents* are closely associated with *dogs*, but they do not stand in a hierarchical relationship. These associated or lateral terms are especially useful in suggesting the most appropriate terms to represent the concept. The search services and the database producers may provide a printed and often online version of the thesaurus used. Thesauri are useful in suggesting other terms which are more focused or broader in scope than the original term.

It has been suggested that after a request has been clarified, a grid may be drawn to denote the different facets of the query. Each column lists terms semantically related to each facet. Depending on the degree of comprehensiveness needed for the search, appropriate Boolean operators may be applied to formulate a search statement for the most appropriate database.

To summarize, inductive reasoning is required for term expansion and the elaboration of concepts. The searcher must be creative in generating ideas and aspects similar to the needed topic in order to articulate and clarify the concept in the context of a question. On the other hand, to formulate a Boolean expression representative of the query, deductive skills are needed to interpret the query content properly. Clearly, there can be a wide range of differences among searchers' expressed interpretations of the query, as well as the way the query is translated into the system's language. Recently researchers have found that the searcher introduces the greatest degree of variability. A research team in conducting an in-depth study of searching behaviors reported that even for the same query searched on the identical database, different sets of retrieved items may be expected from different searchers (Saracevic, Kantor, Chamis, and Trivison, 1988; Saracevic and Kantor, 1988a; Saracevic and Kantor, 1988b). This study used data from searching questions submitted by 40 users. A total of 39 different searchers was involved. Each question was searched by 9 searchers. Thus, there were ample data to study online searching behaviors of a group of experienced searchers and to make pairwise comparisons. One of the major findings was that overlap in retrieved items by different searchers searching the identical question was quite low. In 63.9 percent of cases, searchers appeared to interpret questions differently and thus sought different aspects of the topic. In general, searchers did not use the same search terms. The complexity of online searching is indicated by their findings that in addition to searchers and the time required to search, many other variables affect search results. The root of these problems may be attributable to the use of natural language for expressing, indexing, and searching the same concept, as noted by Doszkocs (1986). Until better natural language processing is achieved, problems will persist.

Citation Search Strategy

With few exceptions, all operating systems accept search statements in the form of Boolean expressions of terms. The citation databases from the Institute for Scientific Information also accommodate Boolean expressions composed of bibliographic citations. This small group of databases may be accessed without representing the search topic by the use of key terms. In the case of citation databases, retrieved items represent papers which have cited a specified paper. This requirement can be relaxed by the use of truncations. For example, one could specify all cited references authored by J. Adams regardless of year of publication. If a variant form of the author's name is also used in the literature, one could specify papers authored by J. Adams as well as by J. A. Adams. To plan a search strategy for citation searching, it is crucial for the searcher to solicit one or more relevant bibliographic citations from the patron. Such information should be as relevant, accurate, and correct as possible for a few specific papers.

Probabilistic Search Strategy

Just as the inverted file structure is perfectly implemented by Boolean algebra, it is also subject to all its limitations. The major flaw of Boolean logic in information retrieval may be traced to its foundation as a two-valued logic (Verhoeff, Goffman, and Belzer, 1961; Bookstein, 1980; Cooper, 1983). In manipulating the sets, elements in the "universe" are either in the resultant set or they are not. In information retrieval, searching the file produces documents which meet the conditions set by the Boolean expression representing the query.

Conversely, those documents not retrieved do not meet those criteria. As a result of each search, each document in the file is either relevant or not relevant to the query represented by the search statement. In other words, the file is divided into two subsets. Implicitly, documents in the relevant sets are given the same relevance weight.

In a realistic retrieval environment, the reader seldom judges items in a retrieved set as either completely relevant or not relevant at all. Most relevant documents are relevant to a certain degree to the kind of information sought. Ideally, given a query, the user would be well served by a list of documents ranked by their probable relevance to the query. Based on the need for a certain number of documents, the user could determine a critical cutoff point for the list. Since the documents are ranked in a decreasing order of relevance to the query, one could merely read the first two documents, or continue on to the 20th or the 200th item.

Another limitation set by Boolean search logic is that it does not permit the expression of any relevance relationship between documents in the file. Since the Boolean search mechanism virtually matches documents with the criteria set by the Boolean expression, each document retrieved strictly bears a relationship with respect to the query alone. In reality as documents on a certain topic are read, the relevance of the next document to be read is dependent upon the preceeding ones read. For example, although both *Introduction to Pascal Programming* and *Data Structure and File Organization* may both be books on programming, if one has already read and worked through the latter, certainly reading the former would add very little to one's knowledge on the subject. The proper sequencing of documents with respect to their content relevance is an important feature in search strategy.

Solutions to overcoming both of the above limitations have been suggested by researchers. Attempting to improve retrieval results, Salton has experimented with different types of probabilistic retrievals (Salton, 1971). More recently, Bookstein and others have suggested the application of fuzzy set theory in searching, so that the criteria of matching the query with documents may be relaxed (Bookstein, 1985). The notion of partial matching has been introduced. For 20 years, Salton has conducted numerous retrieval testings using a variety of indexing, term weighting, and searching techniques. In the last few years, he has also suggested a method of relaxing and extending Boolean search strategy (Salton, Fox, and Voorhees, 1985). Thus far, retrieval experiments using these alternative search approaches have reported greatly improved results in retrieval performance. Unfortunately, at the present time, their implementation presents insurmountable problems in terms of cost and effort. Nevertheless, a body of sound theoretical issues has emerged from this experimental research that are being considered seriously. For a serious study on the probabilistic approach to retrieval, the following books listed in the reference section at the end of this chapter should be consulted: Van Rijsbergen, 1979; Sparck Jones, 1981; Oddy, Robertson, Van Rijsbergen and Williams, 1981; Salton and McGill, 1983. The remaining section includes a description of the approach first suggested by Goffman (1969) in a paper, entitled, "An Indirect Method of Information Retrieval."

GOFFMAN'S INDIRECT METHOD

Goffman's indirect method of searching is based on a file structure different from the combined use of sequential and inverted files. The following demonstrates how a search could be conducted on a file whose construction is based on a probabilistic principle. It produces retrieval results reflecting varying degrees of relevance among documents as well as producing a chain of documents reflecting their subject relatedness to a query.

The search method utilizes a document file which is organized on the basis of a pre-defined document-to-document relevance relationship. Supposing there are n documents in a given file, the degree of relevance between each document and every other document in the file may be determined. These values may be represented in an n-by-n matrix. The data value in each cell represents a degree of subject relatedness between any two documents, i and j. Operationally, the degree of similarity between every other pair of documents could be quantified by a number of methods. Similarity values could be derived from the number of content-bearing title words shared by every other pair of documents in the file, or from the number of common citations received by the two documents. They could even be laboriously assigned by an indexer or a subject expert. Since this association measure is a percentage figure, it could also be considered the probability of the closeness of document i to document j. Its value must lie between zero and one. Each cell value M_{ij} is also the conditional probability of the relevance of document j given the relevance of document i. This similarity measure is sometimes known in the literature as the association measure. The similarity measure between document i and document j may be denoted by M_{ij}. It may be computed as

$$M_{ij} = \frac{\text{(number of common title words between } i \text{ and } j\text{)}}{\text{(total number of unique title words in } i\text{)}}$$

Since the denominators are different for M_{ij} and for M_{ji}, the values of M_{ij} and M_{ji} are also different. The resulting matrix is asymmetric. In other words, the cell values appearing in the two halves of the matrix divided by the diagonal are not symmetrical. A value of unity at the diagonal simply indicates that a given document is perfectly relevant to itself. Conversely, a value of zero indicates that there is no subject relatedness between the corresponding pair of documents. By checking the values in the matrix, one is able to observe how close one document is to another.

Table 9.2 shows a matrix of similarity measures calculated from the number of common descriptors between documents in a file of ten documents $a, b, c, \ldots,$ j. The search strategy may be illustrated by an example. Suppose one wishes to find the probable relevance of document d if document i is known to be relevant. Checking document d in the first column, and moving across to document i, one finds that the probability that document d is relevant to document i is 0.2 or 20 percent, namely, $P(di) = 0.20$, whereas the chance that document i is related to document d is only 2 percent, namely, $P(id) = 0.02$.

Suppose the degree of relevance is specified at 10 percent or more. That is, a critical probability may be established for the search at 10 percent. According to Goffman, at the 10 percent level, document d is said to *communicate* with document i, but document i does not communicate with document d. On the

Table 9.2
A Matrix of Similarity Measures

	a	b	c	d	e	f	g	h	i	j
a	1	0.5	0	0.1	0	0	0	0	0	0
b	0	1	0	0.3	0.25	0.15	0	0	0.3	0.6
c	0.25	0	1	0.5	0	0	0	0	0	0
d	0.15	0	0.6	1	0	0.15	0	0	0.2	0
e	0	0	0	0	1	0	0	0	0	0
f	0	0.25	0	0.5	0.5	1	0	0	0	0.25
g	0	0	0	0	0	0	1	0.14	0	0
h	0	0	0	0	0	0	0.2	1	0	0
i	0	0.2	0	0.02	0.3	0	0	0	1	0
j	0	0.5	0	0	0	0.24	0	0	0	1

other hand, if the critical probability is lowered to zero, documents *d* and *i* communicate with each other. Such a condition is known as *intercommunication*. In other words, document *d* intercommunicates with document *i*. At a specified critical probability, using intercommunication as a criterion, one could partition the documents in the file into intercommunication classes. In each intercommunication class consisting of more than one member, each document intercommunicates with at least one other document in the group. In other words, there are two-way communications among documents in the group.

Intercommunication clusters the documents into nonoverlapping groups or mutually exclusive classes. With this file organization showing the probability of relevance between every other pair of documents in the collection, searching can be based on the probability principle.

Assuming that the searcher is able to clarify and to define a query by a number of terms, the required level of relevance can also be decided. For example, this level could be translated into a critical probability of 0 percent. Namely, documents with any degree of relatedness are desired. For each document, one begins by finding one document with any degree of relevance to the query. By grouping the document file into a number of intercommunicating document clusters and by finding an initial relevant document, one is able to identify other documents communicating with it. This is accomplished by checking the values in the first row and identifying documents associated with document a at any nonzero value. In other words, if document a is related to document d at any nonzero level, there is an indication of at least one-way subject link at this level. This same procedure is followed for all other documents. From Table 9.2, the following relations hold:

a is related to b, d

b is related to d, e, f, i, j

c is related to a, d

d is related to a, c, f, i

e is related to itself only

f is related to b, d, e, j

g is related to h

h is related to g

i is related to b, d, e

j is related to b, f

This is also graphically illustrated in Figure 9.5. Each arrow indicates a single one-way link.

To satisfy the condition of intercommunication, a reciprocal communication relation must exist between any pair of documents. That is, a two-way communication linkage must occur. Thus, checking the list of documents related to document a, document a is found to relate to document d. And among the documents related to document d, document a is also related to document d. Thus documents a and d belong to an intercommunication class. Similarly, documents f and d also intercommunicate. Connecting all the related documents, the file is clustered into three sets:

Group 1: a, b, c, d, f, i, j

Group 2: e

Group 3: g, h

Group 1 contains seven documents. Since document e does not intercommunicate with any other document, it forms a class of one member.

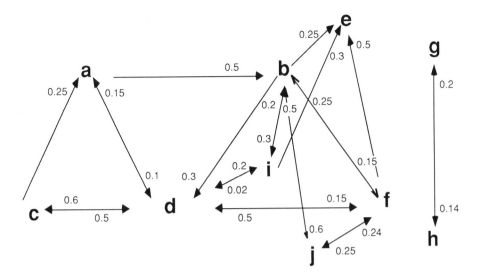

Fig. 9.5. Intercommunication clusters.

However, if the patron wishes to have documents which have at least 50 percent of the descriptors in common with each other, the new file configuration would be quite different. In other words, the critical probability would be raised. This time, document *a* relates only to document *b*, and document *b* on the second row only relates to document *j* at the 50 percent level. The following relationships hold at the 50 percent critical value:

a is related to *b*

b is related to *j*

c is related to *d*

d is related to *c*

e is related only to itself

f is related to d, e

g is related only to itself

h is related only to itself

i is related only to itself

j is related to *b*

The remaining documents *e, g, h,* and *i* only relate to themselves. The following groups are clustered at the 50 percent or higher level:

Group 1: a

Group 2: b, j

Group 3: c, d

Group 4: e

Group 5: f

Group 6: g

Group 7: h

Group 8: i

In other words, the size of the retrieved set may vary according to the degree of relevance required by the user. The example shows that retrieval based on a probabilistic principle can be fine-tuned to the user's needs. Higher recalls may be attained by lowering the critical probability value.

From Figure 9.5, the strength of each link can be ascertained making it possible to rank the documents in Group 1. Additionally, each document in the group may be compared with the representation of the query. The output list may be ranked according to the probability of relevance to the query.

Most experimental results have indicated the superiority of the cluster file used with a probabilistic search strategy. However, this example has also demonstrated that a search strategy based on a probabilistic principle must operate on a different file structure than the existing inverted file. The implementation of new probabilistic search techniques necessitates a major overhaul of the basic file structure. Another obstacle is the requirement of intensive computation in processing a file of any realistic size. Although processing searches is possible, the time required for each search is significant. Large storage requirements are also a nontrivial problem. The matrix size is n by n. Even though a high percentage of the documents are unrelated to each other such that many cells are filled with no value, the memory storage and the storage required for computation is still considerable. At the moment, heavy capital has been invested in all operating document retrieval systems. Thousands of databases are online. All are based on term indexing and structured by an inverted file. In information retrieval as in other fields, adoption of new strategies and technologies tends to be resisted by conservative attitude fostered by large investment in existing technology, as described by Kuhn (1962). A move of this magnitude would require such an extraordinary capital investment that it would be economically impractical.

In this chapter, the complex nature of question analysis has been discussed. Basic elements of Boolean search strategy were presented. Finally, an example of probabilistic search strategy was demonstrated. Clearly, question analysis is of extreme importance to the retrieval effectiveness of information systems. Yet, serious studies in this area have been hampered by the complexity involved. The majority of previous work merely accepted the written form of a request to be the true representative of the requestor's need. Reviewing for the *Annual Review of Information Science and Technology* in 1986, Dervin has noted a shift in new research directions (Dervin and Nilan, 1986). Questions are regarded seriously by some to be driven by information problems which create an anormalous state of knowledge in the requestor. Thus, problem statements together with the motivation and context have replaced the single query statement (Belkin, Oddy, and Brooks, 1982a; 1982b). Useful information is seen as the entity which is capable of changing the image structure and cognitive structure of the receiver. At another level, many research activities have been evident in the area of human-computer interface (Borgman, 1984). Psychological research has been conducted into the features of computer-based systems that could actually facilitate the use of interactive systems.

Since the mental process used in information seeking is generic to both the information consumer and the professional information searcher, much interest has been directed to the online bibliographic database searchers, searching behaviors, and search results. Fidel and Soergel (1983) identified 200 variables relating to information searching. Educational levels, searching experience, cognitive styles, and personal traits have been studied with respect to the degree of search success (Bellardo, 1985; Fidel, 1984; Fenichel, 1981). Cochrane (1981) reported on an analysis of 44 videotape presearch interviews, although no significant pattern was discerned. Massive empirical data have been collected on end-user searching (Sewell and Teitelbaum, 1986). Saracevic and his research team have conducted a comprehensive study of searchers, specific search behaviors, search results, and the type of question searched (Saracevic and Kantor, 1988a, 1988b; Saracevic, Kantor, Chamis, and Trivison, 1987). As a group, these research efforts have produced impressive data. Yet, they represent a first step toward a full understanding of human information processing. Many are struggling in formulating new conceptual frameworks. Nevertheless, these exploratory studies are essential preludes to more definitive investigations.

REFERENCES

Question Analysis

Belkin, N.J., R.N. Oddy, and H.M. Brooks, 1982a. "ASK for Information Retrieval: I. Background and Theory." *Journal of Documentation*, 38(2): 61-71.

Belkin, N.J., R.N. Oddy, and H.M. Brooks. 1982b. "ASK for Information Retrieval: II. Results of a Design Study." *Journal of Documentation*, 38(3): 145-164.

Carter, A. 1936. "Techniques of Library Searching." *Special Libraries*, 27(7): 231-237.

Cochrane, P. 1981. "Study of Events and Tasks in Presearch Interviews Before Online Searching." *Proceedings of the 2nd National Online Meeting*, 133-147.

Hitchingham, E.E. 1979. "Online Interviews: Charting User and Searcher Interaction Patterns." *Proceedings of the American Society for Information Science*, 16:66-74.

Rees, A., and T. Saracevic. 1963. "Conceptual Analysis of Questions in Information Retrieval Systems." *Proceedings of the 1963 Annual Meeting of the American Documentation Institute. Part II*, edited by H.P. Luhn, 175-177. Washington, D.C.: American Documentation Institute.

Saracevic, T. 1983. "On a Method for Studying the Structure and Nature of Requests in Information Retrieval." *Proceedings of the American Society for Information Science*, 20:22-25.

Taylor, R.S. 1962. "The Process of Asking Questions." *American Documentation*, 13(4):391-396.

Taylor, R.S. 1968. "Question Negotiation and Information Seeking in Libraries." *College and Research Libraries*, 29(3):178-194.

Search Strategy

Bates, M.J. 1979a. "Idea Tactics." *Journal of the American Society for Information Science*, 30(5):280-289.

Bates, M.J. 1979b. "Information Search Tactics." *Journal of the American Society for Information Science*, 30(4):205-214.

Bellardo, T. 1985. "An Investigation of Online Searcher Traits and Their Relationship to Search Outcome." *Journal of the American Society for Information Science*, 36(4):241-250.

Bookstein, A. 1980. "Fuzzy Requests: An Approach to Weighted Boolean Searches." *Journal of the American Society for Information Science*, 31(4): 240-247.

Bookstein, A. 1985. "Probability and Fuzzy-Set Applications to Information Retrieval." *Annual Review of Information Science and Technology*, edited by Martha E. Williams. Vol. 20, 117-151. White Plains, New York: Knowledge Industry Publications, Inc.

Borgman, C.L. 1984. "Psychological Research in Human-Computer Interaction." *Annual Review of Information Science and Technology*, edited by Martha E. Williams. Vol. 19, 33-64. White Plains, New York: American Society for Information Science.

Cooper, W.S. 1968. "Expected Search Length: A Single Measure of Retrieval Effectiveness Based on the Weak Ordering Action of Retrieval Systems." *American Documentation*, 19(1):30-41.

Dervin, B., and M. Nilan. 1986. "Information Needs and Uses." *Annual Review of Information Science and Technology*, edited by Martha E. Williams. Vol. 22, 3-33. White Plains, New York: American Society for Information Science.

Doszkocs, T.E. 1986. "Natural Language Processing in Information Retrieval." *Journal of the American Society for Information Science*, 37(4):191-196.

Fenichel, C.H. 1981. "Online Searching: Measures That Discriminate Among Users with Different Types of Experiences." *Journal of the American Society for Information Science*, 32(1):23-32.

Fidel, R. 1984. "Online Searching Styles: A Case-Study-Based Model of Searching Behavior." *Journal of the American Society for Information Science*, 35(4):211-221.

Fidel, R., and D. Soergel. 1983. "Factors Affecting Online Bibliographic Retrieval: A Conceptual Framework for Research." *Journal of the American Society for Information Science*, 34(3):163-180.

Goffman, W. 1968. "An Indirect Method of Information Retrieval." *Information Storage and Retrieval*, 4(4):361-373.

Kuhn, T.S. 1962. *The Structure of Scientific Revolutions*. Chicago: University of Chicago Press.

Oddy, R.N., S.E. Robertson, C.J. Van Rijsbergen, and P.W. Williams, eds. 1981. *Information Retrieval Research*. London: Butterworths.

Salton, G., ed. 1971. *The SMART Retrieval System: Experiments in Automatic Document Processing*. Englewood Cliffs, New Jersey: Prentice Hall.

Salton, G., and M.J. McGill. 1983. *Introduction to Modern Information Retrieval*. New York: McGraw-Hill.

Salton, G., E.A. Fox, and E. Voorhees. 1985. "Advanced Feedback Methods in Information Retrieval." *Journal of the American Society for Information Science*, 36(3):200-210.

Saracevic, T., and P. Kantor. 1988a. "A Study of Information Seeking and Retrieving: II. Users Questions, and Effectiveness." *Journal of the American Society for Information Science*, 39(3):117-196.

Saracevic, T., and P. Kantor. 1988b. "A Study of Information Seeking and Retrieving: III. Searchers, Searches, and Overlaps." *Journal of the American Society for Information Science*, 39(3):197-216.

Saracevic, T., P. Kantor, A.Y. Chamis, and D. Trivison. 1988. "A Study of Information Seeking and Retrieving: I. Background and Methodology." *Journal of the American Society for Information Science*, 39(3):161-176.

Sewell, W., and S. Teitelbaum. 1986. "Observations of End-User Online Searching Behavior Over Eleven Years." *Journal of the American Society for Information Science*, 37(4):234-245.

Sparck Jones, K., ed. 1981. *Information Retrieval Experiment.* London: Butterworths.

Van Rijsbergen, C.J. 1979. *Information Retrieval.* 2nd edition. London: Butterworths.

Verhoeff, J., W. Goffman, and J. Belzer. 1961. "Inefficiency of the Use of Boolean Functions for Information Retrieval Systems." *Communications of the Association for Computing Machinery*, 4(12):557-559.

10
Dissemination and Access

To complete the retrieval cycle, items identified in a search must somehow reach the user. This final function of an information retrieval system is called dissemination. Dissemination is concerned with the process of the transfer of information to those who have need of it. It is closely related to information access, although both terms, *dissemination* and *access*, are used loosely in the literature when addressing a variety of barriers to information transfer.

For the sake of discussion, two different types of dissemination are distinguished. The first is *document delivery* which is associated with all document retrieval services. The ultimate goal is to supply documents whose content may be of value. The job of the retrieval system for each transaction terminates as soon as the identified documents reach the hands of the requestor. Some may be delivered in hardcopies and others in electronic formats. What the patron does with them, and whether the document content produces the desired outcome lie outside the realm of the system's control. Document delivery in libraries is not automatically performed as part of the retrieval procedure. The library patron must take the final step in procuring and taking possession of the physical document. Even the more enterprising systems restrict themselves to adding a pick-up arrangement and/or delivering the printed bibliographies by mail or couriers. A few innovative systems such as the 747-FAST system at the University of Michigan actually deliver the physical document to the requestor within a short time. However, this is the exception rather than the rule.

The second concept is that of the *notification* of documents of potential use to patrons. Notification and alerting go beyond the normal function of an on-demand service where only requests are processed. An alerting service anticipates requests by continuously supplying documents without the user's taking the initiative. The anticipation of needs is based on the notion that even though users may not articulate or take action in requesting information, there are needs which should be met. An information system can best serve its clients by periodically calling to their attention information of probable relevance and then supplying them with the actual materials on a regular basis. Notification is an add-on function to the retrieval system.

DOCUMENT DELIVERY

For any document retrieval system, a two-phase procedure is carried out in document delivery. The first is *location* and the second, actual *delivery*. The following contains a brief chronological account of the development of document delivery.

Throughout history, librarians have forged an impressive array of bibliographic tools which serve to facilitate the location of books and journals. Assuming that the desired items have been identified, catalog entries indicate the locations of individual documents in a single library collection. Such a collection of materials may even be housed in several buildings on a university campus. A union catalog enables the user to find books housed in a group of libraries in different cities or countries. An index to journal literature points to the publishing sources of relevant articles. A union list of serials guides the searcher to the physical sites of the needed journals. These traditional library search tools facilitate the locating of documents.

Libraries also provide a limited service in the delivery and securing of books which are not housed locally. Interlibrary loan service has been a major step towards the procurement of books and journals unavailable on site. It is a cooperative effort undertaken by libraries. Instead of an organizational structure with a central administrative control, coordination and interaction are distributed among member libraries. Each agrees to be both a requestor and supplier of library materials. Transactions are conducted on a case-by-case basis.

Another successful arrangement can be illustrated by the Regional Medical Library Network. Medical libraries in the country are linked to each other in a hierarchical structure for interlibrary loan. This system serves the nation's medical libraries which have been assigned to eleven geographic regions. A resource library is identified for each region. The library acts as the node for coordination and as the resource center for the area. The National Library of Medicine is the central node which can be accessed when resources can not be supplied at the regional level. In pre-electronic days, this document loan service was based on optimal routing for the document transfer.

With the advent of computers and telecommunication, and the widespread use of information utilities, such as Online Computer Library Center (OCLC) and Research Libraries Information Network (RLIN), interlibrary loan service has taken on a new dimension. As one of several modules on these information utilities, the electronic linkage serves well for a number of functions. Messages, requests, orders, and the keeping of statistics are part of the online system. The new version enables a faster turnaround time, and more orderly processing. Service has been greatly improved and systematized in recent years.

Networks

Network is a technical term used in communication and electrical engineering. As a concept, it is used in a broad sense. Networking is taken to mean any cooperative scheme which provides an effective linkage among several sites via a group of individuals, computers, equipment, or organizations. The telephone system is the best example of an effective network. Networks can be implemented on various levels. For example, the Regional Medical Library Network, mentioned previously was formed on the basis of administrative organizational structure. Actual document delivery is dependent on the postal and courier services. A telecommunication network connects a host of computers at different cities and countries, such that data transfer among them is through the existing telephone network. Access speed of data via telecommunication networks has suddenly escalated by several orders of magnitude since the days of postal delivery to a matter of minutes today. The common access to data records and data files is but one of the many benefits derived from a network arrangement. The practical implementation of the networking concept of the seventies has revolutionized the sharing and delivery of information resources.

With dedicated telephone lines or telecommunication network connections, libraries are linked in real-time with central information facilities. Millions of bibliographic records are made available online to libraries, regardless of their locations. They share the use as well as the intellectual preparation needed for data input. This interconnection also enables an easy exchange of information among the members. Many union lists have been replaced by online union catalogs. The locating of library materials is effectively realized by library networking. Some of the impact of networks on document delivery are noted in the following sections.

Online Document Orders

Telecommunication networks have also made possible access to bibliographic citations and full texts of journal literature, directory information, and a host of other nonbibliographic data. Any subscriber can, via a telephone, search the data files of the DIALOG Search Service in Palo Alto, California; of Mead Data Central Incorporated in Dayton, Ohio; of the National Library of Medicine in Bethesda, Maryland; or of any other search service. Online database vendors were quick to see the need for document delivery as an important adjunct to their searching capabilities. Many have enhanced their systems with an electronic document order and delivery function. For example, DIALORDER is an add-on online command to activate the subsystem in DIALOG. So is Quikorder service, an online ordering service from the National Technical Information Service (NTIS). With a retrieved citation set, the searcher is given the option to order a xeroxed copy of any selected item. Companies, such as the Chemical Abstract Service, have advertised that each order will be filled within 24 hours. ISI's Original Article Tear Sheet is another form of document delivery in which articles from the Institute for Scientific Information's library of multiple copies of journals are actually torn. This service has been replaced by its The Genuine Article service. The aim of these services is to supply the physical document with the least amount of time lapse.

Full-text Retrieval

Other applications of electronic document delivery include full-text transmission of documents. Mead Data Central was among the first to allow direct online searching and delivery of full-text. Its flagship, LEXIS, is the largest legal research database in the world with over 3 million cases and statutes. Full-text may be printed at the local printer to provide a hardcopy to the end-user at the conclusion of the search session. Many other full-text databases in the form of electronic equivalents to newspapers, encyclopedias, business and financial reports are added every month. Some well-known examples are *The New York Times, The Wall Street Journal, Forbes Magazine*, and *LEXPAT*, a full-text patent database. Obviously, the immediate availability of these types of current information has an important impact on the way many businesses operate.

With the combination of fast transmission speed, the low cost of compact storage and processing, and the increase of full-text online databases, the gap between the identification and the delivery of needed documents has narrowed considerably. A user may sit at a computer terminal or a multipurpose computer workstation and search the topic online, download the identified citations or full-text onto a local hard disk, view the contents, save, and file them for future use.

For a long time, telefacsimile transmission was not a viable option. Recently many corporations have found it convenient to use the facsimile equipment because of its demonstrated qualitative improvement of output, and lowered costs. This hardware is used in conjunction with the easily accessible microcomputer. Although the equipment is primarily used to transmit documents generated internally in organizations, it has not been used to any extent for published literature. With the eventual resolution of copyright control, this might be another attractive alternative for document delivery.

Optical Laser Technology

Currently, the compact disk, or CD-ROM, represents the storage device of choice. In the last few years, the development of laser technology has opened up a huge market for the commercialization of delivery of all types of information (Herther, 1985; 1987). Databases are no longer limited to bibliographic citations. They are now "document bases." Enormous amounts of text can be compressed into each single optical disk. With a CD-ROM reader attached to a microcomputer, one is able to search, browse, and retrieve literally a modest library of books and journals. Microsoft's Bookshelf consists of a single disk which contains ten databases with an interactive random access memory or RAM-resident link. This desktop electronic library contains the full text of *The American Heritage Dictionary, Roget's Thesaurus, Houghton Mifflin's Usage Alert*, and *Spelling Verifier and Corrector*, the *1987 World Almanac*, the *Book of Facts, The Chicago Manual of Style, Bartlett's Familiar Quotations*, the *U.S. Zip Code Directory*, and Lorna Daniell's *Business Information Sources* (McManus, 1987).

Large data files may also be maintained on compact discs in many local sites. These may be directly linked to a host of local microcomputers by a local area network. The real-time access of databases has fast become an important research aid for many scholars, lawyers, scientists, and physicians. The data can reside in a remote central location and may be accessed via the local telephone connection to a telecommunication network. They can also be reached from a compact laser disk storage attached to one's own microcomputer or from a common file server serving a designated group of users.

This technology has unveiled a new arena for potentially innovative applications, especially in education. The compact laser disk is an effective medium for high resolution images, speeches, and animation, as well as for textual data. Other forms of optical technologies are rapidly coming to the fore. Various interactive versions, voice recognition, and the blending of digital and video in an interactive form are available. The merging of different types of data for effective information delivery is enormously useful for the learner. It is easy to visualize the retrieval of information relating to a type of pulmonary disease in which colored slides, X-ray images, illustrations, graphic displays, charts of statistics, and excerpts from text are brought together and amplified by appropriate voice annotation. With the added capability of an interactive compact disk, or CD-I, learning by active simulation and by role playing can be stimulating. The impact of the effective delivery of information on education, and continuing education can be dramatic.

In 1986, Mead Data Central added the service of MEDIS. It contains the latest medical research developments, diagnosis and treatment techniques, government regulations, cost analysis, and MEDLINE. GENMED, a clinical medical library is composed of (1) text found in 48 journals and 6 medical books; (2) PHARM, a drug information file; (3) ADMIN, a health care administration file; (4) MEDLINE, a bibliographic file; (5) ONCO, an oncology file containing the journals *Cancer, Cancer Treatment Reports, Cancer Treatment Symposia*, the *Journal of the National Cancer Institute*, the National Cancer Institute's *Seminars in Oncology,* and *Physician Data Query* (*PDQ*). All are available through a common query language and searchable online. The last item contains state-of-the-art staging and cancer treatment information, a directory of physicians and organizations providing cancer care, and cancer treatment protocols. Data from these various information sources are integrated so that through an online dialogue, the clinician can locate the institutions where specific procedures are being tested. The display includes the name of the physician with the latest information on the treatment, accompanied by a full-text of appropriate supporting documentation from the latest journal articles.

NOTIFICATION

A service whose primary function is to alert and notify its clients of potentially useful new information on an individualized basis is known as a Selective Dissemination of Information service (SDI) or current awareness service. It provides a continuous and dependable service which often extends to the supply of the actual documents or abstracts which have been screened and filtered by the systems staff. Hans Peter Luhn of the International Business Machines Corporation has often been cited as the first to propose this new concept of information service. He proposed a method of improving the communication of scientific information by the selective dissemination of information assisted by machines (Luhn, 1958). He described SDI as a service "within an organization which concerns itself with the 'machine-assisted' channeling of new items of information, from whatever source, to those points within the organization where the probability of usefulness, in connection with current work or interests is high" (Luhn, 1961). This system extends the conventional library service by alerting and informing patrons through the regular provision of literature.

Many libraries have implemented this concept by routing journal tables of contents or the title pages of papers according to manually maintained subject profiles. Libraries of commercial organizations frequently scan the literature on a regular basis for quality items (Hawkins, 1985). According to the interest of each user, full papers are routed to users for their attention. Instead of providing service only on-demand, this individualized service aggressively seeks out documents of potential use and anticipates its users' information needs. Previously with manual systems, this type of highly customized service was labor-intensive and time-consuming. Since cost is an ever-present constraint, such alerting and delivery services are luxuries ill afforded by most libraries. Therefore, availability of these services has been confined to specialized user groups whose information needs are specifically research or application directed. Furthermore, the organizations that sponsor such intensive, dependable information services tend to view information as directly affecting the quality and quantity of their output products or services.

SDI is one of the most successful services developed in the sixties (Leggate, 1975). Its value for the user is indisputable in terms of savings of time and intellectual effort. Many information centers, information analysis groups, and computerized retrieval systems in industries and government agencies have launched large information systems with powerful computer capabilities to produce data tapes on specialized subject areas to provide SDI services to scientists, engineers, health professionals and social scientists. Numerous organizations have established their internal SDI services. The benefits of current awareness services especially to workers engaged in the physical and biomedical sciences have long been recognized.

The commercial viability of SDI services has also been recognized. The Institute for Scientific Information, in 1965, marketed ASCA (Automatic Subject Citation Alert), a literature alerting service. Periodic literature searches are conducted based on up-to-date user's interest profiles. Indeed, ISI's *Current Contents* together with its recently installed online version have been enormously successful. It is based on a simple current awareness procedure: copies of the table of contents from a group of key journals in a given subject field are regularly sent to its subscribers. By notifying the user of current publication titles on a continuous basis, the user has come to rely on this vehicle to keep up-to-date.

Selective Dissemination of Information

The design of all SDI systems shares several common components (Schneider, 1971; Mauerhoff, 1974). Figure 10.1 shows the essential operations which include the matching of profiles of users and documents, notification, feedback, and the revision of users' profiles with index profiles. The technical difficulties of Luhn's automated intelligence system have been largely overcome by the high performance and general availability of computers. Unfortunately, problems remain with those components which are dependent on humans for processing. Assuming that the document file has been properly processed, the key to the success of a current awareness system is the accuracy of the profiling that is largely dependent on the work performed on profile construction and on profile revision (Sprague and Freudenreich, 1978).

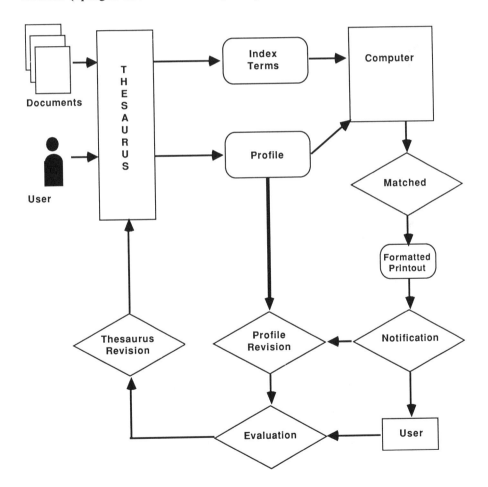

Fig. 10.1. Schema of an SDI system.

PROFILING

Just as networking is the crucial ingredient in document delivery, profiling is the key to any Selective Dissemination of Information service (SDI). A profile is a succinct description of the topical interests of the user. By convention, a profile consists of a listing of keywords joined by Boolean operators characterizing a user's interest. The profile structure is very similar to that of document indexing. The object is to describe the information needs of an individual by a group of keywords. Three aspects are important to profile construction, and determine the precision and accuracy of any profile: (1) the requestor's ability to communicate effectively with the information system, (2) the profiler's interpretation of the user's articulation of his or her needs, and (3) the accuracy with which the identified subject interests are translated to the vocabulary and characteristics of the databases and retrieval systems.

Unfortunately, similar to the process of question analysis, no precise procedure can insure the establishment of an optimal profile. Often an interview is scheduled to probe the subject interests of the client. The interviewer takes note of the topics and the different approaches to topics, types of activities requiring information support, the number of papers needed, whether research reports or patent materials are needed, and the requirements in terms of coverage and languages. As a preliminary step, the profiler might select one or two databases which could be the main sources of information. The requestor's preference and familiarity with potentially useful data files should be ascertained. Finally, an element of education should be incorporated into the interview. The balance between recall and precision requirements and the importance of profile adjustment and maintenance should be explained. In brief, the requestor should come away from the experience with better knowledge of the types of information to be expected from the databases, the kinds of input information useful for effective retrieval, and the requisite feedback needed to improve the quality and quantity of materials retrieved.

In addition to the subject terms, a profile is often supplemented with other requirements. These may be the names of key authors whose works are essential reading, certain sponsoring agencies and journal titles in the fields from which important papers are often found for the user, or key papers or key figures whose works are often cited in this special research area. A list of key references may be used to retrieve all subsequent current papers that cite any one or more of the papers in the starter bibliography.

As an alternative for the researchers, instead of establishing the profile from a user's verbalization of interest, another type of profile may be indirectly established by the user's own publications. One's own writings may be reasonably considered a reliable indication of one's research interest. This may be used in two ways in profile construction. First, index terms assigned to these writings may be used to construct a tentative profile subject to revision by the user. Second, the publications of the users themselves can be used to retrieve other publications similar in subject content. That is, citing papers are relevant to the cited publications. This method of using the user's own publications as an indicator of subject interest is dynamic in that one's record of publications reflects the development of one's research interests. However, this profile establishment method may be only valid for research workers.

MATCHING

With a tentative profile characterizing the user's search patterns, the profiler must then translate these concepts and requirements into the system's vocabulary and syntax. Thesauri are used for keyword translation and amplification. Code books are consulted for the accurate representation of such fields as activities, companies, journal titles, organizations, and product classifications. The searcher may have to determine that certain concepts are to be represented by descriptors from the thesaurus while other keywords are retained for searching in title and abstract fields. After such considerations, the user is consulted for verification of other terms found. The next step is the actual searching online.

NOTIFICATION

The citations, documents, or abstracts retrieved on the basis of the tentative profile are delivered. They may be in the form of hardcopy, or the title page of the paper. Delivery may also be routed through the electronic message system. Electronic text may be viewed and/or hardcopies made. It is crucial that the profile is also included so that the user may check the relevance of the profile with the type of materials included or excluded in the delivered information set.

FEEDBACK

This component of the SDI system evaluates the performance of retrieval systems in terms of the retrieved materials. On the basis of such evaluation, the individual interest profile may be revised and improved for subsequent retrieval. It is also an important mechanism for keeping up-to-date with the user's current and perhaps changing interests. Feedback may take many forms. The reactions to each notification may be either in written or verbal form. At the initial stage of the establishment of the profile, a personal session with the profiler following the delivery of the first retrieval of material may produce the greatest benefit. It is especially crucial if the first few retrieval transactions produce poor results. This is an important element for the success of any SDI service, and full cooperation by the clientele is needed. The feedback mechanism should require the least amount of time and effort on the part of the user. Many organizations enclose a return-requested postcard for feedback information so that a minimal amount of time is required by the user. In the electronic mode, comments before the conclusion of the online session may remind and encourage users' comments.

REVISION AND UPDATE

Finally, most user profiles tend to remain relatively stable. For persons pursuing research in the same area, the profile change is minimal. However, a constant monitoring and adjustment can assure and detect any shift in interest. This may be due to a redirection of the organization's emphasis or product lines. New mergers and acquisitions of the parent organization may necessitate changes in research direction, which may be reflected in the interests of the clientele.

Individual relocation, promotion, or new areas of exploration may also result in the change of one's profile. As the users become more knowledgeable about the capabilities and limitations of the retrieval system, their demands may also change over time. The users' suggestions also need to be given consideration.

Implementation

Before the use of telecommunication networks, SDI services were mostly implemented in-house. Tapes from database producers were subscribed to, and the matching of user profiles with document descriptions were conducted on the local computer. Since then, as computers and the electronic delivery of information have become more common place, SDI service is much less cumbersome and expensive to operate. All major online database search vendors have included facilities for SDI search updates. For example, a user's subject profile in the form of one or more Boolean expressions may be stored on the vendor's computer for a modest fee. Monthly or periodic searching of the relevant files may be performed with an identical search limited to the newly added portion of the data file.

OTHER REFINEMENTS

Two spin-offs resulting from the use of computers and databases have had an impact on information dissemination. They are (1) the ability to capture bibliographic citations and text electronically for incorporation into one's private file and (2) the availability of subsets of specific databases for end-user searching.

Downloading

Downloading is the process of duplicating data contained in a remote computer directly into another file in a local computer via a telephone connection. By the use of communication equipment and a software program, the downloaded file may be saved, sorted, indexed, and merged with another file. The newly created file may be subject to future searching and manipulation. These are essentially electronic citation files or full-text reprint files. A number of software products is available for downloading and organization of personal files. Familiar programs include PRO-CITE, SCI-MATE, STAIR, NLM's GRATEFUL MED, and others. Reviews of the capabilities and limitations of these software are often found in the journals, *Microcomputers for Information Management, Database, Online*, and *Online Review*. The downloaded files are easy to create but more difficult to maintain for easy retrieval. Each is a miniature version of an information retrieval system with its attendant problems of subject organization and retrieval. However, the decentralization of usable online reprint files promotes information access.

End-user Searching

The major online database search services offer reduced searching charges for end-user searching. Dialog's Knowledge Index, and BRS's BRS After Dark are aimed at end-users. PaperChase originated as a research project to test the hypothesis that there is an increased use of biomedical literature by clinicians and biomedical scientists, if current bibliographic data are easily accessible and freely searchable by the users themselves (Horowitz and Bleich, 1981; Bleich, Jackson, and Rosenberg, 1985). The database of PaperChase consisted of articles from the last three years of the MEDLINE database. These papers were taken from the journals available at the library of Beth Israel Hospital in Boston. The data tape was mounted at the local computer. An easy-to-use search interface was installed. Terminals connected to the database were available day and night in the hospital. Similarly, CITE/NLM implemented an easy-to-use user interface on the NLM online library catalog (Doszkocs, 1983). It was found in both projects that availability and accessibility were major contributing factors in the increased use of information systems. Since then local access to subsets of frequently used databases, such as MiniMEDLINE, has been made available in many sites (Broering, 1985). As another type of research tool, institutions can now purchase or subscribe to CD-ROM disks containing large data files. The unlimited online searching available to local users promotes information access. However, a cautionary note is interjected. Although end-user searching is popular, studies by Sewell (1986) have found that the main reasons for the use of online system by end-users are convenience and speed. Other more powerful capabilities are underutilized. Most users perform simple searches. Ease of use is an important factor for the continued use of these systems. Suggestions are made that many areas of the basic online search system could be upgraded to assist the end-user.

Integrated Information Management

Ideally, dissemination means the integrated use of all relevant information by the user, without his or her having to locate various pieces of information from disparate sources. The Integrated Academic Information Management System (IAIMS), an initiative taken by the National Library of Medicine, points in that direction (Matheson and Cooper, 1982). To support clinical and research decisions, the health care professional should be able to call up on his or her desktop computer, relevant patient data, laboratory test results, epidemiological statistics, specialized data files (such as protocols and treatment plans), as well as up-to-date relevant journal literature. Similar ideas of access should be applicable to business and industry. Relevant internal reports, sales and marketing data, trade reports, governmental regulations and restrictions, and published literature should be integrated for ease of use by the decision maker. One is reminded that although there are databases on almost every conceivable topic, the delivery and accessibility of needed information are hampered by the existence of the plethora of information. Productive use of information does not merely depend on its existence but on the preselection, effective coordination, and interlinkage of information sources.

Applications in specialized areas are beginning to appear. Chemical Journals Online provides crossover searching capabilities from CAS Online, which is the online version of *Chemical Abstracts*, to full-text articles in the appropriate journals. As stated earlier, Mead Data Central also offers MEDIS as an integrated information source coordinating a number of medical resources.

Processed Information Services

Today, the public is aware of the existence of more and more information and has found more productive uses for it. Moreover, the level of public expectation of information services has been raised. As many information sources are organized and made available in electronic form, there is greater demand on the actual delivery of information. For example, in the business sector of society, users expect processed information in the form of digests and the tracking of business intelligence from information systems. An increasing number of commercial institutions have offered products targeted for this group of users. For example, independent information brokers offer customized information packages in a highly usable form. They are able to present certain state-of-the-art aspects of a market on a regular basis.

In summary, dissemination and access may be accomplished in many ways. Recent developments in networking activities coupled with advances in information technologies have greatly facilitated document delivery. Electronic delivery of information has brought profound changes on both global and local levels. Traditionally, users in geographically remote areas tended to suffer from information inaccessibility as compared with those living near large, metropolitan, resources-rich centers or academic research libraries. With the wide availability of information utilities and the worldwide online access to thousands of databases, inaccessibility is by and large reduced to a question of whether a modest cost can be tolerated. Information delivery has evolved from strictly decentralized manual operations to centralized, computer-controlled facilities and now to the distributive capabilities offered by optical disks and microcomputers.

Current awareness services are valuable enhancements to on-demand information services. An effective SDI service that supplies useful, up-to-date, new information items to the user can prove to be most cost effective in the long run. The success of SDI lies in the sensitivity and perception with which the subject profiles are drawn, revised, and kept current.

Yet the degree of dissemination offered is also a function of the system's objective and the perceived value of information in the organization. For example, the objective of a hospital library may be the provision of lists of journal article citations, if and when requests are submitted by its health care professional staff. The consistent fast delivery of such lists to the user's department is considered an optimal level of information dissemination. On the other extreme, the goals of a search service at a highly competitive automobile manufacturing company may be entirely different. Its aim may be to provide the maximum informational support for the development, design, production, and marketing of the company's automobiles. In addition to the actual on-demand delivery of documents, the information service may be compelled to sustain an active current awareness service bringing to its users' attention publications and news items of any potential interest. In this case, dissemination and access may extend to encompass the scanning of technical reports from the government and industry, journal articles, monographs, publications from the regulatory agencies, reports from watchdog groups, as well as internal reports which may have been overlooked. This retrieval system may have to deal with problems of locating sensitive information that is not widely disseminated, emanating from competitors and regulatory publications that are restricted in circulation. In another setting such as the public library, dissemination may be concerned with an entirely different set of problems in implementing its goals. Information access may entail the promotion of library service to those who could benefit economically from appropriate data. Effective dissemination in this context may take the form of a community-outreach-education program aimed primarily at the elderly. In other words, dissemination and access may be accomplished on different levels and by various means. More importantly, dissemination must be implemented in accordance with the objective(s) of the retrieval system. The careful articulation of the system's goals and the delineation of its users cannot be overemphasized in the system's design.

REFERENCES

Bleich, H.L., J.D. Jackson, and H.A. Rosenberg. 1985. "PaperChase: A Program to Search the Medical Literature." *MD Computing*, 2:54-59.

Broering, N.C. 1985. "The MiniMEDLINE SYSTEM: A Library-based End-User Search System." *Bulletin of the Medical Library Association*, 73(2): 138-145.

Doszkocs, T.E. 1983. "CITE/NLM: Natural Language Searching in an Online Catalog." *Information Technology and Libraries*, 2(4):364-380.

Hawkins, D.T. 1985. "Use of Machine-Readable Databases to Support a Large SDI Service." *Information Processing and Management*, 12(3):187-204.

Herther, N.K. 1985. "CD ROM Technology: A New Era for Information Storage and Retrieval?" *Online*, 9(6):17-28.

Herther, N.K. 1987. "CD ROM and Information Dissemination: An Update." *Online*, 11(2):56-64.

Horowitz, G.L., and H.L. Bleich. 1981. "PaperChase: A Computer Program to Search the Medical Literature." *New England Journal of Medicine*, 305(16): 924-930.

Leggate, P. 1975. "Computer-based Current Awareness Services." *Journal of Documentation*, 31(2):93-115.

Luhn, H.P. 1958. "A Business Intelligence System." *IBM Journal of Research and Development*, 2(4):314-319.

Luhn, H.P. 1961. "Selective Dissemination of New Scientific Information with the Aid of Electronic Processing Equipment." *American Documentation*, 12(2):131-138.

Matheson, N.W., and J.A.D. Cooper. 1982. "Academic Information in the Academic Health Sciences Center: Roles for the Library in Information Management." *Journal of Medical Education*, 57(10-pt2):1-93.

Mauerhoff, G.R. 1974. "Selective Dissemination of Information." *Advances in Librarianship*, 4:25-62.

McManus, R. 1987. "The Reference ROM." *PC World*, 5(4):236-239.

Schneider, J.H. 1971. "Selective Dissemination and Indexing of Scientific Information." *Science*, 173:300-308.

Sewell, W., and S. Teitelbaum. 1986. "Observations of End-User Online Searching Behavior Over Eleven Years." *Journal of the American Society for Information Science*, 37(4):234-245.

Sprague, R.J., and L.B. Freudenreich. 1978. "Building Better SDI Profiles for Users of Large Multidisciplinary Databases." *Journal of the American Society for Information Science*, 29(6):278-282.

Part III
EVALUATION AND MEASUREMENT OF INFORMATION SYSTEMS AND SERVICES

11

Evaluation and Measurement

THE NEED FOR EVALUATION

To evaluate is to make a judgment of worth or merit. Evaluation is a process involving the evaluator, the object of evaluation, and some underlying assumptions and values associated with the object of evaluation. In evaluating a retrieval system or an information service, one monitors and assesses its operation and performance. As in managing any dynamic organization, one is periodically faced with questions: whether it is at its top performance level, whether it is worth its cost, whether it ought to continue to exist, and whether it can be improved. Four major reasons for evaluation follow.

First, accountability is usually the major reason to conduct an evaluation. For the system's manager, it is a good practice to be ready to produce the evidence necessary to justify the system's operation and to prove its worth. Pressure from their funding source(s) has forced many administrators to examine the operation in terms of quality and quantity of service and to relate the findings to cost. An accepted defense is to demonstrate convincingly the system's output performance in the light of input resources.

Secondly, the assurance of continuous quality service depends on performance evaluation. To evaluate is to relate the present achievements to the goals and objectives of the organization. A good manager knows the difference between what one has versus what one wants. A system's effectiveness can be ascertained by comparing the desired level of performance with the current level at which the system is able to meet users' requirements. The first requirement of good management is a thorough familiarity with the operation of the system. It is imperative to know what is being done at all levels and how well the system is functioning at all times. Consistent monitoring produces descriptive data on the present operation at various levels and the identification of the function of component parts. The analytical process acts as an objective check in identifying functional needs, duplications, or the omission of component parts. Secondly, by developing appropriate performance measures, the level of performance can be more accurately assessed and compared over time. A program of continuous monitoring insures a better understanding and management of existing systems.

Thirdly, evaluation is also critical in solving problems in information systems. Since evaluative activities provide analysis and diagnosis of the systems functions, each component may be scrutinized in terms of strengths and weaknesses with respect to its assigned tasks and functions. Component-specific data as it relates to the system's objectives are useful in planning corrective actions. In the identification of weaknesses, recommendations can be made for specific functions, such as the indexing policy, control of vocabulary, or searching procedure. Particularly in upgrading substandard performance, changes should be introduced in an orderly fashion insuring the least amount of disruption and trauma. Finally, decisions based on quantitative and qualitative data can be made to formulate alternative plans. More importantly, such decisions will be based on a realistic assessment of cost in terms of personnel, effort, and delay time balanced with the expected benefits derived from the system.

Lastly, with well-conducted evaluation studies, data can be obtained to make reasonable predictions and projections of future performance. As a result, evaluation is also valuable in the design and implementation of new systems.

Evaluation may be directed to the entire organization, a subsystem, a specific function, or a component unit. One evaluates in terms of the desired performance level, the finite expenditure, and the benefits derived from the service. In other words, three levels of evaluation are commonly recognized: (1) effectiveness, (2) cost-effectiveness, and (3) cost-benefit (Lancaster, 1977).

Effectiveness. To evaluate the effectiveness of the performance of any unit is to appraise the quality of its output. Quality can be meaningfully addressed only in terms of whether the work unit fulfills a specific set of designated goals. In terms of information services, effectiveness usually measures the extent to which the system or service is able to satisfy the demand placed upon it by its clients. It can also measure the degree to which the system is able to provide pre-set service requirements which may also include system-initiated services, such as a current awareness service in addition to on-demand services. Similarly, if evaluation is directed to an information product, the qualitative measure entails the determination of the extent to which the objectives are actually being attained by the artifact produced.

Cost-effectiveness. The other obvious criterion for evaluation relates to economic issues. Cost-effectiveness is concerned with the operational efficiency of the service or system with respect to cost. It refers to the relationship between the costs incurred and the achievement of a specific level of performance. Its goal is either the least cost to accomplish a stated objective or to achieve the maximum effectiveness for a given cost. Implicitly it asks the questions "Can the system be improved? Can it be operated more efficiently?" Efficiency in terms of effort and time is directly linked to the expenditure.

Cost-benefit. Finally, evaluation relates cost to the value or worth of the service or system. Cost-benefit refers to the relationship between the benefit of the end-product in the form of services rendered and the cost of providing the services. Benefit involves questions such as the following: Does the expenditure justify the benefit derived from the system? Is the payoff worth the economic cost? Frequently, the benefits of information are perceived and stated in a negative way; that is, what is the cost to the organization due to the lack of proper information. What is the cost of duplicating a project due to misinformation? What is the cost of inaccurate information resulting in bad decisions? Although tangible benefits may be articulated, many are hard to define. Benefit as an empirical property is more difficult to capture in quantitative terms except in the commercial sense, namely, the return of one's investment.

From the standpoint of the manager, the performance of an information system and service may be perceived as the classic Input-Processing-Output (IPO) design shown in Figure 11.1.

Fig. 11.1. The IPO model.

Input consists of human, financial, and material resources examined in the light of output in terms of services and benefits (see Figure 11.2). Fixed costs are those derived from equipment purchase, salaries, operating costs, and developmental costs. Variable costs are referred to as functions of a number of transactions, such as the cost per online search or the cost of processing a document in order to make it available to the user. This approach to evaluation, particularly with respect to cost, is of vital concern to managers in terms of the economic viability of the system.

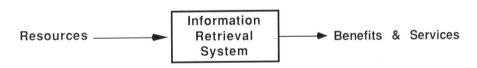

Fig. 11.2. IPO model as applied to an information retrieval system.

On the other hand, the user of an information system is primarily concerned with the evaluation of performance as it relates to the quality of output or the system's effectiveness. In this chapter, evaluation is limited only to the assessment of performance effectiveness. Discussions are centered on evaluation criteria used in document retrieval services and systems, the establishment of appropriate measures, measuring units, and measuring instruments. Focus is directed toward evaluation of performance effectiveness in quantitative terms.

TYPES OF EVALUATION

Evaluation studies of information systems are characterized by two main questions:

1. How well is the system performing?

2. How does the system function?

With regard to the first question, one cannot judge how well the system is working without a preestablished point of reference. Evaluation presupposes the existence of a set of objectives. The precisely defined objectives serve as standards against which measurement and comparison are made. If the objectives are expressible in measurable, observable, and explicit terms, the results of evaluation studies of information systems, services, or even of specific functions are more likely to be reliable and reproducible. It is crucial that one must first determine the desired outcomes of the information system. If the goals cannot be specified, there is no basis for evaluation. Thus, it is nonsensical to evaluate an information system as "an educational system," since educational objectives cannot be stated in unequivocal terms. A function within an information system must also have predetermined objectives serving as goals, against which the actual performance can be assessed. The clear and unambiguous articulation of the system's objectives is the single most important prerequisite for any evaluative activities.

It is important to note that the objectives of the information system or service are different from the objectives of evaluation. To answer the first question "How well is the system performing?", the objectives of the system should capture what the system is supposed to do. If the system's objective is to maximize service to its users, the evaluation objective is to reveal the degree to which the system is able to satisfy users' needs and demands. This is an overall system evaluation stated with respect to an expectation that has been articulated in observable and measurable terms. The results could yield information on the extent to which various significant objectives of the system under study are actually being attained. The aim of this global approach to evaluation is not to find the sources of system's failure, nor to find ways to remedy problems, nor even to identify areas of improvement. King and Bryant (1971) named this *macroevaluation,* which offers an overall assessment of the system's performance.

In contrast to macroevaluation, *microevaluation* is concerned with the second question "How does the system function?" Most service-oriented systems are complex. There are interrelated components, each of which performs one or more specific functions within the overall objective of the system. The objective of this type of evaluation is to analyze the component parts and processes within the system, to understand the function and working of each unit, and to identify specific parts or functions for improvement. Its role is analytical and diagnostic. It offers verdicts on whether the system can be improved, which areas need improvement, whether there is duplication of effort, and whether there are missing components. Its ultimate aim is to offer specific advice when addressing the question "How can the system's performance be improved?" One may equate microevaluation with testing as opposed to evaluation. Unfortunately, the terms *evaluation* and *testing* are frequently used interchangeably with regard to the process of assessment.

One tests a particular function or component of a system to discover if it fulfills its original intent. In testing, one works within the original design and seeks to maximize the various components and functions. The aim is to relate the performance of a particular unit to the level of success in its assigned task. On the other hand, evaluation is also concerned with how well the system has been designed in the first place. The purpose is to determine how well the system has achieved its objectives. Evaluation or macroevaluation may also involve the examination and comparative study of alternative system designs with the aim of identifying the best system for attaining an explicit system's goals. A simple example serves to clarify the difference. An evaluation of the service offered by an online search service may reveal that only 75 percent of all database searches done during the past 12 months were rated as satisfactory by requestors. In testing the performance of searchers who have had training on the frequently used databases against those without training, the results show an average of 95 percent and 60 percent satisfaction rates, respectively. The result of the testing of the searcher's relevant experience may show a positive correlation between training and search success. Thus, on the basis of the test results, a specific source of failure is identified, and a remedy may be instituted.

NECESSARY ELEMENTS
OF EVALUATION

Several essential components should be present in any evaluative study (Unisist, 1978).

Hypothesis

As in any experimental study, an evaluation study must begin with a hypothesis or an evaluation objective. A hypothesis is a tentative solution to a problem. The limits of an evaluation study are defined in a well-formulated hypothesis. For example, "The retrieval effectiveness of an automatic indexing method based on word frequency count equals that of a manual indexing method."

Criteria for Evaluation:
What to Measure?

A key question in evaluative studies is identification of what to measure. Lancaster (1977) and King and Bryant (1971) presented a number of performance criteria for information services. Among those often used in evaluation studies are:

(a) coverage of subject content in the collection or database

(b) ability to retrieve, or recall

(c) ability to avoid nonrelevant documents, or precision

(d) accuracy of data

(e) novelty ratio

(f) response time

(g) time lag, or the interval between the publication of a document and its availability to the user

(h) output display format.

Most information centers collect statistics on the number of users served, the size of the collection maintained, the amount of new materials added annually, and the number of information transactions completed. Such quantitative measures are fairly straightforward. They give an overall description of what is happening at the organization.

However, the ultimate goal of a retrieval system is to bring about a desired change in the knowledge state of the user resulting from the information content of each retrieved document. As a consequence, one hopes that problems are solved, better decisions are made, difficult situations are resolved, insights are gained, goals are clarified, knowledge is synthesized, attitudes are changed, capabilities are extended, or solutions are found. Unfortunately, the attainment of these outcomes is mostly subjective and expressible mainly in qualitative terms. The cognitive processes in humans are too complex to be investigated. There is no direct way to measure knowledge. The transformation process from information to knowledge in an individual cannot be observed. The criteria by which knowledge is attained cannot be measured nor easily externalized. Thus, one of the major problems in evaluating information retrieval systems or processes is that those criteria truly reflective of the quality of service are characterized by attributes that are not readily quantifiable.

Although qualitative performance criteria are not easily measurable, there are a number of indicators reflective of quality of service. Performance criteria are selected to reflect adequately the true purpose of the system. However, it is not likely that all of the purposes of the information retrieval system are represented by one criterion. Qualitative criteria may often be partially captured by quantitative indicators. For example, the aesthetics and comfort level of the physical setting of an information center as variables contributing to the use of the center are qualitative criteria. However, the concept of aesthetics may be represented by several attributes, such as lighting intensity, the presence of cooler colors visible from the interior of the public areas, the placement and presence of paintings, and the spacing of furniture, shelves, and lighting fixtures. These do not totally capture the essence of the notion of aesthetics, but they are reasonable, measurable qualities of the concepts under study. At issue is the importance of the criterion chosen relative to those objectives perceived by the system's manager.

Another important consideration of criterion selection is the measurability of the characteristics under study. In recent years, the quantification of performance of information services has received much attention. Writings by Lancaster (1977), Hamburg, Clelland, Bommer, Ramist, and Whitfield (1974), Kantor (1982), King and Bryant (1971), and others have developed many useful operational definitions of quality and quantity of information service. Along with these criteria, they have also offered specific procedures to measure various aspects of information services. Some investigators measure characteristics of users of information service. One could count the borrowers, users, registered patrons, and the number of library visits as a form of output. Other researchers examine the *system's usage*. Circulation figures, reference questions answered, interlibrary loan transactions, and exposure time of documents are some indications of the usage of the system. Still others investigate the *usefulness* or *contributions* of the system. The relative number of return visits indicates the degree of perceived usefulness of a system's use. Patrons' subjective assessment in terms of user satisfaction is also a valid quality indicator. Although these objective performance measures may not capture the totality of the quality and quantity of information service, they do provide useful tools for the system's manager.

Performance criteria may also be categorized into two distinct classes. The first is directed toward capturing the efficiency and effectiveness of system processes. Many criteria have been developed to test a system's components. The second originates from the user's standpoint. A partial list of criteria include:

- cost

- comprehensiveness of subject coverage

- retrieval effectiveness of indexing languages

- retrieval effectiveness of indexing process (exhaustivity and depth of indexing)

- searching effectiveness by the use of data elements in different fields

- searching effectiveness by the use of key terms and bibliographic citations

- efficiency of loan policy

- retrieval effectiveness and efficiency of searchers in relation to training and background

- retrieval effectiveness of query analysis and formulation procedures

- utilization rate

- users' studies

- user satisfaction

- retrieval effectiveness as measured by user feedback

- effectiveness of end-user searching.

Kantor (1976) believes that there are three important qualitative dimensions to information service. These criteria can be used in evaluation studies of retrieval systems and services. They are (1) relevance, (2) availability, and (3) accessibility.

The concept of *relevance* has been discussed at length in Chapter 4. Although it is key to evaluating information retrieval systems, it is an abstract notion. It measures the system's ability to retrieve those documents that have useful content and to suppress those that do not. As a performance criterion, the more relevant retrievals produced by the system, the more it can satisfy the system's users. Relevance is the property of effective contact between an information source and a destination. Unfortunately, "effective contact" is difficult to define. Basically, one considers relevance as "informativeness," a subjectively determined property dependent on the individual who acts as the judge, or as a relatively objective property assessed with respect to a particular topic. In order to measure relevance, "useful content" must be established for comparison.

1. Many consider the requestor as the sole qualified judge of relevance. Consequently, for an identical query submitted by two users, it is possible that each retrieved document may be judged differently by the two individuals based on different requirements.

2. Other researchers treat relevance as a property found in the content contained in the document and in the query. As such, relevance is independent of the user. A panel of subject experts on the topic is properly regarded as the best judge of the relevance and accuracy of documents. Cooper (1973a, 1973b) defines relevance in terms of "logical consequence." This definition of relevance promises to remove the concept of relevance as a strictly subjective consideration. However, this approach to relevance has not been applied to any operating system.

3. Still others consider relevance a characteristic of a document's quality that can be determined by the utility of its informational content. Thus, a cited paper is considered relevant to the citing document, because it is "used" by the more recent paper. Consequently, if a key paper on a topic is regarded as the requested topic, all publications citing the key paper can be considered relevant to the query.

To operationalize the concept of relevance, effectiveness is regarded as the degree to which the system is able to satisfy requests by identifying relevant documents (White, 1977). The two most common relevance measures are recall and precision ratios, which will be discussed in a later section.

The concept of *availability* as a performance criterion was suggested by Hamburg and his colleagues (1974). It is based on the assumption that the effectiveness of one type of information service, such as borrowing books from a library, is dependent upon whether the desired document is physically available in the expected location at the time the item is sought. It is a more concrete concept than relevance. With respect to availability, the objective of a library is to maximize the exposure of documents to the user. This notion of document exposure time can be operationalized as the number of hours spent with a borrowed document. In-library exposure time can be computed as the average time a user spends in the library per visit during which library materials are used. For documents used outside the library, it is reasoned that since a longer loan period would tend to produce a longer duration in which the book is removed from the library, the document exposure time for patrons other than the borrower could be reduced. Hence, the duration of the loan period has a direct affect on maximizing document exposure time.

Kantor generalizes availability as the fraction of all expressed needs for specific documents that are promptly satisfied. In other words, it is the average output per demand.

$$\text{Measurement of availability} = \frac{\text{Number of items found}}{\text{Number of items sought}}$$

This measure can be interpreted as a probability of success in satisfying a specific demand. Furthermore, Kantor isolates the different causes for failure in order to determine the probability of availability.

Another performance criterion — *accessibility* — is expressed in terms of the barriers experienced in seeking the desired materials. For example, Cooper (1968) suggests the "expected search length" as a possible measure of how well the system is able to divide the file into a "probably relevant" from a "probably not relevant" set. It is measured by the average number of nonrelevant documents the user would be expected to search before finding the number of relevant documents needed. In online database searching of bibliographic records, the measure of accessibility is of practical value. Online printing of the retrieved citations incurs both the actual online connect cost and the cost in terms of the user's effort.

Accessibility may be expressed as the degree of inconvenience in expended effort, delay time, and/or cost incurred for the service. Although measures such as the degree of aggravation and frustration can be used, accessibility in terms of expended effort may be conveniently measured in the number of minutes spent in waiting and in searching. Delay time is the time between the completion of the necessary searching procedures and the actual securing of the document.

Another factor, the actual dollar cost, has been found to contribute inaccessibility to information service, especially to online database searching. Some quantifiable measures of accessibility are:

- the average time spent in looking up the location of a book

- the average time spent in searching a topic online

- the average time spent in processing a book via the interlibrary loan service

- the average time spent in obtaining a satisfactory answer from a reference librarian

- the average cost per online search of a topic.

The benefits of both availability and accessibility analysis are many. One can derive rational policies on the optimal number of duplicate copies needed, the optimal time needed for processing, length of loan periods resulting in maximum availability for specified classes of users, and the best time for the binding of journals. In the management of high demand materials, journal retention, weeding, effective use of space, and the identification of low demand materials for secondary storage are only a few of the many problems found in document retrieval systems.

Performance Measures

THE NEED FOR MEASUREMENT

Suppose the objective of a document retrieval system is that "the majority of its users can find and retrieve those publications that they need and want with a minimum amount of delay and frustration." As a criterion for evaluation, this statement is too broad to be useful. Specifically, how much is "minimum amount of delay"? What constitutes "delay and frustration"? What is a reasonable figure for "the majority of its users"? A reliable evaluation requires specification of empirical properties such as "delay" and "frustration" in observable forms, and such values as "minimum" and "majority" in measurable terms. To exemplify this, a library staff through years of experience can conclude that "Library A is able to satisfy most of the information needs of its users quickly." This statement conveys a general notion of how Library A is performing as compared to the desired objective. However, it is imprecise. One concrete approach is to transform the quantity of "minimum amount of delay" into operational terms such as "the delivering of the needed document within one hour of the request made by every user." This then enables the observation to be made that "On the average, Library A is able to satisfy 85 percent of its users by delivering needed documents within one hour of each request." Such information gives the reader a more precise idea of how well this particular library is performing in terms of document delivery and in satisfying users' requests. In other words, the evaluation is more meaningful. Additionally, quantifying the evaluation allows for comparison. Precision in performance evaluation may be more useful for the decision maker. Measurement forms a strong foundation for evaluation (Campbell and Stanley, 1963).

CHARACTERISTICS OF GOOD MEASURES

Measures are based on the performance criteria identified. A good measure is one that reflects the essence of the criterion and that implies a unit for quantification. Validity and reliability are the two most important qualities of measure. However, in measuring the performance of an information service, another important characteristic must also be considered: the degree of intrusiveness required for data-gathering.

Validity relates to the accuracy and representativeness of the data measured. It is the property linking what is actually measured to what the concept purports to measure. In other words, the measure should reflect the real meaning of the concept to be measured. It attempts to answer two questions. Do the obtained scores accurately measure what the researcher claims to measure? As a requirement, is the sample data obtained typical of the total population under consideration? In other words, is it a representative sample? Is there detected bias or distortion? For example, if an investigator asked every student in a dormitory to name the number of hours he or she spent reading during the preceding week, the scores are not likely to represent the number of hours actually spent in reading. The reason is simply that students normally do not keep an accurate account of the time spent in such activities. Furthermore, they may not be willing to admit to not reading at all. Therefore, the measure taken has low validity.

Reliability is the degree of stability or consistency of the data collected over time. That is, if the same data collection procedure is repeated under the same conditions, would the same scores be obtained? It is the property of stability in recording the results of measuring. It is directly concerned with the accuracy and precision of the measuring instrument. For example, in collecting search results to compute a recall ratio, the relevance of any retrieved document may be established by a human judge. The performance criterion is dependent upon subjective assessment. Over a period of time, questioning the same individuals on the same set of documents is likely to produce different relevance scores. Therefore, recall as a measure is also unlikely to be very reliable.

Intrusiveness relates to the degree to which the data collecting process interferes with the normal operation of the subjects in the information facility. If the process of collecting data disturbs the normal activities of the user, his or her behavior or answers may be influenced by reaction to the presence of the experimenter. Low validity may result. The same is true if intrusive measures are used in collecting data from the staff of the information facility. The presence of the experimenter becomes an undesirable disruptive factor that may alter the normal behavior of the subjects. Even worse, if the experiment is presented as a threat to the careers of staff members, such as a comparative evaluation of the staff in terms of their work, cooperation could even be withheld. Finally, if data collection is overly disruptive to the routine operation of the organization under study, obtaining representative data would not be possible.

MEASURING UNITS

The two most commonly used measures of relevance are the ratios of recall and precision. Cleverdon was the first to conduct extensive testing of retrieval systems using recall and precision as performance measures. *Recall* is the percentage of relevant documents actually retrieved from the total available pool of relevant documents in the file. It measures how well the system is able to retrieve relevant documents. *Precision* is the ratio of the relevant documents actually retrieved to the total set of retrieved documents, which may consist of both relevant and nonrelevant materials. It gives an indication of how well the system provides relevant documents from among those retrieved.

$$\text{Recall} \quad = \quad \frac{\text{what was obtained and was considered useful (hits)}}{\text{total useful documents in the file (hits + misses)}}$$

$$= \quad \frac{\text{number of relevant documents retrieved}}{\text{total number of relevant documents in the file}}$$

$$\text{Precision} = \quad \frac{\text{what was obtained and was considered useful (hits)}}{\text{total of what you got from the file (hits + false drops)}}$$

$$= \quad \frac{\text{number of relevant documents retrieved}}{\text{total number of documents retrieved from the file}}$$

Suppose a data file contains 100 documents. In a search, ten documents are retrieved, of which only four are found to be relevant to the question. However, there are two other documents in the file that are known to be relevant to the topic and are not retrieved. In calculating the recall and precision ratios, the following table is often used.

	Relevant	Not relevant	Total
Retrieved	Hits $a = 4$	False drops $b = 6$	10
Not Retrieved	Misses $c = 2$	Dodged $d = 88$	90
Total	6	94	100

Hence

$$\text{Recall} = \frac{a}{a+c}$$

$$= \frac{4}{4+2}$$

$$= 0.66$$

$$\text{Precision} = \frac{a}{a+b}$$

$$= \frac{4}{4+6}$$

$$= 0.40$$

In probabilistic terms, recall is an estimation of the conditional probability that an item will be retrieved given that it is relevant to the query. Precision is an estimation of the conditional probability that an item will be relevant given that it is retrieved.

In examining the elements in the table shown, the number of dodged items d, which is the number of nonrelevant documents not retrieved from the search, is not taken into account by either recall and precision. Thus, it is conceivable that in two data files of widely different sizes, such as one with 100 papers versus one with 1,000,000 papers, the same query could produce the identical set of recall and precision values. That is, for the collection of 1,000,000 documents, the values in all four categories can be shown in the following table:

	Relevant	Not relevant	Total
Retrieved	Hits $a = 4$	False drops $b = 6$	10
Not Retrieved	Misses $c = 2$	Dodged $d = 999,988$	999,990
Total	6	999,994	1,000,000

The recall and precision ratios from both tables are identical. To cull through a collection of 1,000,000 items to retrieve 66 percent of all relevant materials on a given topic surely indicates a better system's performance when compared to the same 66 percent recall retrieved from a small collection of 100 items!

To take account of the size of the collection from which retrieval is conducted, specificity was another measure proposed by a Western Reserve University research group in the 1960s. Specificity measures how well the systems is able to reject nonrelevant documents with respect to the size of the collection.

$$\text{Specificity} = \frac{\text{\# of nonrelevant documents not retrieved}}{\text{total \# of nonrelevant documents in the file}}$$

$$= \frac{d}{b + d}$$

Thus, the specificity ratios for the above two examples of the 100 document file and the 1,000,000 document file are 94 percent and 99.9 percent, respectively. The system with the larger collection performs extremely well. The specificity is nearly 100 percent.

Fallout has also been suggested as another parameter of a search. It is the probability of a false drop. It is another measure attempting to incorporate the effects of the file size. Unfortunately, both specificity and fallout are fairly insensitive measures when the retrieved set is quite small in comparison with large files.

$$\text{Fallout} = \frac{\text{\# of nonrelevant documents retrieved}}{\text{total \# of nonrelevant documents in the file}}$$

$$= \frac{b}{b+d}$$

Finally, efficiency was proposed as a single measure of system effectiveness on retrieving relevant and only relevant documents. This composite measure incorporates all elements in the table, and its values range from -1 to +1.

$$\text{Efficiency} = \text{Recall} + \text{Specificity} - 1$$

Under ideal conditions, perfect scores for each of the five measures would be derived from the following:

(1) $c = 0$ in that no relevant item would be missed in the search and recall would be unity since all relevant items in the file would be retrieved.

$$\text{Recall} = \frac{a}{a+c}$$

$$= 1$$

(2) $b = 0$ in that no nonrelevant document would be retrieved. Thus,

$$\text{Precision} = \frac{a}{a+b}$$

$$= 1$$

(3) Since $b = 0$,

$$\text{Specificity} = \frac{d}{b+d}$$

$$= 1$$

(4) Since $b = 0$,

$$\text{Fallout} = \frac{b}{b+d}$$

$$= 0$$

(5) Consequently, if and only if all relevant documents were retrieved,

$$\text{Efficiency} = \frac{a}{a+c} + \frac{d}{b+d} - 1$$

$$= 1 + 1 - 1$$

$$= 1$$

Similarly, the worst condition would produce the following scores:

(1) $a = 0$ in that no relevant document would be retrieved.

$$\text{Recall} = \frac{a}{a+c}$$

$$= 0$$

(2) Since $a = 0$,

$$\text{Precision} = \frac{a}{a+b}$$

$$= 0$$

(3) $d = 0$ in that not only can the system not retrieve any relevant document, but also all nonrelevant documents would be retrieved. Thus,

$$\text{Specificity} = \frac{d}{b+d}$$

$$= 0$$

(4) As $d = 0$,

$$\text{Fallout} = \frac{b}{b+d}$$

$$= 1$$

(5) As a result, if and only if all nonrelevant documents were retrieved,

$$\text{Efficiency} = \frac{a}{a+c} + \frac{d}{b+d} - 1$$

$$= 0 + 0 - 1$$

$$= -1$$

However, one must bear in mind that for each search, the desirable scores of these performance measures depend entirely on the user's retrieval objectives. Naturally, a comprehensive search would aim to have the best score possible for each of the four measures. Yet, a very high recall from a large data file with comprehensive coverage could probably be accompanied by fairly low precision. One must be prepared to examine many documents of dubious value for the search. On the other hand, to identify one or two relevant citations, one need only to aim for high precision. In special cases, such as a search to check a proposed doctoral topic, one must tolerate low precision with relatively low specificity in the hope that the recall is zero. In other words, one must expect to scan a comprehensive list of citations with any possibility of relevance to the proposed topic and hope not even one is on the topic of study.

There are two major problems associated with the use of the most common performance measures, recall and precision. The first is the absence of a reliable method to obtain objective relevance assessments. The second problem has to do with the lack of a valid procedure in obtaining a total set of relevant documents for any search topic. The precision measure is often used either formally or informally by the patron and by the searcher. The user, in scanning the results of a search, easily evaluates the search in terms of the precision ratio since all the necessary data to calculate precision are contained in the retrieved set. On the other hand, the key unknown piece of data for the computation of the recall ratio is the total number of relevant items to the search topic contained in the file. For any topic, there is no easy way to examine the entire file to estimate the total number of relevant documents. Operationally, true recall is a measure impossible to establish.

Most experimental studies have adopted one of the following three methods to estimate the value for the denominator of the recall ratio.

1. *Prepared answer sets.* Prior to any searching, answer sets are prepared for a number of queries to be searched in the experimental data set. The known relevant documents may then be 'planted' in the sample collection. The queries are then processed through the system to obtain retrievals which are then compared with each known relevant set. As a result, one tests the system's ability to retrieve planted relevant documents.

     A second variation is also possible. Document sets are selected from the file. These are examined by a subject expert who formulates a query for each of the known document sets. Although these synthetic requests may be used in small experimental databases, this is impractical for experimentation on operating retrieval systems.

2. *Pooled relevant retrieved sets.* Real requests are collected and each is searched by a searcher. The result for each search is evaluated and recorded. Then each query is searched again by parallel searches. The search may be submitted to a number of other experienced searchers. Each query is searched again by the group of experienced searchers. Their search results are pooled. The pooled set of retrieved documents is evaluated again. This group of pooled relevant retrieved documents for each query is considered the total relevant set and is used to compute the recall ratio for the query. The parallel searches may be searches done at another search system, or they may be derived from other information sources.

3. *Cited references as relevant sets.* A third scheme succeeds in bypassing the process of subjective relevance assessment and the arbitrary establishment of a total relevance set. In many search forms, it is customary to ask the patron for one or more publications that are representative of the topic of the search. Since cited documents are assumed to be relevant to the citing document, this provides a set of ready-made known relevant documents for the query in retrieval experimentation.

Kantor (1976) suggests that the concept of availability can be operationalized in empirical studies by determining the probability of success in finding the desired document at the time of the search. Data to be collected include the total number of demands or inquiries (W), and the number of failures due to each of the dissatisfaction categories:

DA = dissatisfaction due to the books never having been acquired

DC = dissatisfaction due to the books having been in circulation

DL = dissatisfaction due to the books having been misshelved, lost, etc.

DU = dissatisfaction due to user's error.

Using Kantor's branching diagram in Figure 11.3 (see page 234), the number of failures due to DA, DC, DL, and DU is determined by data collected in libraries. Consequently, of 100 books sought, the probability of finding the desired document in the library promptly is computed as follows.

Assuming that $W = 100$, i.e., there is a total of 100 inquiries used in the study,

- the probability of user satisfaction is 90/100 percent, if, ten of the books were never acquired

- the probability of user satisfaction is 85/90 percent if, of the books acquired, five were out in circulation

- the probability of user satisfaction is 70/85 percent, if, of the books acquired and not in circulation, 15 were misshelved

- the probability of user satisfaction is 60/70 percent, if, of the books acquired, not in circulation, and not misshelved, ten were not found by users.

As shown in Figure 11.3, the probability of user satisfaction in spite of all these sources of failure is the product of all of the probabilities. The probability of actually finding the item promptly at the time it is sought is indicated by PS:

PS = PA x PC x PL x PU

= 90/100 x 85/90 x 70/85 x 60/70

= 60%

The reader is referred to Kantor's book *Objective Performance Measures for Academic and Research Libraries* for further details on methods of availability analysis (Kantor, 1984). Procedures for measures such as "document exposure time" for availability and "access delay time" in interlibrary loan service for accessibility are also provided in his book.

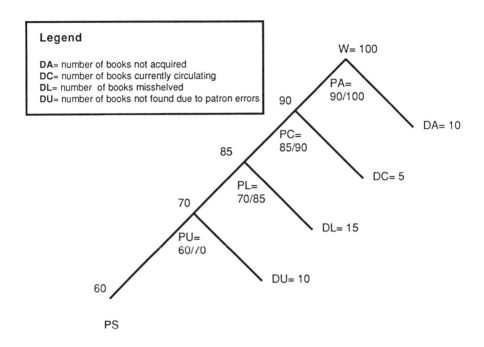

Legend

DA= number of books not acquired
DC= number of books currently circulating
DL= number of books misshelved
DU= number of books not found due to patron errors

W= 100

PA=
90/100

DA= 10

PC=
85/90

DC= 5

PL=
70/85

DL= 15

PU=
60//0

DU= 10

PS

$$PS = PA \times PC \times PL \times PU$$
$$= 90/100 \times 85/90 \times 70/85 \times 60/70$$
$$= 60\%$$

Fig. 11.3. Kantor's branching diagram for availability analysis.

MEASURING INSTRUMENTS

In social research, the measuring instrument often refers to the questionnaire used in surveys, the interviewing schedule, the personality and psychological tests used, or other types of measuring devices. In retrieval experimentations, many of these measuring instruments are also used. As in other measuring instruments, there are limitations. The range of experimental errors is greater than those found in empirical scientific studies conducted in the controlled conditions of a laboratory. Moreover, the measuring units of weight and length have greater precision as compared with measures that depend on expressed opinion or feedback based on experience.

Not all measuring instruments used in retrieval experimentations are dependent on opinion and subjective interpretation. Data from observations are also used in retrieval studies. In collecting unobtrusive data such as those from documentary sources, the measuring instrument is the simple recording of observable characteristics in publication, citations, and other records. These measures can be more reliable. Yet, whether this documentary evidence is a faithful indicator of "influence," "use," "worth," and "utility," which are the criteria sought, should be carefully examined.

In summary, all measurements are imperfect. The true score exists only in theory. Deviations always exist between the observed scores and the corresponding true scores. The difference between them is the deviation caused by errors of measurement, the chosen measure, and the nature of the measuring instrument. All measuring instruments produce some errors. The researcher attempts to minimize the differences by using the most appropriate instrument and measure, and by consistent and careful measuring. However, errors are unavoidable and normally there is an accepted range of experimental errors contributed by such deviations found between the true and measured scores in each field of study. For the physical sciences, the margin of error may be minimal when compared with that found in social science research. The accuracy of each instrument is, nevertheless, of prime importance. The accuracy of measurement depends on the measuring instrument as well as on how the measuring unit is defined.

METHODS OF MEASUREMENT

It subsequently follows that the ability to quantify evaluation criteria is dependent on the ability to formulate an operational procedure designed to assign symbols or numbers to the empirical properties to be measured. Measurement is the procedure by which numerals, numbers, or other symbols are assigned to empirical properties according to a set of predetermined rules. A variable is an empirical property which can take on two or more values. Measurement is defined by the presence of numerals, assignments, and rules. Numerals are symbols used to label objects and indicate properties. For example, in the calculation of a Grade Point Average, 4 is commonly used to indicate excellent performance by students; 3 is an indication of good work; 2 of average performance; and 1 of below average work. These four numerals act as labels. Although they have relative values, they do not possess the quality of a true quantitative ratio scale.

When numerals are given quantitative meaning, they become numbers, amenable to mathematical and statistical manipulations for more precise descriptions. For example, the salary level of librarians may be labeled by the actual dollar amount received annually by each librarian. Salaries may be represented by actual dollar figures, but the types of libraries in which they work may only be indicated by labels such as A for public libraries, B for school libraries, and so on. The quality of measurement is greatly enhanced if assignments are consistently applied to map numerals onto objects, events, or variables. Measurement is also defined by explicit rules that explicate the way in which numerals or numbers are to be assigned to objects or events. A rule might state: "Assign the numerals 1 through 5 to the level of satisfaction according to the user's perception of reference service received during the seven days prior to the receipt of the questionnaire. If the user is not at all satisfied, let 1 be assigned; if the user is well satisfied, let 5 be assigned."

Finally, an evaluation study differs from all other kinds of research only in its special purpose. It aims to evaluate the impact and/or the efficacy of a system, or a system component. Thus, good research design is assumed. Any scientific inquiry must be planned according to two basic considerations. First, one must specify precisely what it is one wants to find out. Second, one must determine the best way to accomplish this goal. The first consideration is crucial to the success of the study in that, in the clear articulation of the purpose of the research, one is formulating a workable hypothesis. Furthermore, a carefully worked out study purpose often implies what types of data to be collected and how they are to be gathered as well as methods of analysis.

Ultimately evaluation studies, as in other scientific studies, involve making some kind of observations and interpreting what has been observed. However, depending on the research purpose, the planned study could be exploratory, descriptive, explanatory, or predictive with corresponding degrees of increasing rigor in the study design. The choice of the most appropriate research design is dependent on the research aim, budgetary and time constraints, available expertise, data access, and even political expediency. The reader should consult the classic text by Campbell and Stanley (1963) for the details of experimental designs.

Evaluation studies in the field of information retrieval have been criticized for the lack of rigor. This is due in part to the difficulties inherent in any studies that are dependent on evaluation criteria based primarily on subjective assessment. Nevertheless, there is a long history of evaluation experiments in which much has been learned about evaluation methods, performance measures, measurement, measuring units, and the identification of the notion of relevance as the true if not implicit performance criterion for all document retrieval systems. The following section presents some of the accomplishments in evaluation research in the field of library information science.

SELECTED RESEARCH RESULTS

There is a large body of literature on evaluation and testing of information retrieval systems. The reader should consult review articles that appear regularly in the *Annual Review of Information Science and Technology.* Two recent texts, Sparck Jones' *Information Retrieval Experiments* (1981) and Vickery and Vickery's *Information Science in Theory and Practice* (1987) contain thorough reviews of evaluative experimentations in information retrieval. This chapter concludes with some highlights of major evaluation efforts.

Historically, the first major evaluation and testing effort was conducted by Cyril Cleverdon in two series of experiments, known as Cranfield I and II. The first series was performed in 1957 and reported in 1962. The objective of Cranfield I was on the comparison of post-coordinated indexing with more traditional indexing languages using 18,000 documents and 1,200 search topics. Surprisingly, specificity of the indexing vocabulary and the degree of exhaustivity of indexing were much more significant than the differences in the indexing languages used. Human factors were found to exert a major influence on retrieval. For the first time, recall and precision were used consistently throughout, and their inverse relationship was clearly shown. As more carefully controlled tests on the components of indexing languages were performed in the second group of experiments, uncontrolled vocabularies were found to produce better retrieval results. This landmark work laid the foundation for subsequent evaluations and experimentations. Its impact on research methodology in information retrieval is substantial.

Elaborately controlled retrieval experiments were performed at the Comparative Systems Laboratory at Case Western Reserve University (Saracevic, 1971). Different indexing procedures, vocabularies, and search strategies were tested. Again, under equal conditions, the performance of most indexing languages was found to be similar.

The SMART system at Cornell University is the best-known experimental automated retrieval system in existence (Salton and McGill, 1983). For twenty years, Salton performed extensive experimentation on automatic indexing with various term weighting schemes, search strategies with different clustered techniques, automated query formulation based on relevance feedback, and more recently extended Boolean searches. Elaborate semantic and syntactic analyses were employed. In addition to numerous articles and reports, Salton reported his findings and insights in several books (Salton, 1971; 1975; Salton and McGill, 1983). Among his findings was the fact that retrieval and information processing using natural language was enormously complex. Without a deep understanding of linguistic theories, realistic semantic maps and syntactic structures could not be implemented for effective retrieval. At this stage, simpler indexing methods produced slightly better results. His results also showed dramatically the application and improved results of the probabilistic approach to retrieval. In cluster files, documents were grouped according to their content similarity. Without searching the entire file, each incoming query was made to first check the centroid or the most representative member of a document group before checking the other group members. Although the SMART project has had little effect on operating retrieval systems, it has provided a sound theoretical framework for examining the retrieval process.

Lancaster (1969) was responsible for the first large-scale study on the effectiveness of an operating system, MEDLARS. Subsequently, several other studies on online biomedical retrieval systems were conducted (Lancaster, 1977). In particular, the experience on MEDLINE has been valuable. Lancaster's writings offer many practical considerations on conducting evaluation studies. He has added novelty as another important performance criterion in retrieval. The novelty ratio is the number of relevant items in the retrieved list not previously known to the requestor. Evaluation studies were treated in a more technical level in Van Rijsbergen's 1979 book.

Much knowledge has been gained in the conduct of experimentation, testing, and evaluation since the late 1950s when information professionals became aware of the need for the application of the scientific method to serious experimentation. Researchers have been confronted with issues of control, experimental design, variables, sampling, and other research questions.

In the last decade, retrieval evaluation has centered upon online systems. The first large-scale impact study of online search services was performed by Wanger and her team (Wanger, Cuadra, and Fishburn, 1976). Two reviews on the research of online systems by Fenichel (1981) and Bellardo (1981) are recommended for further reading. One notes that the process of searching, attributes associated with the searcher, the degree of elaboration of the query, different search systems, the use of search features, and the effect of cost are among the many variables investigated and tested.

Major findings of several decades of evaluation and testing activities are summarized below.

There is confirmation from every study that the recall remains in the medium range. That is, no matter what search keys or searchers are employed, the retrieval results in terms of recall and precision are bound to lie within the range of 40 to 60 percent. Although not definitively established, the inverse relationship between recall and precision is commonly noted. In other words, higher recall is associated with lower precision and vice versa.

Findings also show the overall effects of a number of variables. Simple indexing schemes and natural language are shown to be as good as elaborately structured and controlled vocabularies. Exhaustive indexing (which is roughly translated into more terms used in indexing) tends to produce more effective, narrower searches. Specificity of the indexing vocabulary also provides more retrieval precision. In recent years, research has moved away from focusing on the input characteristics of the system to those of the searcher. There is substantial evidence that the searcher may be the major variable in any retrieval transaction. Since there is a minimal overlap of items among the sets retrieved by different searchers when searching the identical query, it is unlikely that any single searcher is able to produce the maximum recall.

Along a different track, several investigators have independently examined the retrieval resulting from searching with data elements from different fields of the record. In searching the same topic by using one or more of the following search keys, namely, title words, abstract words, descriptors, and/or text words in the full text, few common items were found among the different retrieved sets (Katzer, McGill, Tessier, Frakes, and DasGupta, 1982). The comparison of term searching and citation searching of the identical topic has also produced little overlap among the two equivalent search results (McCain, 1989; Pao and Worthen, 1989). The variations introduced by different searchers and different search keys have major implications for retrieval.

Since online data searching has become widely available, much attention has centered on the performance of online systems. The professional searcher has often been the object of study, specifically with regard to his or her search success as related to training, experience, personality traits, and other factors. Although no single characteristic has been detected to be associated strongly with performance, query analysis and elaboration have been found to vary widely with individual searcher.

Direct searching of bibliographic information without the help of professional searchers has been seen to promote literature use. Many biomedical researchers and scientists have been introduced to online searching using user-cordial interfaces and those search softwares designed for the professional searcher. Thus, end-user searching for the occasional searcher has been studied with a view to improve system design, to modify easy-to-use online help features, and to identify frequently used literature subsets. Finally, the characterization of information requests appears to exert more weight on retrieval than document indexing efforts. In particular, the area of question analysis has been identified as a major source of problems in poor performance.

Research has amassed considerable empirical data. As yet, the complexity of information retrieval systems has eluded our understanding. The nature of the information user is little understood. The attempt to incorporate the element of "informativeness" which is individualistic with topicality in relevant retrieval is in its infancy (Boyce, 1982). The profession is only at the beginning in the process of explaining the nature of the way users express their information requirements, the retrieval transaction, or the system's behaviors. It is interesting to note that since the early works of Cleverdon, the profession has come full circle to the acknowledgment and rediscovery of the complexity of the information user as an individual.

REFERENCES

Bellardo, T. 1981. "Scientific Research in Online Retrieval: A Critical Review." *Library Research*, 3(3):187-214.

Boyce, B.R. 1982. "Beyond Topicality: A Two Stage View of Relevance and the Retrieval Process." *Information Processing and Management*, 18(3): 105-109.

Campbell, D.T., and J.C. Stanley. 1963. *Experimental and Quasi-Experimental Designs for Research*. Chicago: Rand McNally College Publishing Co.

Cooper, W.S. 1968. "Expected Search Length: A Single Measure of Retrieval Effectiveness Based on the Weak Ordering Action of Retrieval Systems." *American Documentation*, 19(1):30-41.

Cooper, W.S. 1973a. "On Selecting a Measure of Retrieval Effectiveness. Part I." *Journal of the American Society for Information Science*, 24(2):87-100.

Cooper, W.S. 1973b. "On Selecting a Measure of Retrieval Effectiveness: Part II. Implementation of the Philosophy." *Journal of the American Society for Information Science*, 24(6):413-421.

Fenichel, C.H. 1980-81. "The Process of Searching Online Bibliographic Databases: A Review of Research." *Library Research*, 2(2):107-127.

Hamburg, M., R.C. Clelland, M.R.W. Bommer, L.E. Ramist, and R.M. Whitfield. 1974. *Library Planning and Decision-making Systems*. Cambridge, Massachusetts: MIT Press.

Kantor, P.B. 1976. "Availability Analysis." *Journal of the American Society for Information Science*, 27(5):311-319.

Kantor, P.B. 1982. "Evaluation of and Feedback in Information Storage and Retrieval Systems." *Annual Review of Information Science and Technology*, edited by Martha E. Williams. Vol. 17, 99-120. White Plains, New York: American Society for Information Science.

Kantor, P.B. 1984. *Objective Performance Measures for Academic and Research Libraries*. Washington, D.C.: Association of Research Libraries.

Katzer, J., M.J. McGill, J.A. Tessier, W. Frakes, and P. DasGupta. 1982. "A Study of the Overlap Among Document Representation." *Information Technology: Research and Development*, 1(4):261-274.

King, D.W., and E.C. Bryant. 1971. *The Evaluation of Information Services and Products.* Washington, D.C.: Information Resources Press.

Lancaster, F.W. 1969. "MEDLARS: Report on the Evaluation of Its Operating Efficiency." *American Documentation*, 20(2):119-142.

Lancaster, F.W. 1977. *The Measurement and Evaluation of Library Services.* Washington, D.C.: Information Resources Press.

McCain, K.W. 1989. "Descriptor and Citation Retrieval in the Medical Behavioral Sciences Literature: Retrieval Overlaps and Novelty Distribution." *Journal of the American Society for Information Science.* In press.

Pao, M.L., and D.B. Worthen. 1989. "Retrieval Effectiveness by Semantic and Citation Searching." *Journal of American Society for Information Science.* In press.

Salton, G., ed. 1971. *The SMART Retrieval System: Experiments in Automatic Document Processing.* Englewood Cliffs, New Jersey: Prentice Hall.

Salton, G. 1975. *Dynamic Information and Library Processing.* Englewood Cliffs, New Jersey: Prentice Hall.

Salton, G., and M.J. McGill. 1983. *Introduction to Modern Information Retrieval.* New York: McGraw-Hill.

Saracevic, T. 1971. "Selected Results from an Inquiry into Testing of Information Retrieval Systems." *Journal of the American Society for Information Science*, 22(2):126-139.

Sparck Jones, K., ed. 1981. *Information Retrieval Experiment.* London: Butterworths.

UNESCO. United Nations Educational, Scientific and Cultural Organization. 1978. *Guidelines for the Evaluation of Information Systems and Services.* Paris: Unesco.

Van Rijsbergen, C.J. 1979. *Information Retrieval.* 2nd edition. London: Butterworths.

Vickery, B.C., and A. Vickery. 1987. *Information Science in Theory and Practice.* London: Butterworths.

Wanger, J., C.A. Cuadra, and M. Fishburn. 1976. "Impact of On-line Retrieval Services: A Survey of Users, 1974-1975." Santa Monica, California: Systems Development Corporation.

White, G.T. 1977. "Quantitative Measures of Library Effectiveness." *Journal of Academic Librarianship*, 3(3):128-136.

Part IV
NEW DIRECTIONS
FOR
INFORMATION SYSTEMS

12

Toward Intelligent
Information Retrieval

Information retrieval research has made impressive gains. Library and information science researchers have done pioneering work in improving the content representation of documents and queries. Especially in the study of document representation with controlled languages, natural languages, automatic indexing, and content extraction, there is no equal. Years of experience have been accumulated from extensive and elaborate experimentations in alternative retrieval strategies which incorporate the elements of uncertainty and partial match instead of a strictly relevant or not-relevant outcome. A theoretical foundation has been established based on probabilistic principles. Another significant contribution of information retrieval research has been in the investigation of term relationship, document/term relationship, document/document relationship, and author relationship, most of which are generated from the analysis of textual materials. Library information science also has a long history in evaluation and testing of systems and systems components.

In the arena of operational systems, information retrieval activities have been fueled by the recent incredible advances in computing, telecommunication, laser, and other emerging technologies. Information retrieval researchers pioneered in the design and development of computer-based retrieval systems. Suddenly, the question is no longer whether computers are affordable, but how they can be deployed effectively in the retrieval process. Today, information searching is linked with online searching. In addition to the unknown thousands of private databases, there are commercial databases on every conceivable topic. The number of searches performed has also grown accordingly.

Yet, in spite of the optimism of these computer-aided searching devices, subject retrieval on any database in whatever media is still based on keyword indexing and searching is still conducted on the principle of Boolean logic. In other words, the content representation of documents and the basic file structure have not changed since the days of manual systems. It is discouraging to speculate that even with the help of today's powerful technologies, the same low level of retrieval performance is achieved, but at a faster speed. Aside from the inadequacy of the internal structure of operational retrieval systems, there is increasing uncertainty concerning the best way to elicit accurate queries from the inquirer. The lack of knowledge on how information needs are expressed hinders substantive progress in a better match of the request with relevant documents. To add to this picture, wide variability has been shown on the retrieval results of professional searchers as well as from those of the actual users of information. In other words, retrieval reliability is still elusive.

Fortunately, recent literature indicates new research directions in addressing these persistent problems of mediocre retrieval. In the forefront are efforts to utilize new techniques to design and develop "intelligent" information systems. Increasingly interest is shown in the study of human information processing as it relates to how problems are solved, how one understands and makes use of information, how people evaluate information, and how people learn and apply knowledge. If these issues sound similar to those of concern to researchers in artificial intelligence (AI), they are. Basic problems in cognition and learning are intimately linked with how questions are formulated in the human mind, how information problems are characterized by natural language, and how strategies evolve in the process of information searching. These questions are central to the works of AI workers, cognitive scientists, designers of question-answering systems, and information scientists. Currently since AI researchers have produced promising results in many application areas, there is great optimism in applying similar techniques in information retrieval. In particular, a number of prototypical expert systems performing various document retrieval functions have been under development. They vary greatly in terms of subject scope and in the complexity of functions performed. The potential applications of AI research in a wide range of information retrieval functions could vastly alter the present way of life with immense economic, social, and even political implications. Several relevant items are listed in the bibliography. In particular, the reader is directed to the two special issues of volume 23 of *Information Processing and Management* (Borko, 1987b and Croft, 1987). The subject has also been reviewed by Linda Smith in *Annual Review of Information Science and Technology* (1987). A description and a brief survey article by Vickery and Brooks (1987a) is also recommended.

ARTIFICIAL INTELLIGENCE

AI is a new and complex subject area. Even among the experts, there is no agreement on what AI is and on what its subfields are. However, the object of AI research is clear. It is to discover the thought processes that are associated with intelligent behaviors, and to find ways to program the computer to perform functions which normally require human intelligence. In a highly readable book for the nonspecialist, Roger C. Schank (1984), one of the foremost AI researchers, states that there are two approaches taken in artificial intelligence research – product-directed and theory-directed. Robotics and expert systems are derived from the product-directed approach to AI. These products are designed to respond to certain demands such as providing robots for the disabled to perform a host of chores around the house and expert systems to help an individual in determining if he or she qualifies for a bank loan. The builders of expert systems try to capture a body of expert knowledge and to reduce the reasoning needed to a set of if/then rules in a series of computer programs. For example, in using a medical diagnostic program, an individual is guided through its chain of rules until it reaches a tentative differential diagnosis. There is an explosion of expert systems developed for medicine, geology, engineering, manufacturing, financial services, diagnostical servicing of machinery, and many other areas. These represent incredible technological advancements.

On the other hand, theory-directed AI research is concerned with how knowledge is represented in human mind, how humans process thoughts, what people know, how they use what they know, and how they learn what they know. To build an expert system with any degree of complexity, the system designer should also know in detail what goes on in the mind of the human counterpart. That is, he or she must understand how people think and reason in order to perform intelligently. Obviously, AI probes the age-old problems of the philosophy of mind. For example, in formulating a theory of learning, the theory-directed researcher constructs computer models to represent these mental processes. The accuracy of the theory is then tested by computer programs. Since computer programs can only execute exactly according to the instructions given, these theories must be rigorous and must incorporate everything involved in any specific range of human tasks. The computer serves a valuable function in AI research in that nothing can be assumed. As a result, getting the computer to understand language, to learn from experience, to associate meanings to symbols, and to establish linkages among relevant concepts based on what has been input sheds light on how humans perform these tasks. Conversely, learning more about human information processing also helps AI researchers in the study of the mind. Any incremental knowledge gained represents scientific advancement. To perform like an intelligent being, the computer must have the ability to understand language. Therefore, work on how a person processes natural language is important for AI and for information retrieval. AI is closely aligned with cognitive science, psychology, linguistics, and philosophy.

EXPERT SYSTEMS

Since expert systems have received massive publicity, many unfortunately associate artificial intelligence with the building of intelligent computer systems only. An expert system is a complex program that emulates the problem-solving process of human experts. It is a knowledge-base system consisting of two essential components: (1) an appropriate knowledge base for the subject domain that incorporates rules of applications and (2) an inference engine that provides the problem-solving mechanism. The knowledge base is built by extracting the knowledge of one or more human experts and representing it in the computer. The knowledge engineer, a skilled programmer, works with the expert to translate what the expert knows and how he or she reasons and solves problems into a form usable by the computer. This process is known as knowledge engineering. It is found that experts, such as professional online searchers, solve problems in their field without following any precise procedure. Instead, they use *heuristics* or *rules of thumb*. This heuristic approach works as a reliable guide to action, even though one cannot prove in a rigorous way that it must work. Usually an expert system captures this heuristic knowledge-base approach to problem-solving in a narrowly defined subject domain.

To enable the communication between the expert system and the user, three other components are usually present. First, an intelligent user interface allows for interaction. It extracts relevant information from the inquirer and clarifies input data. Secondly, an explanatory module presents the justification for the conclusion reached by the expert system. It allows the user to trace the reasoning or rules by which the decision was made. Finally, an optional help module facilitates the use of the system. An expert system is seldom intended as a substitute for a human expert. Rather, it serves as an advisor on the subject, drawing upon the knowledge in the knowledge base with the incorporated heuristics. Two classic examples are MYCIN, an expert system for diagnosis and therapy in infectious blood diseases and INTERNIST, a diagnostic expert system for internal medicine.

Some of the common characteristics of today's expert systems are as follows. First, in making decisions in a chosen domain, many possible alternatives had to be examined. For example, in a diagnostic system, there are many factors to be considered by the physician. Secondly, most of the problems in the subject area do not have a simple yes or no answer. In the medical diagnostic situation, rendering a realistic conclusion, one states with a degree of likelihood rather than with a definitive answer. Thirdly, it follows that expert systems express with such uncertainty because the data on which these conclusions are based are often incomplete, subjective, or even inconsistent. Fourthly, expert systems deal with concepts expressed by language rather than by exact numeric values. Lastly, the type of knowledge in expert systems is valuable in that such knowledge could be useful for others who do not have ready access to experts.

One can easily extrapolate from the above that the process of information seeking could also be emulated by an expert system. The current frontier in the information retrieval community is to design expert systems which could emulate some aspects of information seeking. The approach followed by professional searchers are heuristic and there is a relative defined body of professional knowledge. For example, the computer could be effectively used in lieu of a professional searcher to prod the user for useful ideas in a question negotiation session in which the information inquirer may interact with an intelligent computer system. It could also suggest useful terms during search formulation to the searcher. The application of expert systems techniques to information retrieval systems is very new. Most projects are at the experimental stage. Some have completed prototypes. Three areas of applications in document retrieval could be identified – cataloging, reference work, and search intermediary. Examples of expert systems in each of these areas are presented below.

EXPERT SYSTEMS IN INFORMATION RETRIEVAL

Borko (1987a, p.82) wrote that since "classification, after all, is a basic activity in our field, and if it is possible for an ES (expert system) to classify and diagnose medical diseases, then possibly an ES could be designed to classify and catalog library materials." At the University of California at Los Angeles, he is developing a prototype expert system, MAPPER, to catalog maps. The system is based strictly on the AACR2 cataloging rules and the MARC map format with some consultation from map catalogers. Four interrelated sets of programs, or modules, are planned for MAPPER: A User Interface module provides the user with menu-driven instructions to elicit relevant information about the map to be cataloged. It is designed to be used by persons with different levels of computer and/or cataloging expertise. A Knowledge Base module contains the set of decision rules relevant for map cataloging. They are in the IF/THEN format in that when the condition in the IF clause is satisfied, the conclusion in the THEN clause is reached. These rules are extracted from the AACR2 rules. The Inference module takes the information given by the cataloger and applies and selects the appropriate rules from the knowledge base in order to come up with the main cataloging entry. It also checks if the input data is adequate to satisfy the condition in the IF clause. If not, the system asks for additional information. The Explain module allows the cataloger to understand why particular rules are chosen and to follow the reasoning used for such choices. The main objective of this module is to impart confidence in the use of the system. It also allows the user to suggest other alternative rules and override the system's choice. MAPPER is implemented on an IBM PC/AT.

An ambitious system is the interactive knowledge-base system, Indexing AID Project, which has been developed as a prototype at the National Library of Medicine. AI techniques are utilized as an aid to provide improved quality and consistency in indexing biomedical journal literature at the library (Humphrey and Miller, 1987). This system is intended for use by trained MEDLINE indexers.

An example of an expert system in reference work is PLEXUS, an intelligent referral system on the subject of gardening, which is under development at the University of London (Vickery and Brooks, 1987b). This system has an intelligent interface probing and directing the user to the most likely sources of information. In answer to a query, the system refers to the most likely persons, books, places, institutions, or societies that may help to solve the specific gardening problem. This is an ambitious project. Although it appears that limiting the subject to gardening entails a circumscribed domain, the types of knowledge required are complex. A major accomplishment is the way PLEXUS perform semantic processing. An elaborate scheme has been developed to represent knowledge. In order for PLEXUS to "understand" queries in natural language, a set of semantic categories are established with hierarchical subcategories. These categories represent the relevant concepts in this subject domain. A dictionary is maintained to screen user input, to classify terms, to normalize, and to associate terms with semantic categories. Capabilities are built in to sort out synonyms and homographs. Classes of terms are linked. A complex network is set up. A number of semantic contexts are also created for each term, even though an exhaustive enumeration is impossible. In summary, PLEXUS has a rich knowledge base with a sophisticated semantic network. Another interesting reference expert system not included in the 1987 volume of *Information Processing and Management* is the ANSWERMAN developed at the National Agricultural Library (Waters, 1986). It helps the patron to identify likely reference books to answer questions in agriculture.

The third type of expert systems is in the development of intelligent search interfaces. A wide variety of these systems exists. They range from the commercially available gateway softwares, such as PRO-CITE and SCI-MATE to the more elaborate CONIT which is described below. Not one of them qualifies as truly *intelligent*. Online searching involves a complex of mental processes and tasks. Several attempt to contain their systems to specific subsets of retrieval strategies. CONIT (COnnected Network for Information Transfer) is an automated search intermediary. It has been developed by Marcus at MIT over a number of years (Marcus and Reintjes, 1981a, 1981b). At the early stage of the system's development, it can automatically execute logon procedures for different search systems. Marcus then developed capabilities for database selection for any given topic and a host of other online suggestions (Marcus, 1983). Although it is not a true expert searcher, the work has provided a deeper understanding of the complexities of the retrieval process.

As AI research enters its next phase, several problem areas present themselves. In the AI community at large, there is increasing awareness of the difficulties in capturing the knowledge and experience of human experts. The process of knowledge acquisition is difficult, elusive, and expensive. In the keynote address at MEDINFO 86, the Fifth Conference on Medical Informatics, Edward A. Feigenbaum of Stanford University, a renowned AI researcher, predicted that knowledge acquisition and knowledge representation would be the important areas on the next agenda for AI research. He noted that recent years of experimental work have demonstrated that expert systems can be successfully built. At the moment, it is known that it is not the inference engine, but the knowledge base which controls the quality and power of the expert system. He termed it the Knowledge Principle. He put it simply: "If a program is to perform well, it must know a great deal about the 'world' in which it operates. In the absence of knowledge, reasoning won't help." (Feigenbaum, 1986). He anticipated that it will be commonplace for knowledge systems to interact with users in actual natural language in voice in addition to keyboard input, since the nature of such characteristics that would entice the user in using these system is well understood. He asserted that the real challenge lies in understanding how humans acquire and structure information so that the process of knowledge acquisition can be improved to the point of building a realistic knowledge base emulating that of a real expert. The representation and structure of knowledge have been the central concerns of information retrieval researchers. They found that representing and structuring information must necessarily lead to the important related issue of the development of dynamic semantic networks with linkages to related concepts and terms. Since information retrieval research has had considerable experience in the area of natural language processing, the complex research areas of knowledge base and semantic net are of interest to information scientists and researchers in expert systems.

Evaluation is another area of concern. Although systems evaluation has been addressed by researchers, the issues have not been resolved. The main question is what constitutes the standard to which performance of the expert system is to be compared. In other words, can there be a norm for expert behaviors?

At the basic level in the field of library information science, information scientists are currently grappling with the issues surrounding the information consumer as an individual with individualistic characteristics. Knowledge from psychology and cognitive sciences is liberally used in the search for better understanding of how queries are formulated and what takes place in the human mind during a question negotiation session. At the practical level, manageable problems are being solved. An example is the study of features which could contribute toward user friendliness of interacting with online systems so that online systems can be better designed and configured.

However, so far expert systems have been domain-specific. Some have noted that searching of information is not limited to any topic and to any contextual base. Design problems are substantial since application in this area is new. Even if feasible, others speculate that the introduction of AI techniques on a non-domain-limited basis is likely to be a long-term goal since the market is not yet ready to afford the significant overhead required for additional large and complicated processing systems. Still others contend that it may not be possible to build expert search systems. In online searching, strong evidences have shown that different search sets result from different expert searchers. In the past, expert systems have been built on areas in which human experts are actually found. If professional searchers could not agree on the search strategy of any given search, it might be difficult to capture expert knowledge.

For the time being, some interim solutions have been offered to optimize the present operational retrieval systems. Several systems have been developed with some "intelligent" characteristics to aid the searcher/user of the online search system. CITE/NLM (Doszkocs, 1983) is the only operational system with advanced features to aid the searcher. It produces an online list of terms based on stemming of the search term entered by the user and on other syntactical analysis so that other useful search terms are displayed. The search may then be recycled to produce better results. PaperChase contains a subset of frequently consulted journal citations with a user-cordial interface (Horowitz and Bleich, 1981). A number of helpful features are incorporated to aid the user in executing a search. The SIRE retrieval system displays a list of citations ranked by probable relevance (Noreault, Koll, and McGill, 1977; Koll, Noreault, and McGill, 1984). CONIT (COnnected Network for Information Transfer system), an automated search intermediary, is able to perform a host of useful online tasks (Marcus and Reintjes, 1981a; 1981b). Pao (1987) is developing a procedure to combine the retrieval from term searching and citation searching to improve recall and precision. Add-on devices to optimize existing search features can serve to improve retrieval results of today's systems.

Finally, in the far side of Feigenbaum's dream, his vision of information retrieval could take the form of his "Library of the Future." In his words (1986, p.xlv),

> Now imagine the library as an active, intelligent "knowledge-server." It stores the knowledge of the disciplines in complex knowledge structures (perhaps in a formalism yet to be invented). It can reason with this knowledge to satisfy the needs of its users. These needs are expressed naturally, with fluid discourse. The system can, of course, retrieve and exhibit (the electronic textbook). It can collect relevant information; it can summarize; it can pursue relationships.
>
> It acts as a consultant on specific problems, offering advice on particular solutions, justifying those solutions with citations or with a fabric of general reasoning. If the user can suggest a solution or a hypothesis, it can check this, even suggest extensions. Or it can critique the user viewpoint, with a detailed rationale of its agreement or disagreement.

In conclusion, the field of information retrieval remains a fertile ground for both basic and applied research.

REFERENCES

Borko, H. 1987a. "Getting Started in Library Expert System Research." *Information Processing and Management*, 23(2):81-87.

Borko, H., ed. 1987b. "Expert Systems and Library Information Science." *Information Processing and Management*, 23(2):75-154.

Croft, B.C. 1987. "Artificial Intelligence and Information Retrieval." *Information Processing and Management*, 23(4):249-382.

Doszkocs, T.E. 1983. "CITE/NLM: Natural Language Searching in an Online Catalog." *Information Technology and Libraries*, 2(4):364-380.

Feigenbaum, E.A. 1986. "Autoknowledge: From File Servers to Knowledge Servers." *MEDINFO 86: Proceedings of the Fifth Conference on Medical Informatics*, xliii-xlvi. (Washington, D.C., October 26-30, 1986). Amsterdam: North-Holland.

Horowitz, G.L., and H.L. Bleich. 1981. "PaperChase: A Computer Program to Search the Medical Literature." *New England Journal of Medicine*, 305(16): 924-930.

Humphrey, S.M., and N.E. Miller. 1987. "Knowledge-Based Indexing of the Medical Literature: The Indexing AID Project." *Journal of the American Society for Information Science*, 38(3):184-196.

Koll, M.B., T. Noreault, and M.J. McGill. 1984. "Enhanced Retrieval Techniques on a Microcomputer." *Proceedings of the 5th National Online Meeting*, 165-170. Medford, New Jersey: Learned Information, Inc.

Marcus, R.S. 1983. "An Experimental Comparison of the Effectiveness of Computers and Humans as Search Intermediaries." *Journal of the American Society for Information Science*, 34(6):381-404.

Marcus, R.S., and J.F. Reintjes. 1981a. "A Translating Computer Interface for End-user Operation of Heterogeneous Retrieval Systems. I. Design." *Journal of the American Society for Information Science*, 32(4):287-303.

Marcus, R.S., and J.F. Reintjes. 1981b. "A Translating Computer Interface for End-user Operation of Heterogeneous Retrieval Systems. II. Evaluation." *Journal of the American Society for Information Science*, 32(4):304-317.

Noreault, T., M. Koll, and M.J. McGill. 1977. "Automatic Ranked Output from Boolean Searches in SIRE." *Journal of the American Society for Information Science*, 28(6):333-339.

Pao, M.L. 1987. "Developing a Front-End Integrating Keyword and Citation Retrieval." *Proceeding of the 8th National Online Meeting*, 379-386. Medford, New Jersey: Learned Information, Inc.

Schank, R.C. 1984. *The Cognitive Computer: On Language, Learning, and Artificial Intelligence.* Reading, Massachusetts: Addison-Wesley Publishing Company, Inc.

Smith, L.C. 1987. "Artificial Intelligence and Information Retrieval." *Annual Review of Information Science and Technology,* edited by Martha E. Williams. Vol. 22, 41-78. White Plains, New York: American Society for Information Science.

Vickery, A., and H. Brooks. 1987a. "Expert Systems and Their Applications in LIS." *Online Review,* 11(3):149-165.

Vickery, A., and H. Brooks. 1987b. "PLEXUS — The Expert System for Referral." *Information Processing and Management,* 23(2):99-117.

Vickery, A., H. Brooks, and B. Robinson. 1987. "A Reference and Referral System Using Expert Systems Techniques." *Journal of Documentation,* 43(1):1-23.

Vickery, B.C. 1986. "Knowledge Representation: A Brief Review." *Journal of Documentation,* 42(3):145-159.

Waters, S.T. 1986. "Answerman, the Expert Information Specialist: An Expert System for Retrieval of Information from Library Reference Books." *Information Technology and Libraries,* 5(3):204-212.

Bibliography

Addis, T.R. "Expert Systems: An Evaluation in Information Retrieval." *Information Technology: Research and Development*, 1(4):301-324, 1982.

Aitchison, J., and A. Gilchrist. *Thesaurus Construction—A Practical Manual.* 2nd edition. London: Aslib, 1987.

American Library Association. *Library Effectiveness: A State of the Art: Papers from a 1980 ALA Preconference.* New York: Library Administration and Management Association/ALA, 1980.

American National Standards Institute. *American National Standard for Writing Abstracts. ANSI Z39-14-1979.* New York: American National Standards Institute, 1979.

American National Standards Institute. *Guidelines for Thesaurus: Structure, Construction & Use.* New York: American National Standards Institute, 1980.

Bates, M.J. "Idea Tactics." *Journal of the American Society for Information Science*, 30(5):280-289, 1979.

Bates, M.J. "Information Search Tactics." *Journal of the American Society for Information Science*, 30(4):205-214, 1979.

Belkin, N.J. "Information Concepts for Information Science." *Journal of Documentation*, 34(1):55-85, 1978.

Belkin, N.J., R.N. Oddy, and H.M. Brooks. "ASK for Information Retrieval: I. Background and Theory." *Journal of Documentation*, 38(2):61-71, 1982.

Belkin, N.J., R.N. Oddy, and H.M. Brooks. "ASK for Information Retrieval: II. Results of a Design Study." *Journal of Documentation*, 38(3):145-164, 1982.

Belkin, N.J., T. Seeger, and G. Wersig. "Distributed Expert Problem Treatment as a Model for Information System Analysis and Design." *Journal of Information Science*, 5(5):153-167, 1983.

253

Bellardo, T. "Scientific Research in Online Retrieval: A Critical Review." *Library Research*, 3(3):187-214, 1981.

Bellardo, T. "An Investigation of Online Searcher Traits and Their Relationship to Search Outcome." *Journal of the American Society for Information Science*, 36(4):241-250, 1985.

Bernstein, L.M., E.R. Siegel, and C.M. Goldstein. "The Hepatitis Knowledge Base: A Prototype Information Transfer System." *Annals of Internal Medicine*, 93(1 pt2):169-181, 1980.

Blair, D.C. "Indeterminacy in the Subject Access to Documents." *Information Processing and Management*, 22(3):229-242, 1986.

Blair, D.C., and M.E. Maron. "An Evaluation of Retrieval Effectiveness for a Full-Text Document-Retrieval System." *Communications of the Association for Computing Machinery*, 28(3):289-299, 1985.

Bleich, H.L., J.D. Jackson, and H.A. Rosenberg. "PaperChase: A Program to Search the Medical Literature." *MD Computing*, 2:54-59, 1985.

Bobinski, G.S., ed. "Current and Future Trends in Library and Information Science Education." *Library Trends*, 34(4):535-787, 1986.

Bookstein, A. "Relevance." *Journal of the American Society for Information Science*, 30(5):269-273, 1979.

Bookstein, A. "Fuzzy Requests: An Approach to Weighted Boolean Searches." *Journal of the American Society for Information Science*, 31(4):240-247, 1980.

Bookstein, A. "Probability and Fuzzy-Set Applications to Information Retrieval." *Annual Review of Information Science and Technology.* Edited by Martha E. Williams. Vol. 20, 117-151. White Plains, New York: Knowledge Industry Publications, Inc.

Bookstein, A., and D.R. Swanson, eds. "Operations Research: Implications for Libraries." *Library Quarterly*, 42(1):1-158, 1972.

Booth, A.D. "A 'Law' of Occurrences for Words of Low Frequency." *Information and Control*, 10(4):386-393, 1967.

Booth, A.D. "On the Geometry of Libraries." *Journal of Documentation*, 25(1): 28-40, 1969.

Borgman, C.L. "Psychological Research in Human-Computer Interaction." *Annual Review of Information Science and Technology.* Edited by Martha E. Williams. Vol. 19, 33-64. White Plains, New York: American Society for Information Science.

Borko, H. "Information Science: What Is It?" *American Documentation*, 19(1): 3-5, 1968.

Borko, H. "Trends in Library and Information Science Education." *Journal of the American Society for Information Science*, 35(3):185-193, 1984.

Borko, H. "Getting Started in Library Expert System Research." *Information Processing and Management*, 23(2):81-87, 1987.

Borko, H., ed. "Expert Systems and Library Information Science." *Information Processing and Management*, 23(2):75-154, 1987.

Borko, H., and C.L. Bernier. *Abstracting Concepts and Methods*. New York: Academic Press, 1975.

Borko, H., and C.L. Bernier. *Indexing Concepts and Methods*. New York: Academic Press, 1978.

Boyce, B.R. "Beyond Topicality: A Two Stage View of Relevance and the Retrieval Process." *Information Processing and Management*, 18(3):105-109, 1982.

Boyce, B.R., and K. Primov. "Pao's Selection Method for Quality Papers and the Subsequent Use of Medical Literature." *Journal of Medical Education*, 52(12):1001-1002, 1977.

Bradford, S.C. *Documentation*. London: Crosby Lockwood, 1948.

Branscomb, L.M. "Information: The Ultimate Frontier." *Science*, 203(4376): 143-147, 1979.

Broering, N.C. "The MiniMEDLINE SYSTEM: A Library-based End-User Search System." *Bulletin of the Medical Library Association*, 73(2):138-145, 1985.

Brookes, B.C. "Bradford's Law and the Bibliography of Science." *Nature*, 224(5223):953-956, 1969.

Campbell, D.T., and J.C. Stanley. *Experimental and Quasi-Experimental Designs for Research*. Chicago: Rand McNally College Publishing Co., 1963.

Cherry, C. *On Human Communication*. Cambridge, Massachusetts: MIT Press, 1978.

Churchman, C.W. *The Systems Approach*. New York: The Dell Publishing Co., Inc., 1968.

Cleveland, D.B., and A.D. Cleveland. *Introduction to Indexing and Abstracting*. Littleton, Colorado: Libraries Unlimited, 1983.

Cleverdon, C.W. "Design and Evaluation of Information Systems." *Annual Review of Information Science and Technology.* Edited by Carlos A. Cuadra. Vol. 6, 41-73. Chicago: Encyclopaedia Britannica, 1971.

Cleverdon, C.W. "Optimizing Convenient Online Access to Bibliographic Databases." *Information Services and Uses*, 4(1/2):37-47, 1984.

Cole, J.R., and S. Cole. "The Ortega Hypothesis." *Science*, 178(4059):368-375, 1972.

Collison, R.L. *Abstracts and Abstracting Services.* Santa Barbara, California: American Bibliographical Center-Clio Press, 1971.

Cooper, W.S. "Expected Search Length: A Single Measure of Retrieval Effectiveness Based on the Weak Ordering Action of Retrieval Systems." *American Documentation*, 19(1):30-41, 1968.

Cooper, W.S. "On Selecting a Measure of Retrieval Effectiveness. Part I." *Journal of the American Society for Information Science*, 24(2):87-100, 1973.

Cooper, W.S. "On Selecting a Measure of Retrieval Effectiveness: Part II. Implementation of the Philosophy." *Journal of the American Society for Information Science*, 24(6):413-421, 1973.

Cooper, W.S. "Exploiting the Maximum Entropy Principle to Increase Retrieval Effectiveness." *Journal of the American Society for Information Science*, 34(1):31-39, 1983.

Crane, D. "Information Needs and Uses." *Annual Review of Information Science and Technology.* Edited by Carlos A. Cuadra. Vol. 6, 3-39. Chicago: Encyclopaedia Britannica, 1971.

Crane, D. *Invisible Colleges: Diffusion of Knowledge in Scientific Communities.* Chicago: University of Chicago Press, 1972.

Crawford, S. "Informal Communication Among Scientists in Sleep Research." *Journal of the American Society for Information Science*, 22(5):301-310, 1971.

Cremmins, E.T. *The Art of Abstracting.* Philadelphia, Pennsylvania: ISI Press, 1982.

Croft, W.B. "Clustering Large Files of Documents Using the Single Link Method." *Journal of the American Society for Information Science*, 28(6): 341-344, 1977.

Croft, B.C. "Artificial Intelligence and Information Retrieval." *Information Processing and Management*, 23(4):249-382, 1987.

Daniels, P.J. "Cognitive Models in Information Retrieval—An Evaluative Review." *Journal of Documentation*, 42(4):272-304, 1986.

Dervin, B., and M. Nilan. "Information Needs and Uses." *Annual Review of Information Science and Technology*. Edited by Martha E. Williams. Vol. 22, 3-33. White Plains, New York: American Society for Information Science.

Dhawan, S.M., S.K. Phull, and S.P. Jain. "Selection of Scientific Journals: A Model." *Journal of Documentation*, 36(1):24-41, 1980.

Doszkocs, T.E. "CITE/NLM: Natural Language Searching in an Online Catalog." *Information Technology and Libraries*, 2(4):364-380, 1983.

Doszkocs, T.E. "Natural Language Processing in Information Retrieval." *Journal of the American Society for Information Science*, 37(4):191-196, 1986.

Doyle, L. "Semantic Roadmaps for Literature Searches." *Journal of the Association for Computing Machinery*, 8(4):553-578, 1963.

Drott, M.C. "Bradford's Law: Theory, Empiricism and the Gaps Between." *Library Trends*, 30(1):41-52, 1981.

Drott, M.C., and B.C. Griffith. "An Empirical Examination of Bradford's Law and the Scattering of Scientific Literature." *Journal of the American Society for Information Science*, 29(5):238-246, 1978.

Dubois, C.P.R. "The Use of Thesauri in Online Retrieval." *Journal of Information Science*, 8(2):63-66, 1984.

Dyer, E.R. "The Delphi Technique in Library Research." *Library Research*, 1(1):41-52, 1979.

Fenichel, C.H. "Online Searching: Measures That Discriminate Among Users with Different Types of Experiences." *Journal of the American Society for Information Science*, 32(1):23-32, 1981.

Fenichel, C.H. "The Process of Searching Online Bibliographic Databases: A Review of Research." *Library Research*, 2(2):107-127, 1980-81.

Fidel, R. "Online Searching Styles: A Case-Study-Based Model of Searching Behavior." *Journal of the American Society for Information Science*, 35(4): 211-221, 1984.

Fidel, R. "The Probable Effect of Abstracting Guidelines on Retrieval Performance of Free-text Searching." *Information Processing and Management*, 22(4):309-316, 1986.

Fidel, R. "Writing Abstracts for Free-text Searching." *Journal of Documentation*, 42(1):11-21, 1986.

Fidel, R., and D. Soergel. "Factors Affecting Online Bibliographic Retrieval: A Conceptual Framework for Research." *Journal of the American Society for Information Science*, 34(3):163-180, 1983.

Fischer, R.G. "The Delphi Method: A Description, Review, and Criticism." *Journal of Academic Librarianship*, 4(2):64-70, 1978.

Ford, G. *User Studies: An Introductory Guide and Select Bibliography.* (Occasional Paper No. 1). Centre for Research on User Studies, University of Sheffield, England, 1977.

Garfield, E. "Citation Analysis as a Tool in Journal Evaluation." *Science*, 178(4060):471-479, 1972.

Garfield, E. *Citation Indexing — Its Theory and Application in Science, Technology, and Humanities.* New York: John Wiley & Sons, 1979.

Garfield, E. "The Epidemiology of Knowledge and the Spread of Scientific Information." *Current Contents*, 35:5-10, 1980.

Garvey, W.D., and B.C. Griffith. "Communication and Information Processing Within Scientific Disciplines: Empirical Findings for Psychology." *Information Storage and Retrieval*, 8(3):123-136, 1972.

Goffman, W. "On Relevance as a Measure." *Information Storage and Retrieval*, 2(3):201-203, 1964.

Goffman, W. "An Indirect Method of Information Retrieval." *Information Storage and Retrieval*, 4(4):361-373, 1968.

Goffman, W., and V.A. Newill. "Generalization of Epidemic Theory." *Nature*, 204(4955):225-228, 1964.

Goffman, W., and M.L. Pao. "Retrieval of Biomedical Information for Emerging Interdisciplinary Problems." *Proceedings of the 4th International Congress on Medical Librarianship*, 39-50. Belgrade, Yugoslavia: GRO "M. Gembarovski" — Nova Gradiška, 1980.

Goffman, W., and K.S. Warren. *Scientific Information Systems and the Principle of Selectivity.* New York: Praeger Press, 1980.

Griffith, B.C., ed. *Key Papers in Information Science.* New York: American Society for Information Science, 1980.

Griffith, B.C., and A.J. Miller. "Networks of Information Communication Among Scientifically Productive Scientists." *Communication Among Scientists and Engineers*, 125-140. Edited by C. Nelson and D. Pollack. Lexington, Massachusetts: D.C. Heath Company, 1970.

Griffith, B.C., and N.C. Mullins. "Coherent Social Groups in Scientific Change." *Science*, 177(4053):959-964, 1972.

Griffith, B.C., P.N. Servi, A.L. Anker, and M.C. Drott. "The Aging of Scientific Literature: A Citation Analysis." *Journal of Documentation*, 35(3): 179-196, 1979.

Griffith, B.C., H. Small, J.A. Stonehill, and S. Dey. "The Structure of Scientific Literature. II: Toward a Macro- and Micro-Structure for Science." *Science Studies*, 4(4):330-365, 1974.

Griffith, B.C., H.D. White, M.C. Drott, and J.D. Saye. "Tests of Methods of Evaluating Bibliographic Databases: An Analysis of the National Library of Medicine's Handling of Literatures in the Medical Behavioral Sciences." *Journal of the American Society for Information Science*, 37(4):261-270, 1986.

Hall, H.J. "Patterns in the Use of Information: The Right to Be Different." *Journal of the American Society for Information Science*, 32(2):103-112, 1981.

Hamburg, M., R.C. Clelland, M.R.W. Bommer, L.E. Ramist, and R.M. Whitfield. *Library Planning and Decision-making Systems*. Cambridge: MIT Press, 1974.

Hawkins, D.T. "Use of Machine-Readable Databases to Support a Large SDI Service." *Information Processing and Management*, 21(3):187-204, 1985.

Hawkins, D.T., and R. Wagers. "Online Bibliographic Search Strategy Development." *Online*, 6(3):12-19, 1982.

Hayes, R.M., and E.S. Palmer. "The Effects of Distance Upon Use of Libraries: Case Studies Based on a Survey of Uses of the Los Angeles Public Library — Central Library and Branches." *Library Research*, 5(1):67-100, 1983.

He, C., and M.L. Pao. "A Discipline-Specific Journal Selection Algorithm." *Information Processing and Management*, 22(5):405-416, 1986.

Herner, S. "Brief History of Information Science." *Journal of the American Society for Information Science*, 35(3):157-163, 1984.

Herther, N.K. "CD ROM Technology: A New Era for Information Storage and Retrieval?" *Online*, 9(6):17-28, 1985.

Herther, N.K. "CD ROM and Information Dissemination: An Update." *Online*, 11(2):56-64, 1987.

Hirst, G. "Discipline Impact Factors: A Method for Determining Core Journal Lists." *Journal of the American Society for Information Science*, 29(4): 171-172, 1978.

Hitchingham, E.E. "Online Interviews: Charting User and Searcher Interaction Patterns." *Proceedings of the American Society for Information Science*, 16:66-74, 1979.

Hogeweg-de Haart, H.P. "Social Science and the Characteristics of Social Science Information and Its Users." *International Forum on Information and Documentation*, 8(1):11-15, 1983.

Hoover, R. *Online Search Strategies.* White Plains, New York: Knowledge Industry Publications, 1982.

Horowitz, G.L., and H.L. Bleich. "PaperChase: A Computer Program to Search the Medical Literature." *New England Journal of Medicine*, 305(16): 924-930, 1981.

Humphrey, S.M., and N.E. Miller. "Knowledge-Based Indexing of the Medical Literature: The Indexing AID Project." *Journal of the American Society for Information Science*, 38(3):184-196, 1987.

Kantor, P.B. "Availability Analysis." *Journal of the American Society for Information Science*, 27(5):311-319, 1976.

Kantor, P.B. "A Review of Library Operations Research." *Library Research*, 1(4):295-345, 1979.

Kantor, P.B. "Evaluation of and Feedback in Information Storage and Retrieval Systems." *Annual Review of Information Science and Technology.* Edited by Martha E. Williams. Vol. 17, 99-120. White Plains, New York: American Society for Information Science, 1982.

Kantor, P.B. *Objective Performance Measures for Academic and Research Libraries.* Washington, D.C.: Association of Research Libraries, 1984.

Katzer, J., M.J. McGill, J.A. Tessier, W. Frakes, and P. DasGupta. "A Study of the Overlap Among Document Representation." *Information Technology: Research and Development*, 1(4):261-274, 1982.

Kessler, M.M. "Bibliographic Coupling Between Scientific Papers." *American Documentation*, 14(1):10-25, 1963.

King, D.W., and E.C. Bryant. *The Evaluation of Information Services and Products.* Washington, D.C.: Information Resources Press, 1971.

Kochen, M. "Information Science Research: The Search for the Nature of Information." *Journal of the American Society for Information Science*, 35(3): 194-199, 1984.

Kochtanek, T.R. "Bibliographic Compilation Using Reference and Citation Links." *Information Processing and Management*, 18(1):33-39, 1982.

Koll, M.B., T. Noreault, and M.J. McGill. "Enhanced Retrieval Techniques on a Microcomputer." *Proceedings of the 5th National Online Meeting*, 165-170. Medford, New Jersey: Learned Information, Inc., 1984.

Krikelas, J. "Information-Seeking Behavior: Patterns and Concepts." *Drexel Library Quarterly*, 19(2):5-20, 1983.

Kuhn, T.S. *The Structure of Scientific Revolutions*. Chicago: University of Chicago Press, 1962.

Lancaster, F.W. "MEDLARS: Report on the Evaluation of Its Operating Efficiency." *American Documentation*, 20(2):119-142, 1969.

Lancaster, F.W. *The Measurement and Evaluation of Library Services*. Washington, D.C.: Information Resources Press, 1977.

Lancaster, F.W. *Information Retrieval Systems: Characteristics, Testing and Evaluation*. 2nd edition. New York: John Wiley and Sons, 1979.

Lancaster, F.W. *Vocabulary Control for Information Retrieval*. Washington, D.C.: Information Resources Press, 1972.

Lancaster, F.W. *Vocabulary Control for Information Retrieval*. 2nd edition. Arlington, Virginia: Information Resources Press, 1986.

Lawani, S.M., and A.E. Bayer. "Validity of Citation Criteria for Assessing the Influence of Scientific Publications: New Evidence with Peer Assessment." *Journal of the American Society for Information Science*, 34(1):59-66, 1983.

Leggate, P. "Computer-based Current Awareness Services." *Journal of Documentation*, 31(2):93-115, 1975.

Line, M.B. "Half-Life of Periodical Literature: Apparent and Real Obsolescence." *Journal of Documentation*, 26(1):46-54, 1970.

Line, M.B., and A. Sandison. " 'Obsolescence' and Changes in the Use of Literature with Time." *Journal of Documentation*, 30(3):283-350, 1974.

Line, M.B., and A. Sandison. "Practical Interpretation of Citation and Library Use Studies." *College and Research Libraries*, 36(5):393-396, 1975.

Lotka, A.K. "The Frequency Distribution of Scientific Productivity." *Journal of The Washington Academy of Science*, 16(12):317-323, 1926.

Luhn, H.P. "A Statistical Approach to Mechanized Encoding and Searching of Literary Information." *IBM Journal of Research and Development*, 1(4): 309-317, 1957.

Luhn, H.P. "A Business Intelligence System." *IBM Journal of Research and Development*, 2(4):314-319, 1958.

Luhn, H.P. "Selective Dissemination of New Scientific Information with the Aid of Electronic Processing Equipment." *American Documentation*, 12(2): 131-138, 1961.

Lunin, L., ed. "Perspectives on Systems Methodology and Information Research." *Journal of the American Society for Information Science*, 33(6): 373-408, 1982.

Machlup, F. *The Production and Distribution of Knowledge in the United States.* 2nd edition. Princeton, New Jersey: Princeton University Press, 1979.

Machlup, F., and U. Mansfield, eds. *The Study of Information: Interdisciplinary Messages.* New York: John Wiley and Sons, 1983.

MacMullin, S.E., and R.S. Taylor. "Problem Dimensions and Information Traits." *The Information Society*, 3(1):91-111, 1984.

Marcus, R.S. "An Experimental Comparison of the Effectiveness of Computers and Humans as Search Intermediaries." *Journal of the American Society for Information Science*, 34(6):381-404, 1983.

Marcus, R.S., and J.F. Reintjes. "A Translating Computer Interface for End-user Operation of Heterogeneous Retrieval Systems. I. Design." *Journal of the American Society for Information Science*, 32(4):287-303, 1981.

Marcus, R.S., and J.F. Reintjes. "A Translating Computer Interface for End-user Operation of Heterogeneous Retrieval Systems. II. Evaluation." *Journal of the American Society for Information Science*, 32(4):304-317, 1981.

Maron, M.E. "Depth of Indexing." *Journal of the American Society for Information Science*, 30(4):224-228, 1979.

Maron, M.E. "Associative Search Techniques versus Probabilistic Retrieval Models." *Journal of the American Society for Information Science*, 33(5): 308-339, 1982.

Maron, M.E., and J.L. Kuhns. "On Relevance, Probabilistic Indexing, and Information Retrieval." *Journal of the Association of Computing Machinery*, 7(3):216-244, 1960.

Matheson, N.W., and J.A.D. Cooper. "Academic Information in the Academic Health Sciences Center: Roles for the Library in Information Management." *Journal of Medical Education*, 57(10-pt2):1-93, 1982.

Mattessich, R. "The Systems Approach: Its Variety of Aspects." *Journal of the American Society for Information Science*, 33(6):383-394, 1982.

Mauerhoff, G.R. "Selective Dissemination of Information." *Advances in Librarianship*, 4:25-62, 1974.

McAllister, P.R., R.C. Anderson, and F. Narin. "Comparison of Peer and Citation Assessment of the Influence of Scientific Journals." *Journal of the American Society for Information Science*, 31(3):147-152, 1980.

McCain, K.W. "Descriptor and Citation Retrieval in the Medical Behavioral Sciences Literature: Retrieval Overlaps and Novelty Distribution." *Journal of the American Society for Information Science*, 1989. In press.

McGrath, W.E. "The Significance of Books Used According to a Classified Profile of Academic Departments." *College and Research Libraries*, 33(3): 212-219, 1972.

McGrath, W.e. "Relationships Between Hard/Soft, Pure/Applied, and Life/Nonlife Disciplines and Subject Book Use in a University Library." *Information Processing and Management*, 14(1):17-28, 1978.

McGrath, W.E. "Collection Evaluation — Theory and the Search for Structure." *Library Trends*, 33(3):241-266, 1985.

Meadow, C.T. "Matching Users and User Languages in Information Retrieval." *Online Review*, 5(4):313-322, 1981.

Monsell, S. "Representations, Processes, Memory Mechanisms: The Basic Components of Cognition." *Journal of the American Society for Information Science*, 32(5):378-390, 1981.

Morse, P.M. *Library Effectiveness: A Systems Approach.* Cambridge, Massachusetts: The MIT Press, 1968.

Narin, F. *Evaluative Bibliometrics: The Use of Publication and Citation Analysis in the Evaluation of Scientific Activity.* Cherry Hill, New Jersey: Computer Horizon, 1976.

Narin, F., and J.K. Moll. "Bibliometrics." *Annual Review of Information Science and Technology.* Edited by Martha Williams. Vol. 12, 35-58. Washington, D.C.: Knowledge Industry Publications, Inc., 1977.

Narin, F., G. Pinski, and H.H. Gee. "Structure of the Biomedical Literature." *Journal of the American Society for Information Science*, 27(1):25-45, 1976.

Noreault, T., M. Koll, and M.J. McGill. "Automatic Ranked Output from Boolean Searches in SIRE." *Journal of the American Society for Information Science*, 28(6):333-339, 1977.

Oddy, R.N., S.E. Robertson, C.J. Van Rijsbergen, and P.W. Williams, eds. *Information Retrieval Research.* London: Butterworths, 1981.

Paisley, W.J. "Information and Work." *Progress in Communication Sciences.* Edited by B. Dervin and M. Voigt. Vol. 2, 113-166. Norwood, New Jersey: Ablex Publishing, 1980.

Pan, E. "Journal Citation as a Predictor of Journal Usage in Libraries." *Collection Management*, 2(1):29-38, 1978.

Pao, M.L. "A Quality Filtering System for Biomedical Literature." *Journal of Medical Education*, 50(4):353-359, 1975.

Pao, M.L. "Automatic Text Analysis Based on Transition Phenomena of Word Occurrences." *Journal of the American Society for Information Science*, 29(3):121-124, 1978.

Pao, M.L. "An Empirical Examination of Lotka's Law." *Journal of the American Society for Information Science*, 37(1):26-33, 1986.

Pao, M.L. "Lotka's Law: A Testing Procedure." *Information Processing and Management*, 21(4):305-320, 1985.

Pao, M.L., and D.B. Worthen. "Retrieval Effectiveness by Semantic and Citation Searching." *Journal of the American Society for Information Science*, 1989. In press.

Price, D.J.D. *Little Science, Big Science.* New York: Columbia University Press, 1963.

Price, D.J.D. "Networks of Scientific Papers." *Science*, 149(3683):510-515, 1965.

Price, D.J.D. "A General Theory of Bibliometrics and Other Cumulative Advantage Processes." *Journal of the American Society for Information Science*, 27(5):292-306, 1976.

Pritchard, A. "Statistical Bibliography or Bibliometrics?" *Journal of Documentation*, 25(4):348-349, 1969.

Rappoport, A. "What Is Information?" *ETC: A Review of General Semantics*, 10(4):5-12, 1953.

Rohde, N.f. "Information Needs." *Advances in Librarianship*, 14:49-73, 1986.

Rolling, L. "Indexing Consistency: Quality and Efficiency." *Information Processing and Management*, 17(2):69-76, 1981.

Salton, G. "Automatic Text Analysis." *Science*, 168(3929):335-343, 1970.

Salton, G., ed. *The SMART Retrieval System: Experiments in Automatic Document Processing.* Englewood Cliffs, New Jersey: Prentice Hall, 1971.

Salton, G. *Dynamic Information and Library Processing.* Englewood Cliffs, New Jersey: Prentice Hall, 1975.

Salton, G. "Another Look at Automatic Text Retrieval Systems." *Communications of the Association for Computing Machinery*, 29(7):648-656, 1986.

Salton, G., C. Buckley, and E.A. Fox. "Automatic Query Formulations in Information Retrieval." *Journal of the American Society for Information Science*, 34(4):262-280, 1983.

Salton, G., E.A. Fox, and E. Voorhees. "Advanced Feedback Methods in Information Retrieval." *Journal of the American Society for Information Science*, 36(3):200-210, 1985.

Salton, G., and M.J. McGill. *Introduction to Modern Information Retrieval*. New York: McGraw-Hill, 1983.

Salton, G., C.S. Yang, and C.T. Yu. "A Theory of Term Importance in Automatic Text Analysis." *Journal of the American Society for Information Science*, 26(1):33-44, 1975.

Salton, G., W.H. Wu, and C.T. Yu. "The Measurement of Term Importance in Automatic Indexing." *Journal of the American Society for Information Science*, 32(3):175-186, 1981.

Sandison, A. "Densities of Use, and Absence of Obsolescence in Physics Journals at MIT." *Journal of the American Society for Information Science*, 25(3):172-182, 1974.

Saracevic, T. *Introduction to Information Science*. New York: Bowker, 1970.

Saracevic, T. "Selected Results from an Inquiry into Testing of Information Retrieval Systems." *Journal of the American Society for Information Science*, 22(2):126-139, 1971.

Saracevic, T. "Relevance: A Review of and a Framework for the Thinking on the Notion in Information Science." *Journal of the American Society for Information Science*, 26(6):321-343, 1975.

Saracevic, T. "On a Method for Studying the Structure and Nature of Requests in Information Retrieval." *Proceedings of the American Society for Information Science*, 20:22-25, 1983.

Saracevic, T. "Measuring the Degree of Agreement Between Searchers." *Proceedings of the American Society for Information Science*, 21:227-230, 1984.

Saracevic, T., and P. Kantor. "A Study of Information Seeking and Retrieving: II. Users Questions, and Effectiveness." *Journal of the American Society for Information Science*, 39(3):177-196, 1988.

Saracevic, T., and P. Kantor. "A Study of Information Seeking and Retrieving: III. Searchers, Searches, and Overlaps." *Journal of the American Society for Information Science*, 39(3):197-216, 1988.

Saracevic, T., P. Kantor, A.Y. Chamis, and D. Trivison. "A Study of Information Seeking and Retrieving: I. Background and Methodology." *Journal of the American Society for Information Science*, 39(3):161-176, 1988.

Schank, R.C. *The Cognitive Computer: On Language, Learning, and Artificial Intelligence.* Reading, Massachusetts: Addison-Wesley Publishing Company, Inc., 1984.

Sewell, W., and S. Teitelbaum. "Observations of End-User Online Searching Behavior Over Eleven Years." *Journal of the American Society for Information Science*, 37(4):234-245, 1986.

Shannon, C.E., and W. Weaver. *The Mathematical Theory of Communication.* Urbana, Illinois: University of Illinois Press, 1949.

Shaw, W.M., Jr. "Loan Period Distribution in Academic Libraries." *Information Processing and Management*, 12(3):157-159, 1976.

Shera, J.H., and D.B. Cleveland. "The History and Foundations of Information Science." *Annual Review of Information Science and Technology.* Edited by Martha E. Williams. Vol. 12, 249-275. White Plains, New York: Knowledge Industry Publications, Inc., 1977.

Shoval, P. "Principles, Procedures and Rules in an Expert System for Information Retrieval." *Information Processing and Management*, 21(6):475-487, 1985.

Singleton, A. "Journal Ranking and Selection: A Review in Physics." *Journal of Documentation*, 32(4):258-289, 1976.

Small, H. "Co-citation in the Scientific Literature: A New Measure of the Relationship Between Two Documents." *Journal of the American Society for Information Science*, 24(4):265-269, 1973.

Small, H., and B.C. Griffith. "The Structure of Scientific Literature. I: Identifying and Graphing Specialties." *Science Studies*, 4(1):17-40, 1974.

Smith, L.C. "Citation Analysis." *Library Trends*, 30(1):83-106, 1981.

Smith, L.C. "Artificial Intelligence and Information Retrieval." *Annual Review of Information Science and Technology.* Edited by Martha E. Williams. Vol. 22, 41-78. White Plains, New York: American Society for Information Science, 1987.

Soergel, D. *Indexing Languages and Thesauri: Construction and Maintenance.* Los Angeles, California: Melville Publishing Company, 1974.

Soergel, D. *Organizing Information: Principles of Database and Retrieval Systems.* New York: Academic Press, 1985.

Sparck Jones, K. "A Statistical Interpretation of Term Specificity and Its application in Retrieval." *Journal of Documentation*, 28(1):11-21, 1972.

Sparck Jones, K. "Search Term Relevance Weighting Given Little Relevance Information." *Journal of Documentation*, 35(1):30-48, 1979.

Sparck Jones, K., ed. *Information Retrieval Experiment*. London: Butterworths, 1981.

Sprague, R.J., and L.B. Freudenreich. "Building Better SDI Profiles for Users of Large Multidisciplinary Databases." *Journal of the American Society for Information Science*, 29(6):278-282, 1978.

Stone, S. "Humanistic Scholars: Information Needs and Uses." *Journal of Documentation*, 38(4):292-313, 1982.

Swanson, D.R. "Searching Natural Language Text by Computer." *Science*, 132(3434):1099-1104, 1960.

Swanson, R.W. "Design and Evaluation of Information Systems." *Annual Review of Information Science and Technology*. Edited by Carlos A. Cuadra. Vol. 10, 43-101. Washington, D.C.: American Society for Information Science, 1975.

Taylor, R.S. "The Process of Asking Questions." *American Documentation*, 13(4):391-396, 1962.

Taylor, R.S. "Professional Aspects of Information Science and Technology." *Annual Review of Information Science and Technology*. Edited by Carlos A. Cuadra. Vol. 1, 15-40. Chicago: Encyclopaedia Britannica, 1966.

Taylor, R.S. "Question Negotiation and Information Seeking in Libraries." *College and Research Libraries*, 29(3):178-194, 1968.

Taylor, R.S. *Value-Added Processes in Information Systems*. Norwood, New Jersey: Ablex Publishing Corp., 1986.

Townley, H., and R. Gee. *Thesaurus-Making: Grow Your Own Word Stock*. Lexington, Massachusetts: D.C. Heath Company, 1980.

Trueswell, R.L. "Some Behavioral Patterns of Library Users: The 80/20 Rule." *Wilson Library Bulletin*, 43(5):458-461, 1969.

Unisist. United Nations Educational, Scientific and Cultural Organization. *Indexing Principles*. Paris: Unesco, 1975.

Unesco. United Nations Educational, Scientific and Cultural Organization. *Guidelines for the Evaluation of Information Systems and Services*. Paris: Unesco, 1978.

Urquhart, J.A., and R.M. Bunn. "A National Loan Policy for Science Serials." *Journal of Documentation*, 15(1):21-25, 1959.

Van Rijsbergen, C.J. "File Organization in Library Automation and Information Retrieval." *Journal of Documentation*, 32(4):294-317, 1976.

Van Rijsbergen, C.J. *Information Retrieval.* 2nd edition. London: Butterworths, 1979.

Verhoeff, J., W. Goffman, and J. Belzer. "Inefficiency of the Use of Boolean Functions for Information Retrieval Systems." *Communications of the Association for Computing Machinery*, 4(12):557-559, 1961.

Vickery, A., and H. Brooks. "PLEXUS—The Expert System for Referral." *Information Processing and Management*, 23(2):99-117, 1987.

Vickery, A., and H. Brooks. "Expert Systems and Their Applications in LIS." *Online Review*, 11(3):149-165, 1987.

Vickery, A., H. Brooks, and B. Robinson. "A Reference and Referral System Using Expert Systems Techniques." *Journal of Documentation*, 43(1): 1-23, 1987.

Vickery, B.C. "Thesaurus—A New Word in Documentation." *Journal of Documentation*, 16(4):181-189, 1960.

Vickery, B.C. "Knowledge Representation: A Brief Review." *Journal of Documentation*, 42(3):145-159, 1986.

Vickery, B.C., and A. Vickery. *Information Science in Theory and Practice.* London: Butterworths, 1987.

Virgil, P.J. "The Psychology of Online Searching." *Journal of the American Society for Information Science*, 34(4):281-287, 1983.

Virgo, J.A. "A Statistical Procedure for Evaluating the Importance of Scientific Papers." *Library Quarterly*, 47:415-430, 1977.

Wanger, J., C.A. Cuadra, and M. Fishburn. "Impact of On-line Retrieval Services: A Survey of Users, 1974-1975." Systems Development Corporation, Santa Monica, California, 1976.

Warren, K.S., ed. *Selectivity in Information Systems: Survival of the Fittest.* New York: Praeger Press, 1985.

Warren, K.S., and W. Goffman. "The Ecology of Medical Literature." *American Journal of Medical Science*, 262:267-273, 1972.

Wasserman, A. "Information System Design Methodology." *Journal of the American Society for Information Science*, 31(1):5-24, 1980.

Waters, S.T. "Answerman, the Expert Information Specialist: An Expert System for Retrieval of Information from Library Reference Books." *Information Technology and Libraries*, 5(3):204-212, 1986.

Weil, B. "Standards for Writing Abstracts." *Journal of the American Society for Information Science*, 21(5):351-357, 1970.

White, G.T. "Quantitative Measures of Library Effectiveness." *Journal of Academic Librarianship*, 3(3):128-136, 1977.

White, H., and B.C. Griffith. "Author Cocitation: A Literature Measure of Intellectual Structure." *Journal of the American Society for Information Science*, 32(3):163-171, 1981.

Wilkerson, L., and A. Paul. "Every System Should Have One: A Collection of Propezrties Which Can Be Used as a Criterion for Evaluating the Quality of a System." *Information Processing and Management*, 21(1):45-49, 1985.

Wilson, P. "Situational Relevance." *Information Storage and Retrieval*, 9(8): 457-471, 1973.

Wilson, T.D. "On User Studies and Information Needs." *Journal of Documentation*, 37(1):3-15, 1981.

Wood, D.N. "User Studies: A Review of the Literature from 1966 to 1970." *Aslib Proceedings*, 23:11-23, 1971.

Ziman, J. *Public Knowledge: An Essay Concerning the Social Dimension of Science*. London: Cambridge University Press, 1968.

Ziman, J. "Information, Communication, Knowledge." *Nature*, 224:318-324, 1969.

Zipf, G.K. *Human Behaviour and the Principle of Least Effort*. Cambridge, Massachusetts: Addison-Wesley, 1949.

Zuckerman, H. "Nobel Laureates in Science: Patterns of Productivity, Collaboration, and Authorship." *American Sociological Review*, 32:391-402, 1967.

Zunde, P., and M.E. Dexter. "Indexing Consistency and Quality." *American Documentation*, 20(3):259-267, 1969.

Index